GOVERNING
THROUGH TURBULENCE

GOVERNING
THROUGH TURBULENCE

Leadership and Change
in the Late Twentieth Century

David F. Walsh
Paul J. Best
Kul B. Rai

THE HONG KONG POLYTECHNIC
UNIVERSITY   LIBRARY

PRAEGER

Westport, Connecticut
London

Library of Congress Cataloging-in-Publication Data

Walsh, David F.
    Governing through turbulence : leadership and change in the late
twentieth century / David F. Walsh, Paul J. Best, Kul B. Rai.
      p. cm.
    Includes bibliographical references and index.
    ISBN 0–275–95166–9 (alk. paper).—ISBN 0–275–95167–7 (pbk.)
    1. Political leadership—Case studies. 2. Comparative government.
I. Best, Paul J. (Paul Joseph) II. Rai, Kul B. III. Title.
JC330.3.W35 1995
306.2'4'09048—dc20   95–6945

British Library Cataloguing in Publication Data is available.

Library of Congress Catalog Card Number: 95–6945
ISBN: 0–275–95166–9 (hardcover)
      0–275–95167–7 (paperback)

First published in 1995

Praeger Publishers, 88 Post Road West, Westport, CT 06881
An imprint of Greenwood Publishing Group, Inc.

Printed in the United States of America

The paper used in this book complies with the
Permanent Paper Standard issued by the National
Information Standards Organization (Z39.48–1984).

10 9 8 7 6 5 4 3 2 1

Contents

Preface   vii

Acknowledgments   xiii

1 Global Turbulence: Political Change at Century's End   1

2 The New Political Environment: Six Changed Relationships   25

3 Margaret Thatcher: Economic Decline and Turbulence in the
   United Kingdom   45

4 Helmut Kohl and the German Reunification Project   83

5 Lech Walesa and the Emergence of Postcommunist Poland   123

6 Mikhail Gorbachev, Boris Yeltsin, and the Democratization of
   Russia   147

7 Rajiv Gandhi: Economic Liberalization in India   169

8 Deng Xiaoping: China's Economic Transformation   195

9 Leadership in the Age of Turbulence   221

Selected Bibliography   237

Index   243

Preface

Recent works have described the last three decades of the twentieth century as an "age of turbulence" in which the speed, frequency, and scope of political change reached unprecedented levels. Driven by innovations in science and technology, turbulent change impacted nearly every political system and created a political environment of extreme complexity and fluidity. In the environment of turbulence, previously dominant leaders, ideas, and institutions were disempowered and a new generation of leaders came to power. However, these leaders confronted a growing number of political and economic constraints, which greatly complicated the tasks of governing and political management.

The seven leaders discussed in the following chapters are members of the first generation of political elites to assume power in the changed political environment of the late twentieth century. As such, they provide important case studies of "governing through turbulence." Two leaders were the heads of government of advanced industrial countries: Margaret Thatcher (Prime Minister of the United Kingdom, 1979–1990) and Helmut Kohl (Chancellor of Germany, 1982–present). Three were government leaders of states that underwent the transition from communist to postcommunist regimes: Lech Walesa (Solidarity movement leader, 1976–1991; President of Poland, 1990–present), Mikhail Gorbachev (General Secretary of the Communist Party of the Soviet Union, 1985–1991; President of the Soviet Union, 1990–1991), and Boris Yeltsin (President of the Russian Republic, 1990–present). Two were leaders of important Third World states: Deng Xiaoping (*de facto* leader of the Communist Party of China after 1977) was China's most powerful political leader in the post-Maoist period, while Rajiv Gandhi was the Prime Minister of India from 1984 to 1989. These leaders were selected as the subjects for this study because of their obvious international significance and also because each is identified with a particular policy response to the new political conditions. Each leader was also propelled to power by a coherent and important political movement.

This work is primarily concerned with the political and economic settings from which the new leaders emerged, the policy prescriptions offered by each to achieve power, and the major policies they instituted after coming to power. Most important, special attention is given to the manner in which each leader attempted to manage the elements of political turbulence and the crisis of political authority that confronted the leaders of all states after the mid-1970s.

The volume is not intended as a series of biographies, psychohistories, or historical chronologies of the seven leaders' tenures in office. Instead, it consists of a series of case studies, each employing the following analytical categories: (1) the political-economic context; (2) the operative elements of political turbulence in the domestic political environment; (3) a profile of the leader and his or her group; (4) the leader's political program; (5) strategies and means selected for achieving power; (6) the policy dimension—implementation of the new political program; (7) the nature and scope of change; and (8) theories and interpretations of the leader and the new political agenda. The case studies emphasize that each of the leaders was required to respond to the same set of changing global conditions and to the same political environment of turbulence and that these environments acted as increasingly powerful constraints on policy makers in the last three decades of the twentieth century.

The public policy orientation of the seven leaders may be summarized as follows. Thatcher and Kohl represented the interests of New Right and center-right political groups in their respective advanced industrial states. Although each leader faced some unique national conditions and some differences existed between them, both represented the core values of conservative capitalism. Economic policy was accorded top priority, and the identification of means by which to increase the nation's competitiveness in the global capitalist economy was defined as the most important national priority. Major public policies sought to achieve the stimulation of market forces, privatization, deregulation, and the reduction of public expenditures and taxation. In the case of Helmut Kohl, however, the traditional German commitment to the social market economy and the need for resources to consolidate the German reunification project forced significant departures from these policies.

Lech Walesa, Mikhail Gorbachev, and Boris Yeltsin were central figures in the drama of the transition from communist to postcommunist regimes in the former Soviet bloc. As leader of a diverse movement, Solidarity, Walesa achieved power with the support of nationalist and Catholic Church interests, as well as that of secular groups dissatisfied with the social and economic policies of the Communist regime. From 1981 to 1989, Walesa played a crucial role in the negotiations with the army and communist party, which culminated in the peaceful transfer of power and the democratic election of June 1989. As president of Poland, he sought the development of economic and social policies that ultimately facilitated the nation's unprecedented transition from a centrally controlled economy to a market economy.

In the Soviet Union, both Gorbachev and Yeltsin were products of the Communist Party bureaucracy, but their rise to power was achieved with the support of reform elements of the Communist Party of the Soviet Union (CPSU). Gorbachev is most often associated with the policies of *glasnost* (political openness), *perestroika* (economic restructuring), and *Novoye Myshlenie* (New Thinking) in foreign policy. Gorbachev's program was designed to overcome the allocative inefficiencies and technological backwardness of the Soviet economy. Following the failed coup by antireformist elements of the Communist Party in 1991, Gorbachev acquiesced to the demands of more radical reform elements for policies that resulted in the end of Communist Party rule and the restructuring of the USSR as a political entity. One reform group was led by Boris Yeltsin, whose program was a "leftist" critique of *perestroika* that called for the immediate end of the Leninist system. Yeltsin, a former leader of the party bureaucracy, was temporarily demoted within the CPSU in 1987, but his support among the Russian general public continued to increase. As president of the Russian Republic after 1990, Yeltsin was confronted with the political turbulence that accompanied the end of the Soviet Union and the emergence of the Commonwealth of Independent States and other successor countries.

The Third World leaders in the study, Deng Xiaoping and Rajiv Gandhi, were confronted by the effects of a decade-long series of adverse developments in the international economy, beginning in the 1970s. Each of the Third World leaders became identified with a unique policy response or adjustment strategy. In China, Deng Xiaoping emerged from the post-Maoist power struggles as the dominant figure in the Chinese Communist Party (CCP). He is associated with economic policy reforms that were the most sweeping in the communist world prior to 1985, but the CCP leadership resisted political reforms and any challenge to the party's dominant political position. Gandhi's heterodox economic policies sought to promote some degree of liberalization and change in India's transitional economy. Gandhi, however, came to power at a time of increasing political turbulence, when new social and political conflicts were building on older ones. His policies provoked resistance from groups committed to the older, socialist tradition as well as from business interests, which believed the pace of change to be too slow.

The subjects of this study, like all political actors at the end of the twentieth century, operated in a new political environment that was both historically unprecedented and qualitatively different from that of the earlier postwar period. This study is in agreement with those works that have variously described the changes since 1980 as constituting a "global revolution," "breakpoint change," historical change, or "an end to history." Such works have demonstrated conclusively that the political relationships of the early postwar period have ended. The ultimate source of this political change was the revolution in technology and the explosion of scientific knowledge, especially in the areas of electronics, microelectronics, communications, and new production technologies. Although political relationships are always undergoing incremental change, the pace of change since the end of the 1960s, and especially since the mid-1970s, has escalated to the point where major global political relationships now differ qualitatively, and not just quantitatively.

The changes in the following six relationships have been especially important in the transformation of the political environment: (1) relations between the Western and Soviet hegemonies (blocs) at the end of the Cold War; (2) the economic relations between states after the breakdown of the Bretton Woods system; (3) the relations between new capital and traditional capital, capital and labor, and capital and the state since the onset of global capitalism; (4) the relations between the domestic political-economic actors (e.g., government agencies, unions, and business groups) in major states following the breakdown of the postwar political-economic order; (5) relations between the new political movements that have developed since the 1970s and traditional interest groups; and (6) relations between citizens who now possess greatly enhanced analytical and political skills and their governments, which have revolutionized politics in every state.

The collective changes outlined here have had the effect of creating a dynamic and complex political environment, which has produced a crisis of political authority in many states. The end of the Cold War has been accompanied by increased conflict among the states of the West as well as the dissolution of the Soviet bloc, as both superpowers were denied a rationale for continued leadership. The breakdown of the Bretton Woods system and the onset of global capitalism produced economic dislocations in a majority of states. These external changes, combined with domestic economic developments, have also resulted in the collapse of the postwar consensus on economic policy in most advanced industrial states, as well as the demise of the neo-Stalinist economic order in the former Soviet bloc.

In addition, the development of new domestic political movements taxed the political leaders of many countries by greatly increasing the number of groups and issues with which they must contend and by creating both supranational and subnational challenges to state authority. Most important, leaders in every state must now contend with mass publics that have available near-instantaneous access to, and detailed knowledge of, events in their own and other countries. These publics also have daily exposure to expert scientific studies about global trends and problems, which have changed the spatial and temporal dimensions of politics. The geographic distance between states and events has been reduced, and present-day levels of political support are frequently affected by concerns for future outcomes, such as world ecological damage or the possible loss of economic competitiveness.

The leaders who are the subjects of the case studies came to power between the late 1970s and mid-1980s, when the pace of change in each of the six relationships accelerated and underwent qualitative change. Programs such as "Thatcherism" and *perestroika* were efforts to deal with the new political, economic, and social realities. As such, they are important not only because they represented the first efforts to deal with the changed political relationships, but also because in part they helped to shape some of those relationships. For example, the policies of Margaret Thatcher contributed to the end of the postwar consensus on the economy in Great Britain.

By employing case studies that analyze the programs and policies of the most prominent political leaders of the last two decades, the scope, depth, and meaning of the recent political changes become comprehensible for intermediate and advanced undergraduate students. The case studies also permit the integration of concepts and findings from recent research on domestic political economy, international political economy, cultural change, interest group formation and behavior, political parties, and political development. This study is intended for courses in international relations and comparative politics in four-year colleges and universities. It may also be appropriate for certain introductory political science courses seeking a challenging format.

Acknowledgments

The authors wish to acknowledge the assistance of the Faculty Development Office of Southern Connecticut State University in the preparation of this book.

Additionally, the authors wish to thank Professor Tal-Ling Lee for his comments on the chapter about Deng Xiaoping, and Professor John O. Iatrides for reading through materials on the United Kingdom and Germany.

Three librarians, Shirley Cavanaugh, Thomas Clarie, and Paul Holmer, are to be thanked for help in obtaining books, journal articles, and other materials for Professor Kul B. Rai.

We also wish to acknowledge that we would never have finished the project without the able assistance of Jean Polka, the Political Science Department secretary at our university, and Mrs. Kathleen Walsh.

David F. Walsh wishes to dedicate this book to his father.

one

Global Turbulence: Political Change at Century's End

In the last two decades of the twentieth century, one issue has dominated political discussion at all levels—political change. While incremental, small-scale change is always occurring, the international and domestic changes that have occurred in the late twentieth century have been of historical magnitude. International events such as the collapse of state socialism in Eastern Europe and the Soviet Union, German reunification, and the end of the Warsaw Treaty Organization and Soviet bloc are well-known examples. All these changes qualify as "historic," breakpoint, and qualitative in nature because they involve a fundamental restructuring of political forces with worldwide significance. To this list must be added a series of more complex international changes that took longer to develop but were of equal importance, including the end of the Cold War, the decline of American economic hegemony, and the breakdown of the Bretton Woods international economic regime. These changes have transformed the basic political relationships and established patterns in international politics that had prevailed since World War II.

Some sources have argued that these recent changes are so profound as to constitute "a global revolution," the onset of a new era of "postinternational relations" in which states are no longer dominant actors, and an "end to history" in that the Cold War struggle between the two superpowers and their allies is no longer a major issue in international politics. While all these arguments must be carefully assessed and some may need to be tempered to conform to prevailing political realities, they correctly call our attention to the rapid pace and broad scope of political change at the end of the twentieth century. They also correctly point out the unprecedented pervasiveness of the change that has penetrated every geographic area of the world and a majority of the world's states.

The changes within many domestic political systems, such as those in the Soviet Union, have also been of a fundamental, historically significant nature. These changes conform to the model that social scientists have developed for "great domestic political reforms."[1] Such reforms must transform four aspects of the political system: (1) the relationship between the state and society, and especially the manner in which the state seeks to achieve support and compliance from its citizens, (2) the relationship between the state and the economy, (3) the distribution of power among governmental institutions of the state, and (4) the political and economic relationship between the state and the outside world.[2] In the case of the Soviet Union, Mikhail Gorbachev's policies of *glasnost* (political openness permitting critical reappraisals of policies and institutions), *perestroika* (the economic policy of restructuring), and New Thinking (a revisionist view of the relationship between the Soviet Union and the noncommunist world) prescribed changes in precisely those areas.

The late twentieth century has also seen the emergence of a group of national political leaders that has gained a greater degree of international attention than any other since the combat years of World War II. Newspaper accounts and popularized studies have referred to Margaret Thatcher as the "Iron Lady" and her policies as "Thatcherism," to Helmut Kohl as the "Second Bismarck" and the "architect of German reunification," and to Mikhail Gorbachev as the "man who changed the world."[3] Scholarly works generally have been careful not to subscribe to the "great man" theory of history by attributing too much power or control over events to any one individual. Studies by social scientists have demonstrated that, rather than cause or create economic, social, and political changes, individual political actors react to them by attempting to exploit them for their own political ends. The findings of these studies also suggest, however, that certain late twentieth-century leaders have demonstrated great skills in electioneering, mobilizing interest groups in support of new policies, and advancing new political agendas. Several studies have attributed to such leaders as Margaret Thatcher and Mikhail Gorbachev a major role in reordering and redirecting the national political agenda, perhaps for all time.

It is not a coincidence that the last decades of the twentieth century have experienced both major political change and notable political leaders—the two developments are related. Change creates opportunities for political actors in the opposition to come to power and, once in power, to implement new policies and ideas. Change also upsets the established power or authority relationships between political institutions and groups, giving major political actors within them unprecedented room for political maneuvering. On the other hand, a political environment that is experiencing rapid political change is an unpredictable and dangerous setting. Such an environment impels actors to develop and implement bold political tactics and strategies in order to remain in power.

LEADERS AND POLITICAL CHANGE

As many students of the political process have observed, political actors live off the conflicts that develop in society.[4] They seek to gain electoral, financial, and moral support by identifying the major problems that exist in society and proposing solutions that are preferred by the majority of the politically relevant population. Everett Ladd has described the process as one of "ordering and arranging" a political agenda, or prioritized list of issues to be addressed by government, that will gain the support of interest groups.[5] Ideally, these interest groups will combine in a coalition that will last long enough to propel the would-be leaders to power. In democratic states in which political power is achieved through elections, victorious coalitions consist of such groups as labor unions, professional associations, farmers' groups, business organizations, and single-issue movements (e.g., for tax reform, antiabortion legislation, or environmental protection). In communist systems before 1985, victorious coalitions consisted of communist party factions representing the military, the party bureaucracy, state-controlled industry, state-controlled collectivized agriculture, and the scientific community. In the late 1980s and early 1990s, communist party rule was ended in the Soviet Union and the states of Eastern Europe by broad-based coalitions consisting of workers' groups, church organizations, regional interests, intellectual dissidents, ethnic groups, and communist party reform elements united in opposition to communist party–directed decision making and economic outcomes. Recent governing coalitions in the less developed countries (LDCs) of the Third World have formed around strategies for economic adjustment to adverse developments in the world economy.[6] Depending on the state in question, such coalitions have contained the representatives of a wide variety of governmental and private institutions with access to technical information about the contemporary world economy.

Despite the type of regime or level of development, all political actors gain and maintain control of government in the same way, by structuring and manipulating the national political agenda. Would-be leaders must convince politically relevant groups that it is in their interests that the leaders' group control government institutions and implement public policies because these will benefit the target groups politically and economically. Two points about this process must be clearly understood. First, both the selection of issues for the political agenda and the policy solutions or prescriptions for dealing with them are never objective; rather, they are always subjective, biased, and arbitrary. At any point in time, a large number of issues exist as potential items for the national political agenda and multiple policy alternatives are proposed for dealing with them. The selection of particular issues and policies reflects the values and expectations of partisan benefit of the political actor or groups structuring the agenda.

Second, political actors never create the issues or national problems of the political agenda, which instead develop from complex societal relationships that form over long periods of time.[7] For example, such issues as unemployment, loss of economic competitiveness, and military vulnerability obviously have origins dating back at least several decades. Political actors inherit potential issues in much the manner that a card player is dealt a hand. Some cards may be disregarded or even discarded, but the player's success ultimately depends on skill at utilizing the cards that were dealt.

NEW AGENDAS: THE PROSPECTS FOR SUCCESS

Certain social conditions and political environments are more conducive to the successful imposition of a new political agenda than others. Numerous studies have documented that new political agendas may follow great national traumas, such as military defeats or economic depressions. In extreme cases, the new agendas may be accompanied by regime changes in which new constitutional orders and political institutions replace old ones. In his study of American political parties, Everett Ladd argued that each of the four political agendas that were implemented between 1789 and the late 1960s in the United States followed transformations of the major social and economic relationships that define society.[8] Such transformations included the transitions from an agrarian to an industrial society and from an industrial to a postindustrial society, whereby the occupations and basic political orientations of a majority of Americans changed. In another study of Western European political economy, Robert Isaak demonstrated that new political issues can develop when large numbers of citizens perceive the potential for severe loss of economic standing or social prestige or anticipate the possibility of extreme change in their lives.

At such times, issues that are normally considered to be of a private economic or social nature are "pushed up" to the political level as citizens seek protection from their government against the threatened adverse developments.[9] As an example, in the 1970s in Western Europe, unionized labor and businesspersons alike sought government assistance in promoting the international competitiveness of national business when faced with increased foreign competition. This issue of industrial policy (promoting the nation's industry) became an important part of an economic agenda, which included several issues that had previously been thought to be the responsibility of private economic actors.

Considered collectively, the existing evidence demonstrates that agenda change is most likely to occur when there is widespread anxiety over the anticipated loss of opportunities, benefits, or rights that were previously enjoyed or when rapid and pervasive social and economic changes disrupt the established patterns of life (see Table 1). Although societal anxiety is often directed toward the possibility of downward economic mobility, it is by no means limited to economic matters. Fear of such diverse issues as military vulnerability, loss of cultural autonomy, and government abuse of power can also act as a catalyst for new agendas. Moreover, agenda change does not automatically follow severe economic downturns or adverse political developments. The reactions of citizens to economic hard times are shaped by a number of factors, including the amount of information they possess about the economy and the prevailing cultural values of the society, which in some cases may place heavy emphasis on noneconomic issues.[10] Even when the economic trends are understood, they are always in competition with other concerns, and important political groups may choose to support existing leadership groups and agendas because of their satisfaction with performance in noneconomic areas.

Conditions at the End of the Twentieth Century

In the last twenty-five years of the twentieth century, conditions were conducive on a global scale for new agenda formation and, hence, the rise of new leadership groups. Both of the most important prerequisites for such formations, rapid socioeconomic change and mass anxiety about the future, were present in nearly every country. Even the citizens of the two superpowers were not exempt from such conditions. For example, by 1991, major social dislocations had occurred in the territories of the former Soviet Union to a point where that country's status as a superpower was in doubt. The extent of the global change that had occurred by 1990 was scarcely imaginable a few years before, and no one could be sure when the pace of change would slow or what form the new social, economic, and political patterns might take.

TECHNOLOGY: THE CATALYST FOR CHANGE

Why did the prerequisites for major political change develop in so many different countries over so short a span of years? The answer must be found in the spread of new technologies, especially those in the fields of electronics, microelectronics, nuclear energy, and molecular biology, and in the new human attitudes and skills that they spawned.[11] The collective effect of these new technologies was to invalidate economic and social relationships that had existed for most of the postwar period and to shrink distances of time and space between people and events to such an extent that an unprecedented degree of international interdependence was created.

Numerous studies have reported on the impact of the new technologies. In one recent work, a senior Canadian government economist summarized the effects of the new technologies in the following way: "When the history

Table 1
Agenda Change, Western Europe (Center-Left to Center-Right)

Social Democratic Agenda (1960–mid-1970s)		Neoliberal Agenda (mid-1970s–1980s)
I. Major Objectives of Government		I.
To provide full employment; to provide citizens with economic protection against the hazards of life; to promote a culture of social peace and social responsibility.	Post-1973 Developments OPEC oil price increases World recessions of the 1970s and 1980s Trend toward protectionism (OECD states)	To increase the competitiveness of national businesses in the world economy; to liberate market forces through the promotion of an enterprise culture.
II. Major Problems Confronting Society		II.
To counteract negative or uneven outcomes of capitalist development; to provide opportunities for low- and middle-income groups; to preserve the postwar settlement.	State-specific Conditions Increased unemployment Deindustrialization; loss of international competitiveness Business failures Mass anxiety about downward mobility	To return economic decision making to the marketplace; to reduce the overload on government; to restructure the national economy in an age of global capitalism; to reduce welfare state spending.
III. Approach to the Economy		III.
Keynesian aggregate-demand management and other steering mechanisms; utilization of neocorporate structures for economic decision making; acceptance of the welfare state and a mixed economy as givens.		Supply-side economic measures; limited monetarist targets; downgrading of neocorporate structures.

6

Social Democratic Agenda
(1960–mid-1970s)

IV. Major Policies

Countercyclical fiscal measures; regulation of market economy; limited nationalization; promotion of industrial democracy; social programs for general and special needs groups.

V. Sources of Political Support

Trade union movement; low- and middle-income wage earners; special needs groups; some political subcultures; left and center-left attitudinal groups.

Neoliberal Agenda
(mid-1970s–1980s)

IV.

Privatization/denationalization of industry; tax reductions; reductions in social spending and entitlements; limitations on immigration in some states; deregulation; increased spending for defense and police in some states.

V.

Major business associations; self-employed persons and some professional groups; "new middle class"; New Right and traditional conservative ideological groups.

of the twentieth century is written, it will be seen as an age of revolution and transformation that, in terms of its speed, pervasiveness, and technological complexity, was greater than any in the history of civilization."[12] This view is shared by many others, including the author of another important study, who noted that "the entire Industrial Revolution enhanced productivity by a factor of about a hundred [but] the microelectronic revolution has already enhanced productivity in information-based technology by a factor of more than a million,"[13] and a major historian, who wrote that "the last two generations have witnessed more scientific and technological achievement than that achieved in all of the previous 798 lifetimes that humans have lived on earth."[14]

Many of the technologies with the most profound effects on social and economic life have been in existence for some time. Commercial radio broadcasting has existed since the 1920s, televisions have been sold to consumers since 1945, and computers developed from simple calculating machines. In the last years of the twentieth century, however, the quantitative proliferation and mass availability of these technologies have changed their meaning in our lives. Today it is appropriate to speak of global television and radio, since between 1965 and 1985, the number of television transmitters increased sevenfold and the number of television receivers in use grew by more than threefold.[15]

The political and economic consequences of technological innovation are everywhere to be seen. From the mid-1960s on, increasing numbers of workers and businesspeople in advanced industrial states faced threats to their economic well-being from foreign and domestic competition. The new level of international economic competitiveness was the result of new production technologies that permitted the making of superior-quality goods in many parts of the world or, in worst-case scenarios, the movement of entire industries to geographic areas where labor costs were lower. Similarly, the development of nuclear energy, both for peaceful and military usage, has resulted in the growth of huge worldwide political movements of persons who fear the possible environmental consequences. It also appears that a major incentive for the economic and political changes preceding the breakup of the Soviet Union was the realization by Soviet leaders that their incremental industrial innovations were not adequate to keep pace with the industrial changes in the West. As one source noted, the Soviet Union found itself in a technological time warp because from the 1970s on, it was unable to absorb relevant innovations in microelectronics, genetic engineering, lasers, and the use of new industrial materials.[16] The concept of a time warp is useful in understanding the present era. In a sense, every contemporary political and economic actor faces the danger of adjusting to change too slowly or with inappropriate measures. The slogan, "here today, gone tomorrow," which is commonly used to describe today's business climate, also accurately portrays the tension present in most areas of modern life and the reason for widespread insecurity.

Perhaps the most important consequence of technology has been the revolution in the field of communications and the manner in which knowledge is disseminated. Modern communications technology has had the effect of shrinking the world and has dramatically altered both the quantity and quality of information available to leadership groups as well as the mass populations of most states. Global radio and television broadcasts transmitted with the aid of satellites provide near-instant information and analysis of economic and political events around the world. World-class newspapers, journals, personal computers, and photocopying processes have made available to wide audiences scientific and technical data that was previously monopolized by small numbers of experts. As a recent study noted, these developments have produced "fundamental and enduring changes in the analytical skills and cathectic capacities of people," giving them an enhanced capacity "to employ, articulate, direct, and implement" the attitudes they hold.[17] These enhanced analytic skills have complicated the problem of governing and maintaining acceptable levels of political support in every country. The problem has been especially acute in states in which governing authorities previously had control over the means of communication.

One aspect of the communications revolution that has complicated the task of governing deserves special attention. In the contemporary "knowledge-based societies" and "computer-mediated environments" that exist in most states, the temporal or time distances between events have been reduced in the same way that spatial distances have been reduced between geographic areas.[18] It has become commonplace for businesspersons, consumers, and voters to treat the future as a part of the present reality and to behave accordingly. This is one of the most significant attitudinal changes to occur during the technological revolution. Workers who are employed may vote for an opposition party because of the fear they may lose their jobs in the future, while consumers and businesspersons may decide not to buy or invest based on future projections of economic performance. In a sense contemporary political leaders are now responsible for conditions in the future as well as in the present, and since projections of the future often conflict, leaders frequently confront very insecure constituencies.

CHANGE AT THREE LEVELS

It is useful to conceptualize the political developments at the end of the twentieth century as the products of three levels of change: long-term, medium-term, and short-term (see Figure 1).[19] Long-term change involves transformations of processes and social formations that predate World War II. The most important long-term change has been the revolution in technology, particularly the developments in areas, such as communications and infor-

Figure 1
Catalysts for Change (Long-term, Medium-term, and Short-term Change)

Long-term Change
(Pre–World War II–1990s)

Technological Revolution: innovations in electronics and microelectronics; nuclear energy; molecular biology; genetic engineering; biomedicine; etc.

Examples: New production technologies; new industrial materials; global radio and television; computer-mediated societies/ personal computers; photocopying; satellite transmissions.

Medium-term Change
(Late 1960s–1990s)

Breakpoint change in six political or political-economic relationships.

Relationships:
1. End of the Cold War
2. Breakdown of Bretton Woods system
3. Onset of global capitalism
4. Fall of postwar economic settlements
5. Proliferation of political movements
6. Powerful and informed citizens confront the state.

Short-term Change (Post-1973)

Adjustments to the six changed relationships; reactions to economic insecurity; political fluidity.

Examples:
Thatcherism—U.K.
Perestroika—USSR
Heterodoxy—India (some liberal reforms)

mation, that have had a clear and pervasive influence on political behavior. Viewed in historical terms, the information revolution was a continuous process that included such milestones as the use of papyrus paper, the invention of the printing press, wireless radio technology, and the invention of television. Of course, these were of monumental significance for the people of earlier periods and had a revolutionary impact in their time. It was not, however, until the development of communications satellites, personal computers, and global radio and television that humankind achieved the capacity for near-instant and near-worldwide communications. These developments of the late twentieth century clearly represented changes of a qualitative, breakpoint, and historic nature. Similarly, the development of nuclear weapons and recent innovations in biomedical technology represent changes of a similar magnitude in their respective fields.

The technological revolution was not directed by any group, and it had no ideological basis.[20] Unlike conventional revolutions, which frequently occur over a short period of time, some of the specific technologies that ultimately came to have the greatest impact existed for decades before their full potential was realized. In addition, unlike political revolutions, there was no period in which the tide of change was reversed. Each technological innovation was built on an earlier one, and the cumulative effect was to impact the lives of a majority of the world's citizens. Although technological innovations are of themselves scientific in nature, and not political, at the end of the twentieth century, they combined with political, social, economic, cultural, and other factors to disrupt and transform the major political relationships that had defined both domestic and international political life since World War II.

Medium-term changes involve transformations of the dominant political and economic relationships that shaped the postwar world.[21] These relationships include both international patterns, such as the Cold War competition between the United States and the Soviet Union, which shaped the world in a military and strategic sense, and domestic patterns that established the political-economic systems or orders within individual nation-states. Unlike the international patterns, the domestic patterns were both regime-specific and, in some cases, state-specific. For example, the postwar political-economic order took the form of the welfare state in the advanced industrial states of the West, with variations between the states in the size of social programs and the scope of government intervention. In the Soviet bloc it took a different form, that of state socialism directed by the communist party, and again there were significant differences between the various states. Collectively, the international and domestic patterns established the political context in which all political actors operated for most of the period from 1945 through 1970. These relationships determined the pattern of military and political alliances, the structure of the international economy, and the nature of the domestic political economy.

Beginning in the early 1970s, many of the major political and economic relationships that had dominated the formative years after World War II began to break down. In every area, the ultimate catalyst for change was the revolution in technology. Developments ranging from nuclear weapons to new production technologies on the assembly line interacted in a complex way to transform the relationships. Viewed from the perspective of the medium term, the political change at the end of the twentieth century brought about the breakdown of the postwar political and economic order, which had produced unprecedented economic growth and successfully avoided war between the superpowers.[22] Changes in the following six relationships were of central importance in bringing about the end of the postwar era: (1) the end of the Cold War, (2) the breakdown of the Bretton Woods system (the postwar international economic regime), (3) the onset of global capitalism, (4) the breakdown of domestic economic arrangements in many states, (5) the proliferation of domestic political movements, and (6) the changed relationship between newly empowered citizens and their governments. Each of these is discussed in some detail in the next chapter.

Short-term changes include those political, social, and economic transformations, at both the international and domestic levels, that occurred in the period after the initial oil price increases by the Organization of Petroleum Exporting Countries (OPEC) in 1973 through 1975. Those increases, which tripled the price of oil, are considered by many sources to be the action that precipitated both the onset of a worldwide recession and a crisis in the international political economy. The recession brought to an end almost three decades of global economic growth and prosperity and persisted into the 1980s.[23] In social science literature, the post-1973 period has been referred to as a period of "world crisis," "contemporary instability and change," "global insecurity," and "politics in hard times."[24] As one recent work pointed out, the term *crisis*, "in its original Greek form[,] . . . means 'decision' and so identifies a critical juncture in a process when a critical decision must be made."[25] The political and economic changes that occurred after 1973 were largely the result of decisions by economic and political actors at all levels to adjust to the immediate conditions of the crisis, such as rising unemployment, increased inflation, and protectionist behavior by trading partners. They were also the result of efforts to adjust to the breakdown of the economic and political relationships that had dominated in the early postwar period, especially the six relationships examined here.

Because the post-1973 economic crisis elicited adjustments at all levels of society, the political and economic changes took a variety of forms. At the level of the general population, voters deviated from traditional patterns of electoral behavior on the basis of their evaluations of the government's past performance in managing the economy or on the expectation that a new party in power would pursue economic policy objectives consistent with their needs.[26] This resulted in both party realignment and party dealignment.[27]

Dissatisfied citizens also provided indispensable support to a wide variety of political movements, ranging from taxpayers' associations to protest movements of angry farmers fearing the loss of subsidies. At the group level, political leaders sought to identify their parties with new issues, new agendas, and new candidates in response to rapid changes in international economic and political conditions. Changes in the international economy also had a profound effect on the balance of power between domestic interest groups, such as that between labor unions and business organizations.

At the governmental level, the global recession produced major shifts in both domestic and foreign economic policies. The urgency of maintaining the competitiveness of the nation's businesses in the world economy created a new set of policy priorities, which differed considerably from those of the early postwar period. It also led to increased politicization and conflict in the area of international trade as some governments sought to protect their citizens from competition by adopting protectionist means.

THE DYNAMICS OF POLITICAL CHANGE AFTER 1973

In much of the social science literature, the concept of political change is discussed as part of a process of socioeconomic development in which societies are assumed to move from one level or stage to the next in an orderly sequence. Such theories of development seek to identify the key units of analysis or variables in the process (e.g., growth in the gross national product, the proliferation of institutions, and changes in the composition of the workforce), the thresholds at which the various levels of development begin and end, and the sequence of levels through which states must pass as they move from traditional to modern societies.[28] While there is considerable disagreement over the measurement of socioeconomic development and the meaning of political change, this literature has made valuable contributions to our understanding of the differences between states and societies. In the case of the political changes that occurred in the period after 1973, however, the theories of orderly and sequential change have little explanatory value. Many of the economic, social, and political developments that occurred after the OPEC oil price increases actually constituted episodes of reverse development. In the economic area, a majority of states experienced deindustrialization (the loss of industrial sectors and jobs), negative economic growth rates, a contraction of the workforce, capital flight, and the loss of international competitiveness. These developments, which were often discussed as part of a dialogue on "national decline," would seem to represent the opposite of social and economic development.

In the political system, reverse development seemed even more pronounced. Instead of structural proliferation, most states reduced the size of the government bureaucracy and the scope of its regulatory activity in an effort to reduce public expenditures. Instead of the expansion of institutions and processes for mediating and resolving conflicts, such as labor disputes, many of these actually broke down under the pressure of the world recession. Viewed from the perspective of the general population, the citizens of most states lost rights and benefits during the period. In the states of the West, conservative governments renounced responsibility for full employment and general economic well-being, and in the postcommunist states, the transition to a semireformed market economy meant the end of economic protection from the cradle to the grave. In extreme cases, the central governing authority of the state broke down under the pressure of popular dissatisfaction with economic outcomes or the secessionist demands of subnational political groups, and the state ceased to exist in its original form. Such was the case with Yugoslavia, the Soviet Union, and the German Democratic Republic. All these developments are incompatible with models of political development that posit an increasing capacity of the state for problem solving and effective governance.

If the social and economic development after 1973 did not lead to political change consistent with conventional theories of development, then how is this period to be interpreted and understood? We believe that the political meaning of the events after 1973 can best be understood by focusing on one dynamic of rapid social, economic, and technological change—the ability to empower and disempower political institutions and political ideas. In a recent study, Peter Katzenstein summarized the possible effects of change on institutions: "A new context can empower institutions that before had been less central politically; it can disempower institutions that had been central; or it can transform the role institutions play in the larger political economy."[29] In the late twentieth century, rapid and simultaneous changes in the technological, economic, and social contexts accelerated the processes of political empowerment and disempowerment.

Empowerment and Disempowerment of Partisan Political Groups

The most immediate result of the post-1973 economic recession was the disempowerment of political actors and governing parties that were in power at the time when the effects of the world recession first became apparent. At least initially, their disempowerment did not follow a consistent ideological pattern but instead seemed motivated by an antiincumbent and antiestablishment impulse. In Western Europe between 1974 and 1983, every political system with a tradition of major party competition experienced an alternation in power. In the major states in the northern half of Europe, including Great Britain, Germany, and Sweden (in the election of 1976), center-right governments replaced center-left, social democratic governments. In the United States and Canada, the victories of the Republican Party led by Ronald Reagan and the Progressive-Conservative Party of Brian Mulroney, respectively, represented a similar shift from center-left to center-right. In the Mediterranean states of Europe, however, including France, Italy (the election of 1983), Spain, Portugal, and Greece, the alternations of power resulted in an opposite shift, from center-right to center-left.

In the 1980s, the empowerment took a more consistent ideological direction, favoring neoliberal party programs and center-right political parties. In the Mediterranean European states where social democratic parties continued to hold political power, including France and Spain, the empowerment of more conservative elements occurred within the context of the factional infighting within those parties.

The most spectacular cases of disempowerment occurred in the postcommunist states of the former Soviet bloc and the states of the Third World. By 1989, communist party rule in Eastern Europe was ended and every former communist party leader was either retired from politics, in exile, or dead. This included Nicolae Ceausescu, the former Romanian strongman whose security forces were considered by some to be invincible, and the German communist party leader, Erich Honecker, who once led the state considered to be the showpiece of state socialism. By 1991, the communist regime had also collapsed in the Soviet Union. In less than a decade, the dynamics of empowerment and disempowerment in the postcommunist states produced transformations of revolutionary magnitude, which changed the world. The processes of empowerment and disempowerment did not end with the fall of the communist parties, but actually accelerated. By the early 1990s, all the political movements that had been in the forefront of the struggle against the communist regimes had either fragmented or disappeared entirely, and even a reformer of the magnitude of Mikhail Gorbachev had suffered an irreversible erosion of his power base.

The negative impact of the world recession was greatest in the states of the Third World. Protectionist measures by the advanced industrial states reduced Third World exports and increased unemployment and economic misery. In addition, in the wake of OPEC oil price increases, many Third World states greatly expanded their borrowing on foreign markets. This ultimately resulted in runaway domestic inflation and the default on foreign debt payments, which provoked a major crisis in the international economic system. With few exceptions, these conditions produced the disempowerment of almost the entire generation of political leaders who had achieved independence from colonizing states, as well as the defeat of military governments, such as those in Latin America, that had come to power in the first two decades of the Cold War. At the same time, parties and leaders with economic views that were more sympathetic to foreign investment and market-based models of economic development were empowered.

Empowerment and Disempowerment of Political Institutions

The rapidly changing economic and social context also impacted political institutions. In the states of the West, the sudden exposure to "hard times" convinced the electorates of many states that the scope of government intervention in the economy had become too great and the welfare state, too expensive. As a result, every Western state experienced a reduction in the size of the government bureaucracy, ranging from moderate "pruning" in West Germany and Sweden to privatization on a large scale in the United Kingdom. The civil service workforces in every state were also reduced. In addition to the reduction in social service and regulatory agencies, national-level, tripartite institutions (composed of organized business, organized labor, and government) also experienced various degrees of disempowerment.[30] In the earlier postwar period, these institutions had been considered essential for the mediation of labor disputes, but after 1973, market solutions were preferred by the new center-right governments. In contrast to the general trend of reducing social services, several Western states, most notably the United States and Great Britain, significantly expanded the capabilities of their police and military agencies.

In the postcommunist states, the abandonment of state socialism meant, at a practical level, the disempowerment of the extensive network of communist party organs and structures of the state bureaucracy, which had previously controlled almost every area of life. The disempowerment ranged from new restrictions and increased public scrutiny of government structures to the complete destruction of party structures after the fall of the communist regimes. Even such previously feared organizations as the Soviet State Security Committee (KGB) and military establishment suffered a disempowerment that would have been unthinkable a decade before. By 1991, the Warsaw Treaty Organization had been dissolved, the German Democratic Republic had become part of the reunified West German state, the communist parties of Eastern Europe had been reduced to a minority status, and the Soviet Union had been transformed from a superpower empire to a loose federation, the Commonwealth of Independent States, which experienced the secession of several of its subunits.

In the West, the postcommunist countries, and the states of the Third World, the groups and associations representing business interests achieved new levels of power and prestige. This empowerment was especially pronounced in the case of multinational corporations, financial institutions, and investment groups, which were seen as essential in maintaining international competitiveness. In the new environment, international organizations charged with coordinating the economic policies of capitalist states, such as the European Community (EC), the Group of Seven, and the International Monetary Fund, also achieved new levels of power and prestige.

Empowerment and Disempowerment of Political Ideas

The most important political change to result from the new economic and social context was the disempowerment of the political ideas that had dominated in the early postwar period. Political ideas are of crucial importance because they are the basis for political action and for judging the political performance of others. They also prescribe a particular role for government and a particular relationship between state and society. If political ideas become pervasive and are accepted by a large majority of the population, an effective consensus on basic public policy is formed. Recent studies of political economy have argued that a further development, the formation of an "active ideological hegemony," may result if the consensus extends to the leaders of all major political groups and is consistent with the nature of major public and private institutions.[31] (One source has called this consistency "the fundamental unity of the ideological, the political, and the economic").[32] Constant effort is required to maintain the condition of hegemony, and there are always rival hegemonic projects in the form of alternative ideologies and political-economic programs seeking to become dominant. In states in which the condition of hegemony has been temporarily achieved, political conflict between major groups will be limited and they will converge around and support similar public policies.

The disempowerment of political ideas after 1973 destroyed the prevailing hegemonies in both the states of the West and those of the former Soviet bloc. Technological change and the world recession created conditions in which it was possible for opponents to challenge and discredit the prevailing economic and political theories. In the West, the consensus had centered on the political and economic ideas of Keynesianism and social democracy. These had taken political form in the Keynesian welfare state. In the new environment, it was possible for critics to argue that the welfare state was too costly, that there was no longer a positive relationship between government spending and increases in productivity, and that excessive government spending had led to serious losses in international competitiveness.[33] The poor, minorities, women, and special needs groups were also depicted as overly reliant on welfare state programs and as a drain on the economy.

The political attack was successful in forcing some reduction of welfare state programs in every state. In several instances, the reductions were of major proportions, while political parties that had been identified with Keynesian programs lost political power. Public opinion surveys throughout the period demonstrated increasing public support for alternative political and economic theories, such as neoliberalism, monetarism, and supply-side economics. While these ideas gained sufficient support to achieve the breakdown of the postwar Keynesian consensus, they have not yet become sufficiently empowered to constitute the basis of a new conservative hegemony.[34] The result has been a prolonged period of intense political conflict, political disillusionment, and policy discontinuity.

In the Soviet bloc, the postwar ideological hegemony took the form of state socialism, whose principles prescribed centralized control over the economy by state planning agencies and communist party domination of the political system. In the area of foreign affairs, the consensus included support for efforts by the Soviet Union to establish an international economic system of socialist states to rival the liberal international order of the West. The state socialist model of development offered to the world an alternative model that was allegedly superior to the market system of the West. While important groups were denied access to meaningful political participation in the Soviet bloc, the consensus on state socialism extended to all elite segments within the communist party and the state bureaucracy.

As part of a rival international economic system, the Soviet bloc states were denied access to the new technologies and new concepts of business that were developed in the West after the 1960s. By the end of the 1970s, it had become clear to important leadership groups in the Soviet Union and Eastern Europe that the economic performance of the Soviet bloc was hopelessly behind that of the West. The general population was soon to learn the same truth from global radio and television. By the end of the 1980s, the concept of state socialism had been discredited and the state socialist hegemony had suffered a historic defeat.[35] Newly liberated political groups presented a bewildering array of political ideologies as alternatives, ranging from democracy and market capitalism to ultranationalism and a return to monarchy. As the Polish electoral results of 1991 seemed to indicate, none of the ideologies was capable of gaining even majority support.

The heterogeneity of the Third World states makes it impossible to speak of a single prevailing hegemony. Within most Third World countries, however, a state-specific form of nationalism, including a national plan for economic development, formed the basis of the national political consensus. By the 1980s, economic growth had either stopped or reversed to negative levels in most of the states of Latin America and Africa, and the subsequent Third World debt crisis reached proportions that threatened to produce international financial collapse.[36] In the wake of these repercussions from the world recession, many Third World models of development were discredited and disempowered. In addition, the decline of the power of the Soviet Union in world affairs after 1985 and the end of communist party rule in the former Soviet bloc served to deny legitimacy to those nationalist ideologies that were based on the Soviet model of development or Marxist-Leninist principles. The disempowerment of ideological hegemonies thus followed the pattern of the First and Second Worlds; the postwar ideological consensus was destroyed, but no new political beliefs were sufficiently attractive to take their place. As a recent study of the Third World pointed out, in the environment of the 1980s, governments were forced to undertake emergency measures to stabilize their economies, as well as to consider long-term structural changes in the economy, which would be necessary for future economic growth.[37] Since both these issues seriously impacted major political and economic groups, they produced prolonged and intense political conflicts.

THE CONDITION OF POLITICAL TURBULENCE

By any criteria, the twentieth century has been a period of great historical significance with frequent episodes of major economic and political change.[38] Each decade has witnessed political and economic developments that dramatically altered the lives of millions of people, many of which can reasonably be classified as major or revolutionary transformations. No serious political history of the world could be written without reference to such twentieth-century events as the achievement of universal suffrage, the "total war" conflicts of World Wars I and II, the Holocaust, the development of nuclear weapons, the onset of the Cold War, and the decolonization of the Third World.

There seems to be compelling evidence, however, that currently, at the end of the twentieth century, the pace and scope of political change have reached unprecedented levels. This evidence exists in three parts. First, unlike earlier periods when political change resulted from finite, single events such as wars or depressions, in the current period, the catalysts for change are the revolutionary technologies, which have transformed almost every area of life. Their effects are not limited to a particular time period or national population, and their impact will progressively extend to all levels of society on a global scale. Second, since the 1970s, each of the major economic and political relationships that defined political life in the early postwar period has undergone change. Fundamental transformations have occurred simultaneously in international economic relations, international security relations, the nature of group competition at the domestic political level, and the relationship between governments and their citizens.[39] Despite the cataclysmic nature of earlier events that served to stimulate change, none of these produced simultaneous change in all areas. Finally, the political changes at the end of the twentieth century involve the mass populations of states to an unprecedented degree. Revolutionary innovations in global communications technology and related areas have greatly enhanced the political skills of ordinary citizens, who are now capable of employing sophisticated comparative criteria in evaluating the performance of government and equipped to play new, more activist roles as members of political movements or other groups.

In addition to the broad scope of change, the pace of change also accelerated in the period after 1973. This was especially apparent in the rapid disempowerment of previously dominant political and economic ideas. In less than two decades, this disempowerment resulted in the collapse of communism in Eastern Europe and the Soviet Union, the breakup of the Soviet bloc, the end of the Cold War, the reunification of Germany, and sustained attacks against the Keynesian welfare state in the West. Each of these major events triggered myriad lesser changes within the affected nations, and it has become clear that efforts to solve one political problem, even if successful, often result in the creation of new, unanticipated problems, which may be even more difficult to resolve. For example, in the former Soviet Union, efforts to address the problems of technological backwardness and poor economic performance resulted in a crisis of political authority that undermined the state's very existence. New problems arose, such as redefining the relationship between the republics, controlling the state's nuclear arsenal, and dealing with secessionist demands, which could not have been anticipated by the reformers.

In a recent study of change in international politics, James Rosenau undertook an analysis of the contemporary period which employs the concept of turbulence.[40] This concept, which is borrowed from the disciplines of physics, chemical engineering, and organizational theory, seems especially useful in explaining the meaning and nature of the post-1973 period.[41] As defined by Rosenau, turbulence is a condition faced by political actors when the political environment in which they interact is characterized by both a high degree of complexity and a high degree of dynamism.[42] The complexity results from the large number of active political groups, as well as from the extensive interdependence that exists between them. The dynamism of the environment results from the great variability in the goals, methods, and organizational structures of the groups. Rosenau identified several characteristics that develop from the condition of turbulence:[43]

1. The political environment becomes less stable and less predictable, and there is a high degree of political uncertainty among political actors about the motivations and behavior of other groups.

2. There is a tendency for the major "interconnections" or relationships between actors, such as diplomatic relations or international economic ties, to fluctuate frequently and rapidly.

3. Political groups are under great pressure to adapt to the fluctuating relationships, and a great deal of intellectual and sociopolitical energy is required for bargaining, compromising, and mobilizing.

4. Given the fluctuating relationships, political behavior often takes the form of quick responses, temporary coalitions, or policy reversals.

5. The degree of interdependence between actors is so great "as to enable any event to give rise to a restless commotion, which reverberates in fast-paced and unexpected ways throughout the environment."[44]

The characteristics of turbulence identified by Rosenau have certainly been present in both the domestic and international political environments since the 1970s. The proliferation of political movements has increased the complexity of both environments, while the interdependence between actors at the international level has increased with the new communications technologies and the onset of global capitalism. In addition, each of the six major postwar political relationships identified in this chapter has undergone fundamental change. Widespread uncertainty and anxiety have also become a part of political life in every state. Governments and ordinary citizens alike are threatened by the loss of competitiveness in the world economy, protectionist practices by other states, the deterioration of the global environment, terrorism, and hundreds of other problems. We began this chapter by noting that political actors benefit from the conflicts in society by utilizing them to convince their fellow citizens that a new political agenda and leadership are needed to resolve the conflicts in an acceptable manner. Anxiety can serve the same purpose; that is, it can also be used to convince those seeking relief that new political ideas and leaders are needed. The concept of turbulence, therefore, goes a long way toward explaining the many alternations of power and regime changes that have occurred since the 1970s.

The concept of turbulence is useful in one final respect—explaining why so many of the new leaders to come to power since the 1970s have failed to achieve their policy objectives or even to remain in power. The condition of turbulence does not end with one election, a new policy approach, or even a change of regime. Generally, the conditions of turbulence that undermined the previous government continue to operate on subsequent leadership groups, which must develop and implement policies and seek to build political support in the same environment of complexity, dynamism, interdependence, relational fluidity, and anxiety. Regardless of nationality or state-specific advantages and disadvantages, the generation of political leaders that came to power after the 1970s faced the same difficult prospect—that of governing through turbulence.

NOTES

1. Michael Oksenberg and Bruce Dickson, "The Origins, Processes, and Outcomes of Great Political Reform: A Framework of Analysis," in Dankwart A. Rustow and Kenneth Paul Erickson, eds., *Comparative Political Perspectives* (New York: Harper Collins Publishers, 1991), pp. 235–261.

2. Ibid., p. 238.

3. Several of these works do provide excellent material on their subjects. See, for example, the excellent biography of Margaret Thatcher by Hugo Young, *The Iron Lady: A Biography of Margaret Thatcher* (New York: The Noonday Press, 1989).

4. Everett Carll Ladd, Jr., *American Political Parties: Social Change and Political Response* (New York: W. W. Norton & Company, 1970), p. 2.

5. Ibid.

6. For a discussion of adjustment strategies in the Third World, see Joan M. Nelson, ed., *Economic Crisis and Policy Choice: The Politics of Adjustment in the Third World* (Princeton, NJ: Princeton University Press, 1990).

7. Ladd, p. 2.

8. Ibid., chapters 3–6.

9. Robert A. Isaak, *European Politics: Political Economy and Policy Making in Western Democracies* (New York: St. Martin's Press, 1980), pp. 2–9.

10. For a theoretical discussion of economic factors and perceived self-interest in electoral decisions, see James E. Alt and K. Alec Chrystal, *Political Economics* (Los Angeles: University of California Press, 1983).

11. For an excellent discussion of the impact of technology, see James N. Rosenau, *Turbulence in World Politics: A Theory of Change and Continuity* (Princeton, NJ: Princeton University Press, 1990).

12. Maurice Estabrooks, *Programmed Capitalism: A Computer-Mediated Global Society* (New York: M. E. Sharpe, 1988), p. 3.

13. Carver Mead, cited in Rosenau, p. 99.

14. Arthur Schlesinger, Jr., cited in Rosenau, p. 99.

15. Ibid., p. 338.

16. W. W. Rostow, "Eastern Europe and the Soviet Union: A Technological Time Warp," in Daniel Chirot, ed., *The Crisis of Leninism and the Decline of the Left: The Revolutions of 1989* (Seattle: University of Washington Press, 1991), pp. 60–61.

17. Rosenau, p. 334.

18. For a discussion of this point, see David Harvey, *The Condition of Postmodernity: An Enquiry into the Origins of Cultural Change* (Cambridge, MA: Basil Blackwell, 1989), pp. 226–259.

19. For a discussion of this scheme, see Henck Overbeek, *Global Capitalism and National Decline: The Thatcher Decade in Perspective* (Boston: Unwin Hyman, 1990), pp. 1–34.

20. Alexander King and Bertrand Schneider, *The First Global Revolution: A Report by the Council of the Club of Rome* (New York: Pantheon Books, 1991), p. xxiii.

21. Overbeek, p. 4.

22. Ibid, pp. 4–5.

23. For an overview of these developments, see R. J. Johnston and P. J. Taylor, eds., *A World in Crisis? Geographical Perspectives* (Cambridge, MA: Basil Blackwell, 1989), pp. 1–15, 16–78.

24. See Johnston and Taylor; Arthur MacEwan and William K. Tabb, eds., *Instability and Change in the World Economy* (New York: Monthly Review Press, 1989); Daniel Yergin and Martin Hillenbrand, eds., *Global Insecurity: A Strategy for Energy and Economic Renewal* (Boston: Houghton Mifflin Company, 1982); and Peter Gourevitch, *Politics in Hard Times: Comparative Responses to International Economic Crises* (Ithaca, NY: Cornell University Press, 1986).

25. Johnston and Taylor, p. 4.

26. For a discussion of electoral trends in the states of the West, see Heinz Eulau and Michael S. Lewis-Beck, eds., *Economic Conditions and Electoral Outcomes: The United States and Western Europe* (New York: Agathon Press, 1985).

27. See Russell J. Dalton, Scott C. Flanagan, and Paul Allen Beck, eds., *Electoral Change in Advanced Industrial Democracies: Realignment or Dealignment?* (Princeton, NJ: Princeton University Press, 1984).

28. See David Jaffee, *Levels of Socio-economic Development Theory* (Westport, CT: Praeger, 1990).

29. Peter J. Katzenstein, ed., *Industry and Politics in West Germany: Toward the Third Republic* (Ithaca, NY: Cornell University Press, 1989), p. 329.

30. For a discussion of the structure and function of such organizations, see Jurg Steiner, *European Democracies* (New York: Longman, 1986), pp. 219–229.

31. For a discussion of hegemony in postwar British politics, see Colin Leys, *Politics in Britain: From Labourism to Thatcherism* (New York: Verso, 1983), pp. 27, 51–57.

32. Overbeek, p. 28.

33. For an excellent analysis of this attitudinal change in the OECD states, see Theodore Geiger, *The Future of the International System: The United States and the World Political Economy* (Boston: Unwin Hyman, 1988), pp. 40–60.

34. For an excellent case study of British politics in this regard, see Andrew Gamble, *The Free Economy and the Strong State: The Politics of Thatcherism* (Durham, NC: Duke University Press, 1988), pp. 174–231.

35. For an excellent discussion, see Bartlomiej Kaminski, *The Collapse of State Socialism: The Case of Poland* (Princeton, NJ: Princeton University Press, 1991), pp. 3–59.

36. Nelson, p. 3.

37. Ibid., pp. 3–32.

38. The use of the concept of political turbulence is based on the work of Rosenau, especially pp. 7–8, 26–27, 53–60, 104–112.

39. The underlying dynamics of these and other changes are discussed in depth in Rosenau.

40. Ibid., chapters 1–4.

41. Ibid., p. 54.

42. Ibid., pp. 7–10, 60–64.

43. Ibid., pp. 7–11.

44. Ibid., p. 9.

──── **two** ────────────────────────────────

The New Political Environment: Six Changed Relationships

Political life always involves relationships between people, usually in large groups, such as political movements or nation-states. The political changes that have occurred since 1970 can best be understood by reference to the transformations that have taken place in six basic relationships. Three of the relationships are international, while the other three involve domestic political-economic patterns. Two of the relationships involve specific issues, the Cold War and the breakdown of the Bretton Woods system, while the other four involve general patterns that are applicable to all international actors or occur in most of the political systems of the world. The six relationships that have been identified and simplified here for analytical purposes actually involve extremely complex patterns of behavior, and the actual effect of each on political actors is reinforced and magnified by the cumulative effect of all six. It was the changes in these six basic relationships that were the immediate catalysts for domestic agenda change in many of the world's political systems and provided a new group of political leaders with the opportunity to come to power.

THE NATURE OF POLITICAL RELATIONSHIPS

Before discussing the transformations that have occurred in each of the six postwar relationships, it is useful to consider the general nature of political relationships and the types of changes to which they are subject. In the sense that we use the term here, a political relationship is a complex association or connection between two or more political actors that persists for a considerable period of time. The relationship actually consists of a continual series of transactions, or action-reaction sequences, between the actors. Over a period of time, the transactions become patterned and predictable. The actors tend to learn and accept loosely defined roles, which results in a degree of predictability in the way they interact with one another. The more precisely the roles are defined and the more clearly they are understood by all the actors involved, the more settled and predictable the relationship becomes. Political relationships frequently include *de facto* or unofficial rules of conduct, which develop from role expectations. Since the relationships under discussion are either voluntary, as in the case of actors in the global marketplace, or international, as in the case of U.S.-Soviet relations during the Cold War, the rules are not based on legal statutes or constitutional prescriptions but rather are derived from practice and custom. The existence of even very general rules contributes to the stability and predictability of a relationship.

The dynamics of a political relationship can best be understood by reference to one of the six cases, the Cold War relationship between the United States and the Soviet Union. The basic nature of that relationship developed in the final two years of World War II and the early postwar period. During that time, the relationship changed from one of reluctant allies fighting a common enemy to one of competition for global power and influence and came to include competitive interactions in political, economic, military, and ideological areas. By 1948, both superpowers had developed broad policies which, in a general sense, defined the roles they would assume in the conflict. For example, the American policy was called containment, and it prescribed for the United States a role of resisting the initiatives of the Soviet Union through the application of a wide variety of countermeasures. Over time, through their actions and communications, both sides further elaborated the roles they would play; their competition would be intense and international in scope, but neither superpower was willing to engage in direct military confrontation with the other. This emphasis on successful crisis management was again given expression in foreign policy pronouncements such as the Soviet doctrine of "peaceful coexistence," which was based on a realistic assessment of the likely outcome of a nuclear war. Thus, the Cold War relationship came to involve *de facto* rules, modified over time, which successfully avoided war between the superpowers and introduced an element of predictability and stability into a potentially dangerous relationship. It is important to realize that both the roles and rules that were developed were observed by successive individual leaders, administrations, and even generations of elites to the point where a patterned relationship developed that we know as the Cold War.

By their nature, political relationships are constantly undergoing change. Every sequence of action and reaction produces some new information about one's adversary or introduces a new element that transforms the relationship, if only in a marginal way. In addition, political relationships of the variety under discussion involve large groups, ranging from interest organizations with hundreds of members to the governments of modern nation-states, which involve huge bureaucracies. Even when the roles and rules are fairly well defined, it is unlikely that all participants will perceive and interpret a sequence of action and reaction in an identical way. Consequently, the group pluralism that characterizes such relationships serves as an agent of change. The type of change that results from group pluralism is usually small-scale or incremental. More significant changes result from other factors, such as the deliberate decision of an actor to alter his or her role to some degree in the expectation that this will produce a more favorable position in the relationship and maximize opportunities for the achievement of his or her objectives. In this work, such transformations will be referred to as interim changes to emphasize that they establish a temporary or provisional stage in the relationship, which lasts until the next round of interim changes. Interim changes commonly take the form of major policy shifts or the adoption of new means for the achievement of objectives.

The most profound and important change is breakpoint or historic change, which completely transforms the fundamental nature of a relationship or terminates it altogether. Breakpoint change may result from the cumulative effect over time of a series of interim changes, from the sudden introduction of some new element in the general political environment of which the relationship is a part, or from sudden changes in the capabilities or resources of one or more of the actors.[1] Referring once again to U.S.-Soviet relations, the Cold War relationship began when the surrender of Germany and Japan created huge power vacuums in Europe and Asia, which fundamentally changed the international political environment and the structure of international power. The Cold War ended in the period between 1985 and 1991, when breakpoint change resulted from both the mutual recognition of the decline of Soviet capabilities and the collapse of communism in the Soviet Union and Eastern Europe.

Unlike incremental change, which is always present, or interim change, which occurs with some frequency, breakpoint change in major political relationships is rare and constitutes a historically significant development. Breakpoint change can be identified only in retrospect, after it has occurred, because it must constitute a lasting, fundamental change in the relationship, which will not be apparent for some time. It must be remembered that the concept of breakpoint change is an artificial tool for analysis; it is impossible to delineate any single moment, day, or event on which a relationship permanently changed, but it is possible to identify several critical years in which qualitative transformations occurred.

In the last twenty-five years, the world experienced breakpoint change in six important political and political-economic relationships that had defined and structured the postwar world. The scope of change was without historical precedent in this century. Moreover, it led to extensive speculation that these changes might be the harbingers of even more fundamental transformations, and possibly even the end of the nation-state era. The cumulative changes are best understood as the breakdown and abandonment of roles and rules that had developed for most of the century but had been most clearly defined in the period from 1945 through 1970. The onset of breakpoint change in all six areas was a major factor in the development of the political environment of turbulence of the 1970s. Since the policies and programs of the leaders of our study were developed in response to changes in these six relationships, the breakdown or transformation of each must be considered in some detail.

THE END OF THE COLD WAR

The most important national security issue of the post–World War II period was the competitive relationship between the United States and the Soviet Union, which became known as the Cold War. The Cold War was a multidimensional conflict involving military, diplomatic, economic, and ideological competition. It developed from the efforts by the United States and the Soviet Union to exploit the geopolitical power vacuums created by World War II and to shape the postwar world in ways compatible with their national values and political and economic interests.[2] The United States sought the preservation of a world of independent nation-states in which conflicts would be peacefully resolved, possibly through the mediation of regional or international organizations.[3] It also sought the creation of a liberal international economic order in which goods, ideas, and capital could move with a minimum of restrictions between countries. Such a system was in the national interest of the United States, which in 1945 was the world's largest military and economic power.

For its part, the Soviet Union sought an international system of socialist states with centralized nonmarket economies and domestic political systems controlled by national communist parties.[4] As the strongest communist state with the oldest communist party, the Soviet Union would be in a position to exercise political control over such states and coordinate their defense policies in ways compatible with Soviet national interest.[5] Although the center of the Cold War was always Eastern and Central Europe (particularly Poland and the two Germanys), the competition ultimately spread to most parts of the world.

The Cold War created an international system that was dominated by two rival blocs, or hegemonies. In each hegemony, the superpower performed the functions of a hegemon, or dominant member, expending sufficient resources and will to maintain the cohesiveness of the bloc.[6] The United States maintained the integration of its hegemony through political influence and by bearing a disproportionately large share of the costs to other members of belonging to the alliance.[7] American foreign aid always exceeded the costs to other countries of belonging to American-sponsored military alliances or supporting the United States in other ways. The Soviet Union also possessed considerable political influence after World War II, which it utilized to maintain its hegemony, but it also employed force. Each of the hegemonies developed formal military alliances (i.e., the North Atlantic Treaty Organization and the Warsaw Treaty Organization) and regional economic organizations (the European Community and the Council of Mutual Economic Assistance) which, as rival institutions, were presented to the rest of the world as alternative systems for economic development.

The most intense period of Cold War hostility occurred in the late 1940s and 1950s, although the single most dangerous event was the Cuban Missile Crisis of October, 1962. Fortunately, throughout the Cold War, the superpowers practiced successful crisis management and direct military confrontation between them was avoided. In several periods, including 1955, 1959, 1967, 1972–1975, and the late 1980s, a marked relaxation of tensions occurred.[8] From 1964 through 1967, the French undertook foreign policy initiatives to improve relations with the Soviet bloc, followed by similar, and more important, initiatives by the German Federal Republic between 1969 and 1970, which included direct negotiations between the rival German governments. This so-called European phase of detente was followed by a series of direct initiatives by the Soviet Union and the United States between 1972 and 1976, which produced several important results, including the first Strategic Arms Limitation Treaty (SALT I). This superpower stage of detente also proved only temporary, and a new period of intensified competition began in the late 1970s and lasted until 1985. It is generally agreed that the Cold War ended in 1989–1990 when the fall of the Berlin Wall, German reunification within the context of the democratic political structures of the Federal Republic of Germany, and German membership in the North Atlantic Treaty Organization (NATO) transformed U.S.-Soviet relations.

Beginning in the 1940s and early 1950s, the Cold War produced a series of political patterns and relationships which, although they began to erode in the 1960s, were nonetheless of great significance. These patterns included political leadership of each bloc by the superpower hegemon; foreign, defense, and economic policy coordination within each bloc; an arms race between the superpowers, with accompanying high levels of defense spending; and an ideological approach to international politics, which included mistrust and hostility toward states claiming a nonaligned or neutral status.[9] The Cold War also legitimated a domestic political order in the Soviet bloc, which excluded participation in government by noncommunist political groups, while in several of the European states of the Western Alliance, left-wing political groups were also marginalized and denied any meaningful role in government.

The Cold War ultimately produced political tensions within each bloc as well as between the two, as the superpowers struggled to maintain their leadership and their allies sought increased independence in economic and diplomatic areas. The end of the Cold War denied any justification for maintaining the earlier relationships, which were rapidly terminated. The end of the Cold War also removed foreign policy constraints on the superpowers and their allies in both blocs and presented all parties with new opportunities for independent action. The demise of the Warsaw Treaty Organization, the application of several Eastern European states for membership in Western-sponsored economic and military organizations, and the American effort to forge a "New World Order" testify to the extent of change. Determining the state's place in this new world order became the most important issue in the foreign policy agenda of most countries.

THE BREAKDOWN OF THE BRETTON WOODS SYSTEM

The promotion of a liberal international economic order was a top policy priority of the American and British governments during and after World War II. This position was based on the assumption that international economic development and postwar reconstruction could best be achieved through the creation of a world market governed by economic logic, such as the laws of supply and demand, and not by the political logic of economic nationalism.[10] The establishment of a liberal international economic order required the progressive removal of restrictions on trade, the movement of capital, and other forms of economic intercourse, as well as the fostering of economic interdependence between states. Of course, such a system was in the interests of both Britain and the United States, especially the latter. Because of the competitive advantage the United States enjoyed at the end of World War II, America's decision makers correctly anticipated that its relative gains would exceed those of any other state.[11] Even before World War II ended, in July 1944, the United States and Great Britain sponsored a conference at Bretton Woods, New Hampshire, to establish the foundation of a liberal economic order. The meeting was attended by the representatives of forty-four nations and led to the creation of the International Bank for Reconstruction and Development (IBRD, or World Bank) and the International Monetary Fund (IMF).

Throughout the 1940s, the 1950s, and most of the 1960s, the United States used its vast and disproportionate share of the world's wealth to successfully promote a trend toward the liberalization of trade and increased world economic interdependence.[12] The American dollar provided a stable medium of exchange with other currencies pegged to it at fixed rates. The World Bank provided loans for development to countries that agreed to abide by the unofficial rules created at Bretton Woods. In addition, other organizations, including the General Agreement on Tariffs and Trade (GATT), with its General System of Preferences (1971), and the institutions of the European Community contributed to the trend toward liberalization. Most important, throughout this period the United States used the lure of its domestic market to promote the Bretton Woods regime. Countries that agreed to keep their economies open to the rest of the world were provided with the greatest of all rewards—access for their products to American consumers, who comprised the most affluent economic group in the world. In economic terms, the United States served as the economic hegemon of the Western alliance by providing its members with economic benefits that exceeded the costs to them of participating in the liberal economic system. Of course, the states of the Soviet bloc remained outside the system, and many Third World states were only marginally involved.

Beginning in the late 1960s and escalating sharply after the mid-1970s, a countertrend developed in the world economy toward protectionism and economic nationalism. This trend was the result of a series of transformations in the world economy, combined with certain cultural and political changes in the major states of the West. The oil price shocks and subsequent recessions of 1973–1975 and 1979–1981 also served as immediate catalysts for the shift from liberal economics to protectionism. As national political leaders were confronted with increased unemployment, business failures, and the miseries of inflation, they sought economic relief for their citizens through protectionist measures designed to lessen competition from foreign goods and services produced abroad.

In pursuit of protectionist goals, states resorted to a wide variety of exclusionary devices, known as nontariff barriers. These included "voluntary" quotas, procurement preferences, product quality standards, and safety and environmental requirements. Collectively, these devices contributed to the trend of protectionist economic behavior known as neomercantilism, in which a nation's economic activity is increasingly determined by government decisions made according to national political criteria (e.g., to protect jobs or promote national security) rather than by normal economic criteria.[13] After 1970, the erosion of America's economic position had reached a point where its economic resources, political influence, and national will were no longer equal to either the task of promoting economic liberalization or that of preventing the spread of neomercantilist behavior.

In the current political environment of growing neomercantilism, protecting the state's interests in the new world economy is the major preoccupation of all national political leaders. Each of the leaders studied in this volume developed a new economic program or strategy for coping with the changed international economic context. Many leaders have sought to identify a point of maximum national benefit in which selected protectionist measures are employed against foreign competitors while at the same time, the demand is made that other states keep their economies open to their own country's exports and economic penetration. Such a position is often referred to as *free-riding*.[14]

THE ONSET OF GLOBAL CAPITALISM

Beginning in the late 1960s, a trend developed in the world economy toward the increasing internationalization of economic activity. This trend, which some have called the "onset of global capitalism," involved the spatial or geographic movement and redeployment of capital, manufacturing facilities, global firms, and financial institutions between different states and regions.[15] Global capitalism was the result of a number of factors, but two developments were especially important. First, developments in transportation and telecommunications technology have served to shrink geographic distances and compress time.[16] It is now feasible for international conglomerates to move parts and raw materials to production facilities anywhere in the world in order to take advantage of favorable local conditions, such as low labor costs and minimal government regulation of business. Second, the general economic slowdown and periods of recession that followed the OPEC oil price increases of 1973–1975 and continued in the 1980s acted as catalysts for the extension of global capitalism. The desire of corporations and financial institutions to protect their profit margins during the slowdown provided a powerful incentive to shift investment capital and operations to those states, and those regions within states, that promised the highest return on investments.

By the 1980s, it was clear that the dynamics of global capitalism had produced a fundamental restructuring of the world economy. Many centers of traditional manufacturing moved first from North America to the states of Western Europe or Japan and then to the Newly Industrializing Countries (NICs) of Asia, Singapore, South Korea, and Taiwan. The label of Newly Industrializing Country was subsequently extended to other Third World states in both Asia and Latin America as the dispersal of manufacturing facilities continued throughout the decades of the 1970s and 1980s. By the early 1980s, new production technologies made it possible to manufacture even high-technology items like sophisticated electronic devices and semiconductors almost anywhere in the world. The movement of these industries to the NICs followed the path taken earlier by textile, steel, and shipbuilding firms. By the 1980s, the extent of industrialization of the NICs was such that these states had left the periphery of the world economy, which now consisted of those Third World states that were primarily suppliers of natural resources.

While global capitalism produced new economic opportunities for some actors and may have represented a newly invigorated form of international capitalism, it also brought widespread economic uncertainty and distress to many older industrial regions.[17] For such regions in North America and the advanced industrial states of Western Europe, the legacy of the 1980s was one of deindustrialization, unemployment, and business failure by small firms that had been dependent on bigger firms that had moved on. Affected communities and the people within them were often left without any real prospects for economic recovery. Even for the firms, regions, and states that had prospered in the decades of the 1970s and 1980s, the new economic reality was clear: new production technologies or changes in the local political economy could lead to economic decline as rapidly as they had brought temporary economic well-being.

The onset of global capitalism had profound effects for the domestic politics of the advanced industrial states of the West, many states of the Third World, and even the postcommunist states of Eastern Europe. In the West, the sudden need to demonstrate the economic competitiveness of the state led governments to reduce regulations on business, privatize previously state-owned industries, lower taxes, and adopt other supply-side policies. The state came to be considered first and foremost as an economic unit, and the measure of national power increasingly became the state's success in the international economy. In addition, the political relationship between business, labor, and government was radically altered.[18] The new international division of labor created by the relocation of financial capital and business firms greatly weakened the position of national unions in collective bargaining. Further, government leaders of all political persuasions became acutely aware of the extent to which their political fortunes could be affected by private business decisions. Social democratic parties and candidates were harmed politically by claims that their policies would weaken the competitive position of the state and result in the movement of business to more favorable environments.

In the NICs and some Third World states, the rapid but uneven economic development produced severe social and political strains. Government policies to promote economic freedom and modernization led to demands for political change and increased democracy. In the postcommunist states, several of the successor governments to the communist regimes attempted to develop policies to achieve the transition from a centralized, nonmarket economy to a market-oriented one. They also sought to promote the integration of their economies into the world of global capitalism, a process that provoked serious economic, social and political tensions.

THE FALL OF THE POSTWAR ECONOMIC ARRANGEMENTS

In the decade following the end of World War II, complex arrangements were developed in the states of the Western alliance and Soviet bloc that determined the relationship between domestic political and economic actors well into the 1970s. These arrangements typically consisted of a national consensus in support of specific economic and political goals, a process for reaching decisions about the national economy, and interest groups and political parties that served as vehicles for converting the national consensus into public policy. In the advanced industrial states of the West, this arrangement, which was sometimes called the *postwar settlement,* took the form of the welfare state.[19] Such welfare state arrangements, including the New Deal order in the United States, the "collectivist polity" in Great Britain, and the social market economy in the Federal Republic of Germany, existed in some form throughout North America and in every major state of western and northern Europe.[20] The foundation of the welfare state was a compromise between organized labor and business interests in which labor abandoned its most radical demand, the nationalization (state ownership) of major industries, in exchange for business support for the goal of full employment and the creation of social programs to benefit lower- and middle-income groups.[21] The benefits provided by the social programs were continually expanded to include, not only protection against the hazards of life, such as unemployment, physical disability, and old age, but also measures that made modest contributions to social mobility, including regular pay increases, housing subsidies, and enhanced educational opportunities.

The government also participated in the postwar settlement as the administrator of the programs of the welfare state and guarantor of the terms of the arrangement. In addition to the expansion of social programs to new areas and population groups, governments also employed Keynesian economic techniques, including economic planning and the manipulation of government spending (fiscal policy), to preserve mass economic well-being.[22] In Europe, governments also undertook state ownership of some weak-performing business enterprises in order to preserve jobs and guarantee the availability of products and services. In these mixed economies, however, private enterprises always outnumbered those owned by the state and the disproportionate size of the private sector guaranteed that the basic characteristics of the capitalist economy were preserved.

It is difficult to exaggerate the significance of the postwar settlement in the West. The compromise between the interests of capital and labor on which the welfare state was based produced a period of social peace that was unprecedented in the era since industrialization. In each state, an overwhelming majoritarian consensus supported the concept of the welfare state and competing political and economic interests were accommodated through collective bargaining or joint consultation between government, business, and labor. Conflicts over the precise scope and goals of government programs were decided in open electoral competitions in which a clear majority usually prevailed.[23] Equally important, the development of the welfare state corresponded to a period of unprecedented economic growth and well-being. Beginning in the late 1940s, several European states averaged growth rates of 4.5 to 6 percent per year for more than two decades, and even in states with substantially lower growth, such as the United Kingdom, the expansion of the economy was sufficient to fund extensive social programs and benefits. Welfare state programs, in turn, contributed to productivity and growth by providing workers with better nutrition, access to health care, enhanced job skills, and higher levels of education.

The economic slowdown of the mid-1970s brought about the fall of the postwar settlement.[24] In this environment of decreasing profits and increasing competition, critics attacked the levels of taxation that were required to fund the welfare state. Neoliberals and supply-side economists argued that social programs no longer contributed to increased productivity but rather weakened the competitive position of the state in the world economy. In the most important Western states, the economic and political theories on which the welfare state rested were successfully challenged at both an intellectual and an electoral level. In states where opponents of the welfare state gained control of the government, policies were implemented to reduce or completely dismantle major welfare state programs. By the mid-1980s, both the postwar settlement and the political consensus on which it was based had collapsed. Political competition in the 1980s was bitter and intense, and no political vision for the future seemed capable of galvanizing the support of a majority of the population in any country.

Postcommunist States of the Former Soviet Bloc

In the states of the former Soviet bloc, the postwar economic arrangement was based on the Stalinist development model, which emerged initially from the Soviet Union in the 1920s and 1930s. The arrangement, which is most often referred to as state socialism, had the following main features: a monopoly on political power by communist party and state bureaucratic elites; extensive state ownership of natural resources and the means of production; central planning of the economy under the direction of a set of dominant national and regional ministries; a policy bias toward heavy industry and large-scale enterprises; and state ownership or collectivization of a large portion of the agricultural sector.[25] As would be expected, significant differences existed in the forms the arrangement took from country to country and within individual states at different periods of time. In the Soviet Union, policy discontinuities intensified from the late 1950s on as communist party elites sought to cope, first, with the military and economic competition from the West and, later, with the increasingly unsatisfactory performance of the economy. While there was no postwar settlement based on a voluntary consensus of the population, by the time of Leonid Brezhnev's leadership of the Communist Party of the Soviet Union (1964–1982), institutional manipulation and economic policy concessions to important segments of the population had assumed an established and predictable pattern.[26]

State socialism was justified domestically within the Soviet bloc as the ideal political-economic order. To the outside world, it was presented as a scientific scheme for economic development that was superior to the market model of the West. According to communist theorists, under state socialism, important economic decisions about the allocation of national resources and manpower, which products to produce, pricing, wages, and output norms for workers were made by state planners on the basis of rational choice rather than by the chaotic dynamics of the marketplace.[27] Communist theorists argued that development under state socialism would avoid the human suffering and high social costs that had accompanied the industrial revolution in the West. They also sought to bolster their case by pointing out that no other state had matched the speed with which the Soviet Union had industrialized and that only Japan had surpassed its long-term growth record.[28] In the period immediately following World War II, the Soviet Union sought to sponsor an international economic system of socialist states to rival the Bretton Woods system of the West.

From the 1960s on, the economic performance of the states of the Soviet bloc declined rapidly and the case for the superiority of state socialism became increasingly less viable. In the Soviet Union, the average annual real rate of growth dropped from 5.1 percent per year in the 1960s to 3.7 percent in the 1970s and 2.2 percent in the first half of the 1980s.[29] The rate continued to drop after that, falling to negative levels by 1989. Throughout the 1970s and 1980s, the existence of major economic problems became increasingly obvious, including the low quality of manufactured goods, obsolete technologies, gross deficiencies in the quality of services, supply-demand imbalances, low worker productivity and morale, and excess demand for investment goods.[30] Equally important from the perspective of the Soviet Union was the link between the economic system and national security.[31] Excluded from the system of global capitalism in the West and the new technologies it had spawned, the Soviet Union could no longer hope to compete economically or militarily with its chief rival, the United States.

The call for *perestroika,* or restructuring, was initially a call for limited structural reform of the state socialist system in the USSR, but the reform movement soon gave way to the demand for an end to both state socialism and Communist Party political rule. This development has been aptly summarized as follows:

> By rejecting a market environment, state socialism put the full burden of economic management on the party-state. As a result, any revealed conflict related to dissatisfaction with economic performance becomes a direct challenge to the state and consequently to the political order.[32]

When the populations of Eastern Europe and the Soviet Union lost faith in the ability of the party-state to manage the economy, they also lost faith in its ability to govern other areas of life.

PROLIFERATION OF MASS POLITICAL MOVEMENTS

In the last three decades of the twentieth century, the established political order has come under attack from an additional source—mass political movements.[33] Mass political movements are not new. Since the French Revolution of 1789, they have played an important political role in many parts of the world. In the states of the West, organized labor, suffragettes, and civil rights groups were instrumental in bringing about change of a fundamental nature. It was also a revolutionary movement, the Bolshevik faction, that was responsible for the establishment of the first communist regime in Russia. In addition, religious movements, ethnic groups, and national liberation fronts have helped to shape the destiny of many Third World states. The importance of mass movements in the late twentieth century comes, not from the fact that they are new, but because they represent a new, worldwide range of political, economic, and social interests.[34] Their current importance is also a result of their large numbers and the fact that they are active in every type of regime and every geographic area of the world.

Mass movements are politically active groups that are not organized as conventional political parties or economic interest groups.[35] Contemporary examples include such diverse organizations as the pro-democracy movement in China, environmentalists or "Greens" in Western Europe, Tamil separatists in Sri Lanka, and single-issue political groups in the United States concerned about, for example, high taxes or the legality of abortion. The diversity of mass movements has led to a number of conflicting theories about their causes and consequences, and especially about whether they ultimately represent a dynamic form of democracy that will promote political stability or a force that will erode loyalty to the state and its institutions.[36] It may well be that the effect of mass movements is influenced by such factors as the prevailing political culture or regime type and will consequently differ from state to state. The numerical proliferation of mass movements is the result of two factors: (1) long-term cultural shifts that have produced a popular concern for new, noneconomic issues (e.g., environmental protection) and (2) the revolution in communications technology, which provides ordinary citizens with access to scientific data and makes possible media reports publicizing the actions of mass movements around the world.

For contemporary political leaders, mass movements represent a serious political challenge and introduce a new element into domestic politics, as they compete for financial resources and political support with political parties, interest groups, and even government organizations. The size of the antinuclear movement in Western Europe and the intensity of the antiabortion campaign in the United States testify to the organizational efficacy of political movements in the West. The financial resources, political skills, and hours of political activism expended in such efforts are denied to the major political parties and economic interest groups that previously dominated the political process. In addition, mass movements raise new issues, such as the morality of abortion, the status of women, and the safety of nuclear energy, which concern "collective goods" relevant to the whole of society and not just issues of economic self-interest.[37] Not only do these issues cut across party lines and draw off significant levels of support, but they also raise political issues of a highly charged and emotional nature, which are frequently treated by participants as moral struggles. Such conflicts are less susceptible to compromise and more difficult to resolve than those involving traditional economic issues. Some Western mass movements also attack the very foundations of Western political power—bureaucracy, hierarchy, centralization, and elitism.[38] Both in theory and through their own organization, they seek to demonstrate the superiority of a more democratic and decentralized style of political organization.

The effect of mass movements on the established political order has been even greater in the postcommunist states of Europe and in some countries of the Third World. In the 1980s, mass movements in Eastern Europe decisively demonstrated the ability of such organizations to undertake successful antigovernment activity. In Poland in the 1980s, Solidarity, a mass movement disguised as a union, first succeeded in paralyzing the economy and ultimately managed to overcome decades of antipolitical education and demonstrate the bankruptcy of Polish state socialism.[39] Similarly, mass movements were instrumental in the overturning of communist rule in Czechoslovakia and the German Democratic Republic. In the Soviet Union, the period after 1985 produced several new forms of political participation that shaped that state's transition to postcommunism. These included so-called informal groups, which introduced new issues to the political agenda; secessionist movements in the Baltic states, which achieved independence for those regions; and the masses that rallied to the support of Boris Yeltsin and Mikhail Gorbachev during the abortive coup of 1991.[40] The mass movements in all the postcommunist states proved to be very loosely organized, lacking in strong leadership, and short-lived. Most disintegrated soon after the fall of the communist regime and thus contributed to the general environment of political instability.

In assessing their challenge to the established political order in any state, it is important to realize that mass movements draw support from two opposing dynamics, subnationalism and supranationalism.[41] Subnational mass movements form around local or regional issues that challenge the national political leadership of the state from below. The demands of such groups range from more funding to address local problems to calls for increased regional autonomy or even outright independence. In addition to those in the postcommunist states, secessionist movements exist in a substantial number of Third World states. Subnational movements seek the decentralization of the state's resources and political authority structure. Other mass movements form around essentially international issues, such as concern for the global environment or the threat of nuclear war. Since such issues require solutions at the supranational level (above the state), these movements seek to force the compliance of the state to supranational standards. In these instances, the constraints on the state's leaders result from potential centralizing tendencies within the international system.

INFORMATION AND THE EMPOWERED CITIZEN

The most important development in the late twentieth century has been the changed relationship between the government and the governed. Although the first important manifestations of this change occurred in Western states in the 1960s, the new relationship has been dramatically demonstrated in a wide variety of areas, from the Lenin Shipyard in Gdansk to the Presidential Palace in Manila and Tiananmen Square in Beijing. The essence of this change has been the development of new analytical skills and a new attitude toward politics by ordinary citizens, which are transforming politics throughout the world.[42] One recent study has referred to the development of "powerful people" who have an enhanced ability "to connect to world politics," are less likely to learn and behave in a habitual way, and actively question authority.[43]

In some extreme cases, the questioning of those in power leads to a search for new sources of authority, new governments, or even new states, which people believe will improve their lives. Such is the case with the Croatians in the former Yugoslavia, the citizens of the former German Democratic Republic, and the people of the Baltic states of the former Soviet Union. Simply stated, ordinary citizens can now discern personal meaning in distant domestic and international political events, and they will give their loyalty and support to their government only if they judge its performance to be satisfactory in dealing with those and other issues. Such citizens take an instrumental approach to politics in which political activity is viewed as a means or an instrument for personal goal achievement rather than an opportunity for a display of patriotism or other forms of traditional loyalty.

The catalyst for the development of more powerful citizens has been the information revolution.[44] Technological developments in electronics and microelectronics, particularly those associated with radio diffusion, global television, and the personal computer, have given ordinary people access to information that previously was the unique preserve of governments. Investigative reporting, live interviews, international newspapers, reports, and magazine and journal articles provide access to an unprecedented amount of specialized economic and political information.

The availability of this information has given rise to many new political issues, which are defined and debated through the use of scientific data. Some of these have resulted in intense and prolonged political conflicts, such as the issues of environmental protection versus the needs of development, nuclear disarmament and national security, and the safety hazards of the nuclear energy industry. The knowledge of political events in other countries has also played an important role in the development of political movements.

The popular demonstrations against communist party rule in Eastern Europe and the Soviet Union, as well as the pro-democracy movements in several Third World countries, stand as important examples. In these cases, the demands for a new type of political authority and a new political-economic system resulted from the desire to emulate the accomplishments of other societies, which most citizens had never visited but had seen depicted in media accounts. In an age of satellite communications, it is impossible for any government to deny its population detailed knowledge of other political systems.

The communications revolution has also contributed to the formation of political movements in another way. By providing nearly instantaneous coverage of their actions to a worldwide audience, groups receive indispensable publicity. In addition, the knowledge they receive about the existence of like-minded groups in other states is an important source of encouragement and support.

It is important to realize how much the relationship between the government and the governed has changed in the past twenty-five years. As late as the mid-1960s, studies of Western Europe and the United States reported the existence of a "permissive consensus" in which political elites were allowed to dominate public debate and the decision-making process.[45] Most citizens had a "subject orientation" to politics rather than a "participant orientation" and largely confined their political activity to voting.[46] However, by the end of the 1960s, the antinuclear movement in Western Europe, demonstrations against the Vietnam War in the United States, and the May 1968 protests in France clearly demonstrated that the relationship between citizens and their governments was undergoing a fundamental change.

In the states of the Soviet bloc, the communist party remained the main source of all political communications throughout the 1960s, enjoying a near-monopoly in some states. Serious public policy debates were confined to the government, organs of the communist party, and officially sanctioned groups. In the Third World, communications were limited and political skills were largely confined to selected groups in urban areas. In most states, the national government controlled or exercised considerable influence over the mass media.

At the end of the twentieth century, the changed relationship between the government and the governed is the most important factor in what has been termed the crisis of political authority. In the long run, the information revolution and the enhancement of citizens' skills may prove to be catalysts for a more rational, participatory, and democratic politics, and certainly, the revolution will not be reversed. In the short run, however, these developments have greatly complicated the process of governing nation-states and contributed to political instability. In the advanced industrial states of the West, the seemingly unending flow of information relevant to political and social life contains messages that are contradictory, alarmist, incomplete, unfactual, or presented out of context.[47] These messages have at least the potential for manipulation by opposition political groups, and they are the lifeblood of political movements and negative electoral campaigns. In many of the states of the West, this potential is increased by the insistence of the public media on doctrines of "fairness" and "equal time," which require that critics or opposition spokespersons be allowed to comment on statements by government authorities.

In the postcommunist states and the Third World, the flow of information is less but the newness of theories of democracy and capitalism, as well as the sudden end of government control of the means of public communication, have made the practical effects even greater. In states like Russia and the other former Soviet republics, the single message of the Communist Party has been replaced by a chorus of conflicting messages from previously suppressed groups and cultures.

Regardless of the area of the world involved, two critical points about the information revolution and the enhancement of citizens' skills are clear: (1) they occurred at a time when fundamental changes were taking place in important economic and political relationships throughout the world, and (2) they occurred at a time when all the world's major ideologies and the political parties that espouse them (e.g., communist, social democratic, neoliberal, etc.) seem unable to solve the most difficult economic and political problems to the satisfaction of their citizens. The result has been a prolonged period of political volatility, which has taken many forms, including alternations of power on a large scale, minority governments, political stalemate, secessionist movements, the rebirth of nationalist rivalries, mass demonstrations, strikes, political movements, and in general, a restless and disillusioned citizenry. The sense of political and economic insecurity, combined with enhanced analytical skills, has given rise to a new type of politics, which has been a major factor in the crisis of political authority in many states.

THE NEW POLITICAL ENVIRONMENT

The changes in the six relationships that had defined the postwar era deprived political actors of the reference points around which domestic and international political patterns had formed for nearly three decades. The loss of these reference points contributed to a worldwide increase in political turbulence and uncertainty, which impacted political leaders in the West, the Soviet bloc, and the Third World. As the relationships continued to erode, changes occurred in three areas vital to incumbent and aspiring political leaders: the political agenda, the balance of power between political constituencies, and the relative position of domestic political institutions.

Regarding the political agenda, the six changed relationships raised new concerns, and especially a preoccupation with international economic competitiveness, which competed with older issues that had dominated political discourse since the early postwar period. Even in states where the new issues did not entirely replace the old, an alternative political agenda was created with which rival political groups could challenge incumbent political leaders. The changed relationships also served to weaken many previously dominant political constituencies while strengthening certain new ones. In the West, economic interests associated with traditional industries, trade unions, and the public sector lost strength, while groups representing the private sector, and especially high-technology business and financial capital, increased their influence. The shifting balance of power between competing constituencies and interest groups proved a decisive factor in many electoral and political competitions. Finally, domestic political institutions experienced various degrees of empowerment or disempowerment as the postwar political era drew to a close. In general, institutions associated with entrepreneurial activity or international economic competition experienced some degree of empowerment. The process of disempowerment, however, was much more common. The most spectacular example of disempowerment was the demise of the Communist Party of the Soviet Union and the Soviet state itself, following failed efforts to achieve its reform.

By the late 1970s, it became clear that the ongoing changes in the six relationships had created constraints on incumbent leaders and new opportunities for their challengers. In the West, the increasing concern for economic competitiveness created "political space" for successful attacks on the levels of taxation and public expenditure required to maintain the welfare state. In Western Europe the outstanding example of such an attack was that of Margaret Thatcher in the United Kingdom. A similar concern for fiscal constraint and economic competitiveness in the Federal Republic of Germany complicated the task of achieving German reunification and increased the political risks to Chancellor Helmut Kohl. Because of the relationship between a state's technological competitiveness and its military capabilities, the leaders of the Communist Party of the Soviet Union were also forced to respond to the revolution in science and technology. The need to improve Soviet economic performance was the catalyst for the program of reform of Mikhail Gorbachev, which ultimately unleashed forces that produced the demise of the Soviet Union. The same general context of Soviet decline at the end of the Cold War made possible the rise of the Solidarity movement and its leader, Lech Walesa, in Poland. Finally, Third World leaders also confronted the new technological, scientific, and economic realities. A major program of economic adjustment was undertaken by the Communist Party of China and its leader, Deng Xiaoping, with profound social and economic ramifications. A more moderate program of liberal reforms was attempted by Prime Minister Rajiv Gandhi in India, which also had important effects on that state's political economy.

NOTES

1. For a discussion of breakpoint change, see James N. Rosenau, *Turbulence in World Politics: A Theory of Continuity and Change* (Princeton, NJ: Princeton University Press, 1990), pp. 82–87.

2. Thomas G. Paterson, *On Every Front: The Making of the Cold War* (New York: W. W. Norton and Co., 1979), p. 25.

3. For an excellent summary of the goals of the United States, see Theodore Geiger, *The Future of the International System: The United States and the World Political Economy* (Boston: Unwin Hyman, 1988), pp. 9–20.

4. Ibid., p. 20.

5. Ibid., pp. 20–21.

6. Ibid., pp. 7, 171.

7. Ibid., pp. 14–15.

8. For a summary of crisis management and a periodization of the Cold War, see Walter C. Clemens, Jr., "Soviet-U.S. Relations: Confrontation, Cooperation, Transformation?" in Michael T. Klare and Daniel C. Thomas, eds., *World Security: Trends and Challenges at Century's End* (New York: St. Martin's Press, 1991), p. 25.

9. For an overview of U.S.-Soviet interactions in the Cold War, see William G. Hyland, *The Cold War: Fifty Years of Conflict* (New York: Random House, 1991).

10. Robert Gilpin, *The Political Economy of International Relations* (Princeton, NJ: Princeton University Press, 1987), pp. 28–31.

11. See Geiger, pp. 11–17.

12. Ibid., pp. 11–20.

13. Ibid., p. 101.

14. Ibid., pp. 5–6.

15. See Robert J. S. Ross and Kent C. Trachte, *Global Capitalism: The New Leviathan* (Albany, NY: State University of New York Press, 1990).

16. For a discussion of the economic ramifications of these developments, see Scott Lash and John Urry, *The End of Organized Capitalism* (Madison: The University of Wisconsin Press, 1987), pp. 1–17, 84–93.

17. On the invigoration of international capitalism, see Ross and Trachte, p. 3.

18. For a discussion of these developments, see Philip Armstrong, Andrew Glyn, and John Harrison, *Capitalism since 1945* (Cambridge, MA: Basil Blackwell, 1991), pp. 305–332.

19. Mark Kesselman and Joel Krieger, eds., *European Politics in Transition* (Lexington, MA: D.C. Heath and Co., 1987), pp. 9–17.

20. For a discussion of these arrangements, see Steve Fraser and Gary Gerstle, *The Rise and Fall of the New Deal Order, 1930–1980* (Princeton, NJ: Princeton University Press, 1989), pp. 1–153; Samuel H. Beer, *Britain against Itself: The Political Contradictions of Collectivism* (New York: W. W. Norton and Co., 1982), pp. 1, 19, 209–220; and Peter J. Katzenstein, *Policy and Politics in West Germany: The Growth of a Semisovereign State* (Philadelphia: Temple University Press, 1987), pp. 86–110.

21. Kesselman and Krieger, pp. 9–12.

22. For an excellent summary of the effects of Keynesianism, see Peter Hall, ed., *The Political Power of Economic Ideas: Keynesianism across Nations* (Princeton, NJ: Princeton University Press, 1989).

23. For a case study of the politics of the collectivist period in Britain, see Beer, pp. 1–76.

24. See Kesselman and Krieger, pp. 17–23.

25. See Graham Smith, *Planned Development in the Socialist World* (Cambridge, England: Cambridge University Press, 1989), pp. 14–34.

26. Kesselman and Krieger, pp. 601–605.

27. Geiger, pp. 80–84.

28. Smith, p. 98.

29. Geiger, p. 80.

30. For a discussion of the weakness of the Soviet economy, see Edward A. Hewett, *Reforming the Soviet Economy: Equality versus Efficiency* (Washington, DC: The Brookings Institution, 1988), pp. 78–91.

31. Ibid., p. 257.

32. Bartomiej Kaminski, *The Collapse of State Socialism: The Case of Poland* (Princeton, NJ: Princeton University Press, 1991), p. 24.

33. Russell J. Dalton and Manfred Kuechler, eds., *Challenging the Political Order: New Social and Political Movements in Western Democracies* (New York: Oxford University Press, 1990).

34. See Russell J. Dalton, Manfred Kuechler, and Wilhelm Burklin, "The Challenge of New Movements" in Dalton and Kuechler, pp. 3–6.

35. Jurg Steiner, *European Democracies* (New York: Longman, 1986), p. 49.

36. For a discussion of the thesis of the possible erosion of support for the state, see Rosenau, pp. 297–314, 388–415.

37. Dalton, Kuechler, and Burklin, in Dalton and Kuechler, p. 8.

38. Ibid., p. 13.

39. See Kaminski, pp. 124–140.

40. On informal groups, see Nicholas Lampert, "Patterns of Participation," in Stephen White, Alex Pravada, and Zvi Gitelman, eds., *Developments in Soviet Politics* (Durham, NC: Duke University Press, 1990), p. 129.

41. For an excellent discussion of this point, see Rosenau, pp. 297–314.

42. Ibid., p. 334.

43. Ibid., p. 335.

44. Dalton, Kuechler, and Burkin, in Dalton and Kuechler, p. 7.

45. See the findings for Great Britain, Germany, and Italy in Gabriel A. Almond and Sidney Verba, *The Civic Culture: Political Attitudes and Democracy in Five Nations* (Boston: Little, Brown and Company, 1965).

46. Ibid., pp. 22–35.

47. For a discussion of the effects of information at the microlevel, see Rosenau, pp. 338–387.

—— three ——————————————————

Margaret Thatcher: Economic Decline and Turbulence in the United Kingdom

For most of the twentieth century, Britain has experienced relative economic decline. Relative economic decline occurs when a nation's economic performance lags behind that of its major economic competitors in such areas as level of investment, worker productivity, job creation, technological change, and growth of the gross national product. The most visible dimension of relative economic decline is the loss of world market share to the firms of competitor nations. Most sources agree that Britain's economic decline dates to the period from 1870 to 1914, with losses in international competitiveness accelerating sharply after 1890. As the world's "first industrial nation," Britain had enjoyed a near monopoly in many sectors as late as the 1840s to 1870s. By 1900, however, Britain's share of world trade in manufactured goods had fallen to 33 percent, and it continued to decline in each of the next four decades.[1] In 1945, Britain's share of world trade in all areas was still 24 percent, but this figure also declined until the mid-1980s, when it finally stabilized at 8 percent.[2] The loss of international competitiveness occurred gradually and was not always visible to the voting public. During several decades, Britain benefited from the expansion of the international economy, and its economic performance was judged by contemporaries as adequate. For example, in the twenty-year period of high growth and economic expansion following World War II, the so-called "Golden Age of Capitalism" from 1945 to 1965, the annual rate of economic growth in Britain was a respectable 2.8 percent.[3] During the same period, however, Germany averaged 6.7 percent growth; Italy, 6.0 percent; and France, 4.5 percent growth.[4] In short, in good times, the British economy grew more slowly than the economies of its major economic competitors, while in recessionary periods, the decline in macroeconomic performance occurred more quickly.

For purposes of analysis, the postwar era of British politics is usually divided into two periods: (1) a period of "consensus politics" from the early 1950s to the mid-1960s, during which major groups converged around the programs and values of the welfare state, and (2) a period of the breakdown of consensus, repolarization, and political crisis extending from the mid-1960s through the decade of the 1980s.[5] In the period of consensus politics, a unique set of domestic and international factors combined to produce an unprecedented "postwar settlement" involving the nation's largest trade unions and most powerful business interests, especially those representing industrial capital. In exchange for a commitment by business and government to the goal of full employment and the construction of a comprehensive welfare state, the trade unions abandoned their historic demand for public ownership or nationalization of major industries and pledged to curtail strikes and other forms of labor disruption. Both Britain's major political parties, Labour and the Conservatives, endorsed and actively supported this settlement. Both parties also accepted, at least in theory, the policies and institutional arrangements necessary to sustain the welfare state, including a mixed economy in which public and private firms coexisted, a vast bureaucratic state to administer social programs, and Keynesian economic principles. Central to Keynesian economics was the belief that during periods of recession, government should increase its spending to stimulate aggregate consumer demand and preserve jobs. The period of consensus politics coincided with two decades of economic growth, low unemployment, and an unprecedented degree of social peace.[6]

Beginning in the mid-1960s, the international and domestic conditions that had produced the postwar settlement began to disappear, bringing the period of consensus politics to an end. The domestic political environment was permanently transformed by such factors as demographic and generational changes, the effects of two decades of social programs that had provided protection to the majority of the population against the hazards of life, and the rise of postmaterialist political values (quality of life issues). The result was a proliferation of new political groups, styles, and interests, which competed with the older ones. Equally important, the programs and commitments of the welfare state were dependent on the continued growth of the economy at or near the rate of 2.8 percent, as was achieved in the first twenty years after World War II. Instead, however, between 1974 and 1978, the economy grew at less than 1 percent, and in the period of the late 1960s and 1970s, Britain achieved the lowest rate of growth of any of the states of the European Community.[7] The changes in the world economy brought on by overaccumulation, the internationalization of industrial markets, and the shocks resulting from the oil price increases of the 1970s aggravated the structural weaknesses in the British economy and directly impacted the standard of living of millions of Britons. In the words of one source, the economic conditions of the 1970s "shattered the postwar settlement and had deep, and quite possibly lasting, consequences for British state institutions and a wide range of social forces."[8] The second era of postwar British politics was characterized by intense distributional conflicts over jobs, wages, profits, state subsidies, and social benefits.

The acceleration of economic decline shaped British politics in the 1960s and 1970s in two important ways. First, reversing the country's economic fortunes was recognized by successive governments as the most pressing national problem and increasingly dominated the public policy agenda.[9] The increasing frequency of episodes of poor economic performance compelled governments to devote more energy and attention to short-term economic conditions. The usual pattern was to respond with Keynesian demand-management techniques in the form of "stop-go" policies intended to either cool or stimulate the economy. Second, the acceleration of decline was the catalyst for a national debate over which factors, institutions, and groups were responsible for Britain's flagging economic performance. Rival political groups produced a wide range of competing interpretations. Left-wing groups argued that Britain had failed to make appropriate changes in its military, political, and financial roles after World War II, and thus was unable to devote sufficient resources to the renewal of its industrial complex.[10] This interpretation emphasized the role of Conservative Party elites, civil servants, and the financial interests in "the City" (London) in the failure to achieve modernization and competitiveness. Right-wing theorists, especially those of the economic New Right and monetarist schools, attributed Britain's lack of competitiveness to the excessive "politicization" of the economy in the era of collectivist thinking and the welfare state. In this view, the British people had become less productive because of an overdependence on welfare state programs and wage increases that were achieved through political negotiations, not hard work. In addition, excessive social spending, government regulation and high taxation had placed British businesses at a competitive disadvantage and overloaded government with excessive tasks and political demands.[11] The blame rested squarely with the British Labour Party, social democratic intellectuals, Conservative Party moderates who supported Keynesian economic theories (labeled "wets"), and especially the trade union movement, which had become too powerful. Both the political left and right recognized the electoral implications of the debate, and the rival interpretations and public policy prescriptions came to dominate the national political discourse.

THE KEYNESIAN WELFARE STATE, 1945-1970

In the 1970s and 1980s, the Keynesian welfare state, like other national political institutions, proved vulnerable to the political and economic pressures generated by Britain's accelerating decline. Although the majority of both parties continued to support its major programs, the welfare state became the target of increasingly sharp attacks from New Right critics, who argued that it had contributed to deindustrialization, economic disincentives, and national demoralization.[12] Since such criticisms were central to the political program of Margaret Thatcher and reached their height during the time she was prime minister, a proper understanding of Thatcher's career requires a brief review of the cultural, institutional, and public policy foundations of the Keynesian welfare state.

Culturally, the Keynesian welfare state was the product of a particular set of attitudes that emerged after World War II. These attitudes favored reconciliation, domestic reconstruction, a sense of common purpose, and acceptance of an interventionist state like that which had prevailed from 1939 to 1945.[13] Attitudes favoring consensus politics and accommodation were strongest among those age groups that had experienced World War II as adults but grew progressively weaker among groups with little or no memory of wartime political cooperation. Support for the welfare state at the time of its creation (1945–1951) also reflected a general attitude of deference toward authority on the part of the electorate, as well as a tendency to view the welfare state as part of a national program of postwar reconstruction.[14] Between the 1940s and the 1960s, a generation of Britons was exposed to the relative affluence and security of the welfare state and became more secular, permissive, and pluralistic than at any time in British history.[15] By the 1960s, support for the welfare state was increasingly based on narrow self-interest, and specifically on the ability of the welfare state to deliver desired outcomes and benefits to various groups in British society.

In political and structural terms, the welfare state rested on a limited consensus involving both major political parties and Britain's largest interest groups. Following the Labour Party's electoral victories in 1945 and 1950, the Conservative Party was compelled to campaign on the pledge not to dismantle the major social programs on which the general population had come to depend.[16] It also accepted the goal of full employment. From 1951 to the 1970s, both major political parties thus converged in their support for the programs and commitments of the welfare state, with each competing for the same voters and utilizing the same electoral appeal—that it could best manage and modernize the welfare state. As the collectivist era progressed, however, it became clear that the convergence between the two political parties and the apparent consensus on which it rested was limited. While Labour Party support for the welfare state had a theoretical foundation in the social democratic model of society and a belief in the goal of equality, Conservative Party moderates (also known as Tories and, later, wets) never accepted socialism and continued to believe in the inevitability of social hierarchy, paternalistic leadership, and social and economic inequality.[17] Their acceptance of the welfare state is best understood as a pragmatic adaptation to the electoral and economic realities of the early postwar years.[18] It was also based on the clear expectation of electoral gains like those experienced between 1951 and 1964, when the Conservatives governed uninterrupted for thirteen years. Following the Conservative electoral defeats in 1964, 1966, and 1974, the fundamental differences between the Labour Party and the Conservative moderates increasingly came to the surface, and from the late 1960s on, a right-wing faction within the Conservative Party rejected outright the welfare state and the principles of the postwar political consensus.

The implementation of new social programs and the increased regulatory tasks associated with the Keynesian welfare state also required the expansion of government institutions. From 1945 to the end of the 1970s, the size and complexity of the national bureaucracy constantly increased. More important, the implementation of the postwar settlement between business and labor required the development of a new type of structure, neocorporate or tripartite institutions, in which the national representatives of business and labor could consult and negotiate with the government on national economic policy. Although Britain's neocorporate structures were weakly developed compared to those of other European states, they were intended to produce optimal policies in important areas and adjust the consensus between business and labor as economic conditions changed.[19] The development of neocorporate institutions combined with the political consensus and convergence between the two major parties produced a unique pattern of politics, which became known in Britain as the *collectivist polity*.[20] With the acceleration of economic decline in the mid-1960s, Britain's institutions became arenas for increasingly intense political conflicts. The bureaucracy was assailed both by groups seeking to maintain or expand social programs, despite the economic downturn, and groups critical of the high levels of spending and taxation. Neocorporate structures were also subject to a wide range of criticisms, including that they had usurped the role of Parliament in national decision making and, later, that they had failed to reverse Britain's economic decline.

Finally, in the area of public policy, the cornerstone or postwar consensus was the acceptance by all major political groups of the Keynesian model of the economy. By the late 1940s, the pledge of full employment had become the central issue of British politics, and subsequent Labour and Conservative governments resorted to Keynesian demand-management techniques to control unemployment. By 1950, the Labour Party had built its identity around a commitment to Keynesianism and the welfare state, and the Conservative Party had embraced Keynesianism as an alternative to public (government) ownership of business and government planning.[21] The Keynesian model emphasized three major points: (1) the private economy is unstable and in need of government intervention, (2) unemployment is a problem of insufficient aggregate demand, and (3) inflation results from excess demand or excessive wage pressure.[22] The Keynesian model thus prescribed government management of the economy to assure sufficient demand in times of increasing unemployment and restrain demand in periods of increasing inflation. Stop-go policies became institutionalized in British government circles, as did the acceptance of deficit spending, which frequently accompanied efforts to combat unemployment.

By the late 1960s, stop-go policies proved unable to control inflation and growing government budget deficits were drawing increasing criticism. In addition, in the 1970s, unemployment and inflation increased simultaneously, a condition for which Keynesian analysis offered no explanation or solution. Both Conservative and Labour governments were compelled to deviate periodically from Keynesian policies in the face of Britain's worsening economic performance. By the late 1970s, an alternative model of the economy, monetarism, had been advanced, which was ultimately adopted by the New Right faction of the Conservative Party.

Economic decision making was also complicated by British membership in the European Community (EC), which effectively began on January 1, 1975.[23] Intended as part of the strategy to promote economic modernization, EC membership added a European dimension to public policy making.[24] Several issues, including Britain's financial contributions to the EC and the possible support for additional steps toward economic and monetary union, subsequently became contentious national issues. The decade of the 1970s proved to be a critical transition period.

ONSET OF TURBULENCE: THE ECONOMIC CRISIS OF THE 1970S

In the 1970s, Britain experienced several developments that are included in the model of political turbulence.[25] These included the proliferation of political groups with widely varying objectives and structures, sudden and profound changes in major political and economic relationships, frequent policy reversals by governments struggling to adapt to changing international economic conditions, and growing mass anxiety over the issue of national political and economic decline. Collectively, these developments produced a political environment of increased instability, increased unpredictability, and rapid change. The onset of turbulence accelerated the processes of empowerment and disempowerment of political ideas, institutions, and individuals. Turbulence was an absolute prerequisite to the emergence of the political program that became known as "Thatcherism" and to the personal political victories of Margaret Thatcher between 1975 and 1987.

From 1970 on, the performance of the economy became increasingly unsatisfactory, and it reached the proportions of a full-blown economic crisis at the end of the 1970s. The economic slowdown was largely the result of developments in the international economy, and especially the emergence of new competitors in Europe and Asia, the decline of the United States as an economic hegemon, and the world economic recession of the 1970s. It also reflected two facts about Britain's position in the world economy: (1) much of Britain's traditional industry was no longer competitive in contemporary world markets, and (2) Britain's neocorporate structures had failed to develop an effective strategy for industrial renewal during the 1960s. In the 1960s, the decline of the British economy was most evident in such categories as the rate of profit, industrial productivity, import penetration, and the share of world exports in manufacturing.[26] Successive governments responded to the flagging economic performance with two decades of stop-go interventionism, or U-turns, in which policy priorities alternated between efforts to stimulate the economy to create jobs and efforts to slow economic expansion to control inflation or protect the value of the pound sterling. After a decade of failure to reverse Britain's economic decline, the effects of the slowdown and deindustrialization became apparent throughout the British economy. From 1973 through 1978, economic growth averaged only 1.1 percent per year, inflation rose at twice the OECD average, and unemployment increased from 2.6 percent in 1974–1975 to 5.7 percent in 1977–1978.[27] In addition, in the 1970s, Britain experienced a form of deindustrialization that was accompanied by heavy social and political costs. In the years between 1968 and 1976, more than 1 million manufacturing jobs were lost, and in the decades of the 1970s and 1980s combined (1970–1989), a net loss of 2.8 million industrial jobs occurred.[28] This loss exceeded that of any other country in Europe. The economic hardship culminated in the "Winter of Discontent" (1978–1979) when, in addition to slowing economic growth and increasing inflation (stagflation), Britain experienced major public sector strikes.

Continued economic growth was an absolute prerequisite to the maintenance of the postwar settlement, which the sharp decline in virtually every category of macroeconomic performance in the mid-1970s shattered.[29] From the 1960s on, British politics were increasingly characterized by what have been called "benefits scrambles," "pay scrambles," and "subsidy scrambles."[30] These were intense conflicts between the most powerful organized interest groups in the country, which sought to maximize their share of the benefits from the welfare state in the new environment of growing economic constraints. These scrambles resulted in what one source has called the "politics of pluralistic stagnation" and the "paralysis of public choice."[31] Interest groups abandoned any conception of long-term interests, including the preservation of the postwar settlement, in the interest of short-term economic payoffs, while political parties under pressure to capture votes at election time were willing to offer increased benefits to these same groups without regard for the long-term economic consequences or the potential incompatibility of their commitments.[32]

In the 1970s, stagnation turned to political turbulence when the declining economy made it impossible to meet the economic demands of major interest groups. The turbulence was also increased by the efforts of the two major parties to escape from the collectivist consensus by reasserting their historic, partisan ties with either the trade unions or organized business.[33] Between

1970 and 1974, the Conservative government of Edward Heath, which was the first to break with the postwar settlement, incurred the wrath of the Trade Union Congress by adopting policies to restrict the activities and power of trade unions. As a result, between 1970 and 1974, more than three million workdays were lost to strikes, including strikes by dockworkers, local authority workers, and the National Union of Mineworkers (NUM).[34] The mineworkers strike was a major contributing factor to the defeat of the Conservative Party in the election of 1974. Between 1974 and 1979, the historic tie between the Trade Union Congress and the Labour Party was also severely strained when international economic constraints forced the government of James Callaghan to adopt wage restraints. The result was a series of crippling strikes by Ford workers, tanker and truck drivers, train engineers, civil servants, local government workers, public utilities employees, and health workers.[35] These strikes, which increased in intensity and duration each year from 1974 through 1978, included strikes both of an official and "wildcat" (unsanctioned) nature. The division between the Labour Party and the trade unions made possible the election of Margaret Thatcher in 1979 and also contributed to sharp conflicts within the Labour Party that ended with the formation of a separate party, the Social Democratic Party, which was led by a group of disenchanted Labour Members of Parliament (MPs).[36]

MARGARET THATCHER AND THE "THATCHERITES"

The woman who was to achieve worldwide stature as a prime minister was born in 1925, the daughter of lower-middle-class parents who resided in the Lincolnshire area of England. It is generally agreed that her basic political beliefs were rooted in both the time and place in which she grew up.[37] Grantham, where her father owned a grocery store, was a small but prosperous market town where "the working class scarcely existed as a sociological entity" and where fear of the working class and antisocialist attitudes were common.[38] Thatcher has frequently reported that World War II left her with a profound sense of patriotism and a strong political identification with the Conservative Party, and especially with its wartime leader, Winston Churchill.[39]

Thatcher's father, Alfred Roberts, proved to be one of the greatest influences in her life. He was a self-taught and self-made man who stressed the values of thrift, hard work, and independence. According to Thatcher, the cultural life of the family centered on the Methodist Church, and her father, a lay Methodist preacher, passed on to his children the simple conviction that "some things are right, and some things are wrong."[40] Alfred Roberts was also active in politics and served Grantham as alderman, justice of the peace, and mayor. Roberts's political affiliation was somewhat ambiguous, and he was elected as an Independent. Most sources agree, however, that both Thatcher's parents held political attitudes that generally corresponded to those of the national Conservative Party. Regardless of his party affiliation, it is clear that Alfred Roberts introduced his daughter to a life of political activism and public service, to involvement with the political and economic leaders of the county, and to the magistrates' court, which ultimately led her to a career in law.[41]

Following graduation from Grantham Girls' School in 1943, Thatcher attended Somerville College, Oxford, and studied chemistry. Although much has been made of the fact that her social background made her an "outsider" in traditional institutions, Thatcher's attendance at Oxford placed her "into the network" that led to a lifetime of activity in Conservative Party politics.[42] At Oxford, Thatcher immediately joined the Oxford University Conservative Association, where she earned a reputation as a highly committed, but "moderate," party adherent. By 1946, Thatcher had risen to the position of president of the Oxford Conservatives, which made her eligible to attend the party's national conference and gave her access to important leadership groups. By this time, the political environment had changed, since the Labour Party had won the 1945 election and was in the process of implementing its social democratic and collectivist program. In 1949, the Dartford Conservative Association chose Margaret Thatcher, then twenty-four years old, to be their candidate for the House of Commons. Dartford was a "safe seat" for the Labour Party, and Thatcher was defeated in the elections of 1950 and 1951. However, in both contests she reduced the Labour Party's margin of victory while waging what a leading biographer has called a campaign "defined by robust simplicities," in which she contrasted the Conservative Party's "proponents of freedom" to Labour's "proponents of slavery."[43] Her performance was sufficiently impressive to Conservatives that in 1957, she was selected by the constituent association of Finchley, a safe seat for the Tories, to run in the next general election. Margaret Thatcher was subsequently elected to Parliament in 1959.

Thatcher's professional activities following her graduation from Oxford in 1946 completed her journey through the network of institutions that ultimately led to the office of the prime minister. Although her initial employment was as a research chemist, first in Essex and then in Hammersmith, London, in 1950 Thatcher enrolled as a part-time law student. She subsequently became a member of the bar in 1954, specializing in tax law, and established a successful practice. While a chemist in Hammersmith, Thatcher met her husband to be, Denis, who was the director of his family's chemical business. He was wealthy and had excellent connections to London's political and business communities. The two were married in 1951 and, as one source noted, "from that day she was untouched by financial worry of any kind" and "materially forever removed from the shop-keeping world in which she had grown up."[44] In summing up her career, biographers and colleagues appear to be in agreement that Thatcher was driven by great ambition and a spirit of acquisitiveness, that Grantham was a place from which she worked to get away, and that initially she was an "outsider" in the tradition-laden institutions (Oxford, the bar, Parliament), which were traditionally dominated by more privileged members of the upper class, most of whom were men.[45]

The Thatcherites

On February 11, 1975, Margaret Thatcher was elected leader of the Conservative Party, a post she was to retain for fifteen years. Thatcher defeated Edward Heath, the former prime minister, and four other candidates following the party's loss in the two general elections of 1974. The faction within the parliamentary Conservative Party that sponsored her election consisted of a diverse group of critics on the party's right wing, which opposed the prevailing Keynesian and collectivist political consensus. This group, most often referred to as the New Right, was part of a tradition within the Conservative Party that had resisted the leadership's acceptance of the postwar settlement and the movement toward the "massive new middle ground in politics."[46] The influence of the party's right wing increased somewhat in the late 1940s and again in the late 1960s under the leadership of Enoch Powell, but it remained in a minority position and was unable to persuade the party to oppose the postwar political consensus. The new environment of economic insecurity and political turbulence that attended the 1970s provided the New Right with a fresh opportunity to achieve ascendancy within the Conservative Party. The victory of Margaret Thatcher in the leadership conference of 1975 represented an important first step toward that ascendancy.

The strength of the New Right faction in the Conservative Party of the 1970s was the result of several factors. Viewed from a sociological perspective, the New Right consisted largely of younger, "self-made" persons of middle-class origin who won election to Parliament following successful careers in public or private institutions. As party backbenchers, they were politically ambitious for greater power and far removed from the traditional leadership of the party, which had acceded to the terms of the postwar settlement in the 1950s. Of the group that publicly supported Thatcher before the first ballot in 1975, only Sir Keith Joseph (later Lord) and Thatcher herself had held positions in Heath's cabinet or shadow cabinet.

At the level of party politics, the New Right faction was also united in its condemnation of Edward Heath. Under his leadership, the party had lost three out of four general elections and, despite the economic traumas of the 1970s, he had failed to convince the electorate of the need for a program of bold, "free-market" reforms.[47] Heath was also perceived as a failure in the area of economic management. The 1970 manifesto promised a program of tax cuts, cuts in public expenditure, and less intervention in industry, but Heath's approach to industrial and economic policy was reversed in the U-turn of 1971–1972.[48] The resulting record-high rate of inflation, budget deficit, and balance-of-payments deficit convinced many on the right that "Britain was more badly governed during the 1970s than in any other decade in its history."[49] Most important, Thatcher's supporters were also united by a commitment to certain political ideas and core values that had deep roots in the conservative tradition. Like the followers of Enoch Powell in the 1960s, they feared the loss of the party's identity as the defender of capitalism, economic freedom, and law and order.[50] In asserting this position, the British New Right joined the conservative reaction against the postwar settlement that was common to other advanced industrial states.

The Conservative Party in Britain has always been a coalition of diverse interests, and the New Right of the 1970s drew support from two different conservative groups, neoliberals and neoconservatives. Neoliberals attacked the Keynesian welfare state from the perspective of free-market, laissez-faire, and minimal-state ideas. Like the classical liberals of the mid-nineteenth century, they emphasized five major points: (1) the importance of the individual, (2) freedom of choice as the only true basis of community, (3) the superiority of the market as a mechanism for the allocation of resources, (4) laissez-faire, and (5) the need for a limited government confined to such basic tasks as national defense, the maintenance of law and order, and protection of the value of the pound through control of the money supply.[51] The neoliberals drew inspiration from American academic defenders of the market, such as Milton Freedman and F. A. Hayek, as well as from the public choice theorists (the most prominent of which were G. Tullock and J. M. Buchanan of the Virginia School). In Britain, neoliberal ideas were advocated by a small but prominent group of writers and journalists (e.g., Samuel Brittan, Anthony Seldon, Lord Harris, and Sir Keith Joseph after 1974), as well as by a number of important political institutes (think tanks) and interest groups. The most prominent included the Institute of Economic Affairs (IEA, established in 1957), the Adam Smith Institute (ASI, established in 1979), the Social Affairs Unit (established in 1980 to critically examine government social affairs programs), the Aims of Industry (established in 1942), and the Institute of Directors (established in 1906).[52]

In August 1974, the Centre for Policy Studies (CPS) was established by Sir Keith Joseph with the permission of the Conservative Party leadership. With Margaret Thatcher as its first president, the center became a forum for the development of free-market policy options and a counterweight to the Conservative Research Department, which reflected the policy outlook of Heath and the party leadership.[53] Regardless of the source, neoliberal critiques of the Keynesian welfare state argued that excessive government intervention had undermined individual initiative and self-reliance, produced excessive levels of taxation and government expenditure, and created a crisis of "ungovernability" as the state became overloaded with economic and social tasks that it could not perform.[54] Political monetarists, including Margaret Thatcher and some of her closest allies, further argued that inflation was the long-term cause of unemployment, and since inflation is largely a monetary phenomenon, Keynesian techniques of demand management and deficit spending actually increased inflation and destroyed jobs.[55] Sources employing public choice analysis added the argument that the absence of profit criteria and other market constraints in the welfare state encouraged the reckless expansion of public expenditures by politicians seeking election and bureaucrats wishing to enhance their budgets and personal salaries.[56]

The New Right also drew support from parliamentary and extraparliamentary groups seeking to reestablish the power of the state to address certain problems. These groups, which are usually labeled as traditional conservatives or neoconservatives, directed their attacks at what they considered to be the negative social and moral consequences of the Keynesian welfare state.[57] Permissiveness, lawlessness, pornography, violence by labor unions, abortion on demand, drug abuse, sexual immorality, and the weakening of the authority of teachers, parents, employers, and the police were common topics of concern.[58] These concerns were often combined with an interest in race, nationhood, national identity, and patriotism.[59] Neoconservative theorists writing in British journals like the *Salisbury Review* called for the reassertion of discipline and authority and emphasized five values different from those of the neoliberals: (1) strong government, (2) social authoritarianism, (3) disciplined society, (4) hierarchy and subordination, and (5) the nation.[60] The influence of the neoconservatives within Thatcher's closest circle of advisors and, later, within her three governments was always clearly secondary to that of the neoliberals, but their presence was still important. In the policies and political ideas that ultimately became known as Thatcherism, references to the superiority of traditional, "Victorian values" and attacks on the societal liberation of the 1960s were commonplace.[61] Beyond that, authoritarian populist appeals against immigration, declining moral standards, increasing crime, irresponsible trade unions, and personal irresponsibility were extremely popular among the issues in the 1979 election.

THATCHERISM: THE NEW RIGHT NATIONAL PROGRAM

The term *Thatcherism* has been the subject of intense intellectual debate. First used by left-wing critics of Thatcher writing in the Euro-Communist magazine, *Marxism Today,* the term has been variously applied to the policies implemented by the Thatcher governments, Margaret Thatcher's personal attributes as a political leader, the leadership style of Thatcher and her ministers in Parliament and Whitehall, the New Right's formula for industrial relations, the political and economic values of the New Right, and the electoral strategy of the Conservative Party during Thatcher's years as party leader.[62] Despite the lack of definitional rigor, each of these descriptions identifies an important element of the New Right's program in the 1970s and 1980s. For the purposes of this study, Thatcherism is defined as the political program of the New Right supporters of Margaret Thatcher within the Conservative Party between 1975 and 1979, as well as the subsequent political program of the Conservative Party in power during the three Thatcher governments of 1979, 1983, and 1987–1990. This program was multidimensional, including not only public policy recommendations but also an electoral strategy, a distinct approach to governing or "statecraft," a blueprint for desired social change, an accumulation strategy for economic renewal, and an ideology that justified the other elements of the program.

Thatcherism is best understood as the New Right's response to the three crises of the 1970s: (1) the crisis of the Conservative Party's electoral decline, (2) the crisis of government authority, and (3) the crisis of accelerated economic decline.[63] The Thatcherite program or national project rested on three pillars: a deintegrative electoral strategy designed to divide the traditional Labour Party vote, a centralist and authoritarian-populist approach to governing, and a neoliberal economic strategy designed to reduce government intervention in the economy. Although there was no Thatcherite master plan in 1975 or 1979 and the emphasis given to individual policies differed over time, the program had largely emerged by the time of the second and third Thatcher governments.[64]

The Crisis of the Conservative Party

In the general election of October 1974, the Conservative Party's share of the popular vote fell to only 35 percent, as the "party of government" experienced its third defeat in four elections. Following the election there was a widespread loss of confidence in the leadership of Edward Heath and an increasing polarization between the moderate, "wet" wing of the party, supporting the collectivist consensus, and the neoliberal, "dry" wing, favoring market-oriented policies. Beginning in 1974, groups within the New Right called for a new strategy for reversing the party's electoral decline. By the 1979 general election, the broad outline of this strategy was apparent. Support for the collectivist consensus had weakened the party's identity among voters as the defender of capitalism and economic freedom. It had also disadvantaged the party by making it compete in a context of social democratic ideas and institutions that favored the Labour Party. Future electoral success required the creation of a new "social base" or electoral coalition formed around a new theme of "popular capitalism."[65] The party had to compete with a new agenda and a new set of political issues that would appeal to upwardly mobile Britons. Popular capitalism would succeed because the popular preoccupation with personal fulfillment and the pursuit of freedom that had manifested in the political movements of the 1960s could be channeled constructively into pursuits such as self-employment and new business ventures.[66] Between 1979 and 1987, conservatives campaigned on the following issues: ending the dependency culture, self-sufficiency, freeing small capital, economic realism, tax relief, deregulation, privatization, freeing individuals from the public sector bias, handing unions back to their members, liberating the wealth-creating sectors, share (stock) ownership, home ownership, and conviction, not consensus, politics.[67]

As implemented, it became clear even before Thatcher's first election in 1979 that the new electoral formula was a deintegrative strategy, which could only succeed through the creation of divisions within the nation as a whole, and especially within the constituencies of the Labour Party.[68] At the national level, the Conservative Party's traditional commitment to national unity gave way to a new program of selective government reintervention, regressive taxation, privatization, and the reduction of subsidies to depressed areas.[69] These actions accelerated the growth of economic inequalities, not only between regions and locations, but also between classes, sexes, and races.[70] By the time of the 1983 and 1987 elections, a strong case could be made for the existence of two geographic nations, the depressed North and the affluent South, as well as a society separated by class, the so-called "one-third–two-thirds society."[71] These groups were separated in both an economic and electoral sense. At the group level, programs and themes were deliberately developed to divide the traditional supporters of the Labour Party. These included immigration and race, the curbing of union power, government intervention in strikes, the sale of public housing, criticisms of the feminist agenda, attacks against welfare "scroungers," attacks against union leaders as "the enemy within," the reduction of benefits to state-dependent people, and opting-out provisions in education and health.[72] As an electoral strategy, the new formula was successful. Although her share of the popular vote never exceeded 43.9 percent, Thatcher was the only prime minister in this century to preside over three consecutive election victories. In 1979, 1983, and 1987, the opposition was ineffective because it was so deeply divided.

The Crisis of Government Authority

Despite the strong antistate bias of the neoliberals, important segments of the New Right expressed concern about the weakening of the effectiveness and authority of government throughout the 1970s. Conservatives attacked the spread of permissiveness, lawlessness, and the declining respect for police, which dated to the political turbulence of the 1960s.[73] Their concern was heightened during the wave of labor militancy in the 1970s, especially following the miners' strike against the Heath government's policy on wage controls in 1973–1974 and Heath's subsequent defeat in the election of 1974. By the time Thatcher assumed the leadership of the Conservative Party in 1975, theories of "state ungovernability" and "government overload" were common themes of the New Right. According to these theories, the authority of Parliament had been undermined by the growth of neocorporate structures in which successive governments had attempted to make national economic policy in consultation with major interest groups representing business and labor. This process had failed because Britain's neocorporate structures were underdeveloped and because it had reduced the government to the status of "just one special interest among others."[74] This also allowed the power of trade unions and selected sectors of industry to grow to dangerous levels, each having the power to disrupt the economic life of the nation. Beyond this, in the age of the Keynesian welfare state, the government had become "overburdened" or "overloaded."[75] In assuming responsibility for full employment, economic growth, and a vast array of social services, the government had become hopelessly overextended.

The Thatcherite theory of statecraft sought the restoration of government authority through the creation of a smaller but stronger state. The foremost task was the reestablishment of the supremacy of Parliament, the cabinet, and the prime minister in national decision making. Around the public theme of a more centralized state, the Thatcherites sought changes in Parliament, the cabinet, Whitehall, neocorporate structures, and the nationalized industries that would accomplish this task. Most of the changes in Parliament, the cabinet, and Whitehall were stylistic or procedural in nature rather than structural because Thatcher personally doubted the usefulness of institutional manipulation.[76] In general, the prime minister's personal control over cabinet decision making was increased, there was greater reliance on informal groups of Thatcher confidants, and political pressure was brought to bear on civil servants to "serve" rather than "advise" their ministers.[77] Sessions of the House of Commons were televised beginning in 1988, reinforcing the popular view of Parliament as a stylized combat between Conservative and Labour Party leaders, and thus increasing its importance.[78]

Important political and institutional changes were made in neocorporate structures, as the Thatcherites sought to disengage the government from tripartite decision making. Neocorporate structures were either placed under the control of Thatcherite ministers, who neutralized them politically, or entirely dismantled.[79] In addition, the policy of privatization succeeded in returning to the private sector a majority of the previously nationalized industries.

The desire to reassert the state's authority over other groups in society led the three Thatcher governments to adopt an activist and interventionist posture. To the Thatcherites, reestablishing the authority of the state meant forcing the compliance of a wide variety of groups with the programs and objectives of the Thatcher government.[80] Target groups included major trade unions, local governments, the British Broadcasting Corporation (BBC), universities and their faculties, local school authorities, the civil service, the Greater London Council, groups within the legal profession, and the National Health Service. These episodes of intervention provoked prolonged and intense political conflicts. Throughout the Thatcher period, the capabilities of the police were constantly expanded. Between 1979 and 1988, the number of police in England and Wales increased by 11 percent, and in the London metropolitan area, it increased by 23 percent.[81] The increase in the size of the police force was accompanied by an extension of police powers and what some have called "the militarization of the police."[82] Their use to an unprecedented degree in industrial disputes, in the interception of communications, and at anti-Thatcher public assemblies was a major feature of the period.

The Crisis of the Economy

Like other postwar elites, the Thatcherites were confronted with the problems of accelerated economic decline, decreasing productivity, and the loss of competitiveness. The strategy they chose for dealing with this crisis was based almost entirely on neoliberal principles drawn from the works of such sources as F. A. Hayek, Milton Friedman, and the Austrian school of political economy. No economic master plan existed in 1975 or 1979, but elements of a neoliberal economic strategy had been presented in the 1960s by factions within the Conservative Party associated with Enoch Powell and had been first introduced in party discussions in the 1950s. Although Thatcher had never personally developed a systematic or detailed economic position prior to 1979, her basic political beliefs, as expressed in speeches and interviews, were consistent with the neoliberal position.[83]

According to the neoliberals, British economic decline was the result of a weakening of the market order, which had been underway for most of the twentieth century but had greatly accelerated in the Keynesian-collectivist era. The complex relationships that constituted the market had been disrupted and distorted by government regulations, increased public spending, high taxes, arbitrary interventions in industry, bureaucratic administration, nationalized industries, and the supplanting of the ideals of individualism with those of collectivism.[84] These same factors had led to structural rigidities in the national economy that impeded or rendered impossible adjustments to changing conditions in the international economy. Britain's trade unions, having been strengthened by legal immunities and neocorporatism, were the most important obstacles to the operation of the market and to structural adjustments because they functioned as coercive and disruptive monopolies in industrial relations.[85]

The Thatcherite economic strategy, which unfolded piecemeal and in stages between 1979 and 1990, reflected neoliberal assumptions about the nature and functioning of both the international and the domestic economies. In general, it sought to reverse Britain's economic decline by liberating entrepreneurial forces and removing all domestic impediments to the adjustment of the British economy to the new requirements of international competition.[86] The strategy accepted as irreversible the multinationalization and internationalization of the British economy, as well as the fact that the economic interests of the nation were no longer the same as those of explicitly domestic capital, and especially Britain's traditional industries. Instead, Thatcherism abandoned the national economic emphasis of Keynesianism and the concept of developing traditional industries for a new accumulation strategy. In the future, Britain would compete for wealth in the world on the basis of internationally tradable services, income from investments overseas by British citizens, and encouragement of inward investment in the United Kingdom by foreign multinational corporations operating in the country.[87] The new objectives required a new pattern of government intervention, a redrawing of the boundaries of state involvement in the economy, and the formation of a new political coalition to support Thatcher and her allies.

The Thatcherite economic strategy included four main sets of policies: (1) policies to achieve financial stability, fiscal discipline, and the reduction of inflation by controlling the money supply; (2) programs to promote supply-side improvements and flexibility (e.g., tax cuts, deregulation, and incentives); (3) programs to restructure and privatize the nationalized industries; and (4) actions and policies to increase "flexibility" in the labor market, including a sustained attack on the political power and legal position of trade unions.[88]

MOBILIZING FOR POWER

Margaret Thatcher's career as a political leader and the rise of the New Right in British politics occurred in five stages. Each stage was characterized by a unique pattern of politics within the Conservative Party, a unique pattern of competition between the Conservative Party and rival parties, and a different set of policy priorities.[89] Several of the periods were also distinguished by marked differences in the performance of the international economy, which not only affected the policy choices of the New Right but also the likelihood of their success. The stages occurred between February 1974 and November 1990.

Stage One: February 1974–February 1975

This stage witnessed the emergence of the Thatcherite faction within the Conservative Party and its active campaign to assume the leadership. The resurgence of the New Right was a direct response to the loss of the general election of February 1974, but it was also a reaction to the perceived loss of the party's identity, the crisis of ungovernability, and the crisis of the British economy. Initially, Sir Keith Joseph was the leader of the New Right faction. In a series of speeches in 1974, he restated the free-market arguments used by the Powellites in the 1960s and directly challenged the traditional party leadership. When Joseph decided not to oppose Edward Heath in the leadership contest of February 1975, Margaret Thatcher agreed to run in his place. Although she achieved victory on the second ballot, the party was severely divided, and the majority of the parliamentary party did not accept the economic principles of the New Right. The majority that voted for change did so only in order to reject the failed party leadership of Edward Heath.

Stage Two: March 1975–May 1979

In this stage, the Thatcherites worked to strengthen their power base within the Conservative Party and develop a political program capable of eliciting electoral support. Since the Conservative Party was a coalition of several strands of conservative thought and seven identifiable factions, the effort to consolidate control proceeded slowly.[90] Most of the members of Heath's shadow cabinet were retained in the first shadow cabinet of Thatcher, and there was a marked continuity in the area of policy. Most of the major issues that comprised Thatcher's program prior to 1979 had been present in the party manifestos of 1970 or 1974. These issues, however, were accompanied by a confrontational political style and radical rhetoric that were unprecedented in the postwar era. The collectivist-Keynesian consensus was denounced, a new era of "conviction politics" was proclaimed, and a new urgency was given to the need for change. The Thatcherite program combined neoliberal economic and material issues (e.g., reduced public expenditures, tax cuts, and antiinflation) with an authoritarian-populist or "strong state" stance on political and social issues (e.g., limits on immigration, hostility to unions, and tougher sentencing of criminals).[91] The program and style succeeded in attracting the support of both middle-class groups dissatisfied with the cost of the Keynesian welfare state and elements of the working class opposed to particular political outcomes like increased immigration.[92]

The national political position of the Thatcherites improved dramatically between 1977 and 1979, when the Labour government lost its majority in the House of Commons and the performance of the economy worsened. The soaring inflation and public sector strikes during the Winter of Discontent, 1978–1979, discredited both the Labour Party's economic strategy and the neocorporatist process on which it was based.[93]

Stage Three: May 1979–June 1983

The Thatcher-led Conservative Party won the 1979 election with 43.9 percent of the popular vote, capturing 339 seats and achieving a 43-seat majority in the House of Commons. The swing to the Conservatives in the popular vote was 5.1 percent, the largest of any election since 1945, and reflected both the success of Thatcher's deintegrative electoral strategy and the internal and electoral weaknesses of the Labour Party following the Winter of Discontent.[94] The first two years were critical in determining that the Thatcherites would have the opportunity to implement their neoliberal economic program. The years 1980 and 1981 corresponded with the onset of a world recession, the cabinet was numerically dominated by members of the former government of Edward Heath, and the implementation of the government's economic policies contributed to a worsening of the domestic recession. Within a year of the election, inflation had risen from 10 percent to 22 percent, and unemployment had increased from 1.3 million to over 2 million by the end of 1981.[95] In December 1981, Thatcher's approval rating with the general public fell to 25 percent, the lowest of any postwar prime minister, and in the summer of 1981, riots occurred in London, Liverpool, and Manchester.[96] Thatcher responded to these difficulties with what was to become a familiar pattern—by asserting that there was no alternative, continuing to pursue unpopular policies, and dominating those members of the party whom she could not convert. The cabinet's "E" (economic) subcommittee was packed with Thatcher's monetarist allies, the cabinet was reshuffled in January 1981 to strengthen her authority, and prominent wets within the cabinet, as well as the party chairman, who had criticized her policies, were dismissed in September 1981. By early 1982, Thatcher's standing in the polls began to improve in response to her determined and inflexible style of leadership. Her reputation for strong leadership was enormously enhanced by her handling of the Falkland Islands War from April to June 1982 and, to a lesser extent, by the policy of "no concessions" to Irish hunger strikers in the Maze prison in 1981.[97]

Stage Four: July 1983–1987

The Conservative party won the 1983 election with 42.4 percent of the vote, capturing 397 seats in the House of Commons and achieving a huge overall majority of 144 seats. The size of the victory reflected the skillful management of Thatcher's campaign; the unpopularity of the Labour Party, which was now dominated by the "hard left"; and approval of Thatcher's "strong state" and authoritarian-populist leadership style. As one analyst noted, "Attitudes to Thatcherism as statecraft had a powerful discriminating impact in the 1983 election," and the lesson of Thatcher's success was that a style demonstrating cohesion, purpose, and success was more important to voters than policy or ideology.[98] In this stage, Thatcher became more assertive in cabinet deliberations and more directly involved in the making of key decisions. In the first two and a half years following the election, Thatcher consolidated her control of the cabinet and party and undertook a more radical policy program. In 1983, ten ministers changed portfolios and three new members entered.[99] Additional reassignments and the cabinet reshuffle of September 1984 also strengthened the position of the Thatcherites and reduced the influence of wets. In this stage of "mature Thatcherism," a number of major neoliberal policy initiatives were undertaken, including the following: a fourfold increase in the privatization of public enterprises, increased deregulation of business, additional regulation of trade unions requiring secret ballots before strikes and for the continuance of union political funds, the defeat of the National Union of Mineworkers' strike of March 1984–March 1985 by the National Coal Board, and aggressive efforts to control the spending of local governments, including the abolition of the Greater London Council in 1986.[100] Many of these programs were extremely controversial (especially the initiatives in education and local government finance) and provoked occasional demonstrations of opposition within the ranks of the Conservative Party, the House of Commons, and the House of Lords.

These events demonstrated once again that Thatcher dominated the Conservative Party but had not converted it.[101] Following the major crisis of the second government (the Westland Affair, in which two cabinet ministers publicly disagreed on the sale of Britain's only helicopter manufacturer to foreign investors), Thatcher undertook a number of concessions to party moderates in preparation for the 1987 election. Limited initiatives to reduce unemployment, which had reached 3.2 million in 1986, were aided by the general expansion of the international economy after 1983.

Stage Five: June 1987–November 1990

The Thatcher-led Conservative Party won the 1987 election with 42.3 percent of the popular vote, winning 376 seats and achieving a majority of 102 seats. Margaret Thatcher thus became the first party leader in the twentieth century to achieve three consecutive election victories. Despite running a professional and effective campaign under the "dream team" of Neil Kinnock (left wing) and Roy Hattersly (right wing), the Labour Party was unable to seriously challenge the Conservatives' electoral dominance. The shock of the 1987 electoral defeat convinced Labour's leadership to undertake what some have called "the great transformation" to the "new model" Labour Party, whose policies and internal structure would be more popular in the changed political context.[102] Although centrist "consolidators" continued to predominate numerically within the Conservative Party, the Thatcherite wing was strengthened by the influx of forty-three new MPs, the majority of whom had backgrounds in business or finance.[103] Encouraged by the election and urged on by New Right ideologues who feared the end of policy radicalism, the Thatcherites undertook an ambitious program in the war against "socialist monopoly."[104] The major policy initiatives in this phase included the following: the transfer of some remaining council housing to private hands, additional privatization of nationalized companies, proposals for the reform of the state education system to facilitate provisions for "choice" and opting out, new curtailments on the legal immunities of trade unions, a comprehensive review of the National Health Service, reductions for the top personal tax brackets, and the replacement of the property-based "rates" tax with the community charge, or "poll tax," for funding local government. With the announcement of this new legislative agenda, Thatcher reached the height of her political power.

The events that were to end Thatcher's dominance over the party and ultimately lead to her resignation began to unfold in 1988. In late 1988 and 1989, in several public appearances, Thatcher intensified her criticism of the leadership of the European Community, and in October, Nigel Lawson, the Chancellor of the Exchequer, resigned in a dispute with Thatcher's personal economic advisor, Sir Alan Walters, over exchange rate policy. Further, in the spring of 1990, riots occurred in protest to the imposition of the poll tax in England and Wales, and in November, Sir Geoffrey Howe, Leader of the House, resigned in protest of Thatcher's position on European monetary union. Three issues, poor political management of the cabinet, opposition to further monetary and political integration in Europe, and the unpopularity of the poll tax, combined with a worsening economic performance after 1987, led to her downfall.[105] In the annual leadership contest of November 1990, Thatcher failed by four votes to achieve the required weighted majority for reelection (15 percent of the total membership of the parliamentary party). Following consultations with party leaders that convinced her that she lacked sufficient support within the parliamentary party, Thatcher resigned on November 22, 1990, prior to the second ballot. In her memoirs, Thatcher made clear her contempt for the party leaders who forced her resignation. Referring to the MPs as "the most slippery of electorates" and complaining of the "lie factor" in her discussion with other ministers, Thatcher argued that resentment against her exercise of cabinet authority and expectations of patronage were the real motivating factors in her defeat.[106] She also emphasized that she had never been defeated by the general electorate and would await the judgment of the bar of history.

IMPLEMENTING THE NEW PROGRAM: THE POLICY DIMENSION

Public policies are courses of action designed to promote, maintain, or prevent particular states of affairs at either the national or international level.[107] Because of the complex and changing domestic and international conditions at which they are directed, the policies of all major states display various degrees of inconsistency over time and within or across selected issue areas. Simply stated, there is an inevitable gap between a government's political and ideological ambitions and its policy achievements. Despite the exaggerated claims of coherence implied by the term "Thatcherism," the policies of the three Thatcher governments were no exception. They also underwent important changes over time as the Thatcherites shifted priorities, adapted to changing conditions, and undertook tactical reversals. Viewed from a comparative perspective, however, the governments of Margaret Thatcher demonstrated a greater degree of policy coherence than any other British government in the postwar era. The high degree of policy coherence resulted from six factors: (1) the nature of the British constitutional and parliamentary systems, which offer relatively few constraints on the power of the central executive; (2) the influence of New Right ideology, and especially neoliberal economic theory; (3) the influence of New Right policy institutes and interest groups; (4) the relative weakness of wet and other moderate factions within the Conservative Party; (5) the popular and electoral weaknesses of opposition parties, especially the British Labour Party; and (6) the strong leadership style of Thatcher and her determination to achieve radical economic and social reform.

The personal influence of Margaret Thatcher was greater in the policy-making area than in any other. Major works have been devoted to the "Thatcher Effect" and the "Thatcher Revolution" in public policy.[108] As prime minister, Thatcher adopted an unusually assertive style and sought to use the full range of constitutional and political powers of the office to increase her control over government decisions. She sought to create a government with a sense of direction, a unity of purpose, and a military-like loyalty to its leader.[109] Thatcher rejected the view of traditional Tory leaders that all factions of the party should be represented in the cabinet and that government policies should reflect group consensus. Under Thatcher, meetings of the full cabinet became less frequent, less collegial, and more directly under the control of the prime minister.[110] In deciding contentious issues, cabinet votes were seldom taken. Instead, Thatcher announced her policy preference at the outset, and this was expected to be the government's official position.[111] In addition, the members of special groups, such as important cabinet committees and the "E" Committee, which dealt with economic policy, were constituted to assure their dominance by Thatcherite ministers. This was especially important in the period before 1983, when those sharing Thatcher's policy outlook comprised a numerical minority in the cabinet. Thatcher also promoted a strongly centralist conception of government which assigned only minimal roles in the policy process to the civil service, royal commissions, and private interest groups.[112]

Neoliberal Economic and Social Policy

Thatcher assigned the highest priority to the implementation of neoliberal economic policies. The stated goal of these policies was to liberate market forces by replacing the "broadly corporatist economy" that had developed during the collectivist era with a "broadly capitalist one."[113] Between 1979 and 1990, the Thatcher government abandoned Keynesian demand management and government-sponsored incomes policies and drastically reduced subsidies to industry. It also renounced the traditional government commitment to full employment and abandoned the system of neocorporate-tripartite consultation in economic decision making that had been the cornerstone of the postwar settlement. Thatcher's program sought to restore Britain's international competitiveness by subjecting consumers and produc-

ers alike to market forces and by implementing the new accumulation strategy based on the service sector, income from foreign investments, and the
attraction of multinational corporations to the United Kingdom.

In the area of social policy, Thatcher sought to reshape the social structure
and transform political and social attitudes in order to promote an "enterprise
culture." The 1979 Conservative manifesto spoke of "working with the grain
of human nature, helping people to help themselves—and others."[114] Social
policy was guided by a set of basic beliefs, including the belief that public
expenditure was too high, the high levels of taxation required to fund social
services restricted choice and freedom, the welfare state had created a self-
serving bureaucracy that promoted a dependency culture, and it was time to
turn back to the traditional family, voluntary effort, and private provision to
meet needs.[115]

The simultaneous commitment to neoliberal and neoconservative political
values gave Thatcherite public policy certain distinctive characteristics. First,
the nearly continuous flow of legislation in such areas as labor relations and
local government finance revealed a trend of continuing intervention and
regulation in the economy and society. As one source argued, the Thatcher
government replaced the postwar "extensive" form of intervention with a
new "intensive" form, in which the issue areas subject to government action
were narrowed but the intervention was deepened.[116] Second, each of Thatcher's major economic and social policies entailed political benefits or subob-
jectives that strengthened the position of the Conservative Party. For
example, the weakening of the trade unions eroded the natural financial and
electoral base of the Labour Party. Third, notwithstanding her claims that
her policy agenda constituted a revolution, most of Thatcher's major policies
were not new and had been proposed or implemented by previous governments. Monetary targets were established by the Labour government of
James Callaghan in 1976, the government of Edward Heath passed legislation
to restrict the legal immunities of trade unions in 1972, and Conservative
Prime Minister Harold Macmillan proposed the spread of home ownership
in the 1960s. The new element of the Thatcher revolution was the distinct
style of confrontation, determination, and centralized leadership that accompanied the policy implementation.

The most radical departures from previous policy occurred in four areas—
economic management, labor relations, local government finance, and housing.[117] Other important policy initiatives were undertaken in the areas of
privatization of nationalized enterprises, taxation and deregulation, and share
ownership.

Macroeconomic Policy: Monetarism and Fiscal Constraint

At the time of Thatcher's first election in 1979, monetarism replaced
Keynesianism as the centerpiece of macroeconomic policy. New policy objectives were announced, including the control of inflation, the management

of sound money, the reduction of the public-sector borrowing requirement, and the promotion of competitiveness and efficiency.[118] The trade-off between lower inflation and higher unemployment was recognized and accepted as Thatcher's macroeconomic policy passed through three phases.[119] In the first stage (1979–1981), strict monetary guidelines were attempted with the adoption of the medium-term financial strategy. In stage two (1981–1985), the deepening recession and pressures from an appreciating pound forced the abandonment of strict monetary guidelines. A more flexible or pragmatic monetary approach was combined with a greater emphasis on reduced government spending. In the third phase (1986–1990), monetary targets were further deemphasized, although the emphasis on sound money remained. High interest rates and the maintenance of a strong exchange rate became the major weapons in the government's efforts to impose monetary discipline.

Labor Relations: Trade Union Policy

The curbing of trade union power was central to Thatcher's economic and political programs. Following several studies of trade union policy while in opposition, Thatcher decided on a policy of confrontation that would include three components: (1) the dismantling of the system of tripartite consultation, (2) changes in industrial relations laws, and (3) changes in the policing of strikes.[120] In addition to denying labor's role in national decision making, seven major employment and trade union acts were passed between 1979 and 1990. The major provisions removed legal support for closed shops, made unions and individual union leaders financially responsible for illegal strikes (protest and secondary strikes), expanded the ability of owners to dismiss strikers, and removed the legal immunities from unions, which authorized otherwise legal strikes but did not follow government-prescribed balloting and governance procedures.[121] Finally, in the first half of the 1980s, the Thatcher government undertook a carefully orchestrated policy of confrontation and resistance to strikes by steel workers, civil servants, railway employees, health workers, and miners. In the crucial episode of the Thatcher government, the year-long strike by the National Union of Mine Workers in 1984–1985, the government sequestered union funds and used aggressive policing tactics to undermine the miners. By the mid-1980s, there was a clear shift of bargaining power away from the trade unions, and in the entire decade, trade union membership fell by more than 3 million, a quarter of its total.[122]

Local Government Finance

Between 1979 and 1990, the Thatcher government passed more than forty acts in a protracted effort to reform the taxing and spending policies of local authorities. The task was complicated by the fact that most of Britain's major cities were governed by the opposition Labour Party, which sought to subvert Thatcher's economic and social policies. In 1986, the Thatcher government abolished the Greater London Council and six metropolitan county councils in response to their refusal to conform to spending guidelines. Also in 1986, at the personal insistence of Thatcher and against the advice of most of her cabinet, the government introduced the now infamous community charge, or "poll tax," as it was dubbed by her opponents. This tax imposed a per capita charge on each adult living in the local authority and was intended to replace the existing system of "domestic rates" or property taxes as the main source of government revenue. Thatcher defended the new tax on the grounds that it was "fairer," would enhance local government accountability, and would be less inflationary. However, the poll tax proved to be a disaster. It was more regressive than rates, raised the tax bill of 55 percent of the electorate, and touched off a national nonpayment campaign.[123] After Thatcher left office, the policy was withdrawn.

Housing

The "spread of home ownership" was a major theme of Thatcher's social program from the beginning. Publicly touted as a program to increase freedom of choice, promote personal responsibility, and increase citizen commitment to the community, the program took several forms. These included the retention of tax relief on mortgage interest, the sale of government land, and the promotion of shared-ownership schemes.[124] The most important measure, however, was the "right to buy" legislation, which offered the tenants of local council housing the opportunity to buy their houses or apartments at discounts ranging from 33 percent to 50 percent and more. Between 1979 and 1988, 1.2 million units of council housing were sold and the number of people owning their own home increased by 3 million.[125] This program legislated away part of the Labour Party's electoral base because Labour tenants who bought their own homes were more likely to vote for the Conservative Party in subsequent elections.[126]

Privatization of Nationalized Enterprises

Although not part of the 1979 program, by 1983 privatization had become a major theme of the Thatcher government. In the decade of the 1980s, the size of the public corporation sector was reduced by about one-half, and the government received £29 billion in proceeds from the sales.[127] The privatized firms included twenty major utilities, British Aerospace, British Airways, British Steel, and British Telecom (51 percent). Combined with the assets from the sale of council housing, public lands, and public buildings, the total proceeds from privatization programs reached £60 billion by the time of

Thatcher's resignation.[128] Critics charged that the shares were undervalued, that increased competition did not result, and moreover, that the privatizations did not lead to improved management.

Taxation and Deregulation

Consistent with neoliberal values, direct taxes were cut, with the top rate being reduced from 75 percent to 40 percent between 1979 and 1988. A reduction in the basic (lowest) tax was also undertaken in 1987. Indirect taxes were increased to compensate for lost revenues, with the VAT (value-added tax) increasing to 15 percent from the old two-tiered system of 8 percent and 12 percent, and a substantial surcharge was applied to national insurance contributions.[129] For the average wage earner, the total tax bill relative to wages earned increased from 45.5 percent in 1979 to 45.7 percent in 1989, as the cuts in income tax were heavily biased in favor of the highest income groups.[130]

Various ministries and offices also undertook reviews of government regulations, with the aim of updating or eliminating unnecessary ones. Financial deregulation, including the abolition of exchange controls in 1979, was a major priority of the Thatcher government and resulted in a rapid growth of profits in the financial services industry.

Share Ownership

In addition to rolling back state control and reducing public sector borrowing, the Thatcher government sought to use the privatization of nationalized enterprises to promote its goal of "popular capitalism." The share issues (stock offerings) of the privatized companies were tailored for modest investors, and the program was touted as a means of spreading wealth and ownership of industry.[131] On the surface, the campaign was successful. Twenty-two percent of the public bought shares, the number of shareholders tripled between 1979 and 1991, and by the time Thatcher left office, shareholders outnumbered trade union members by five to four.[132] Critics point out, however, that during the 1980s, the total proportion of shares owned by individuals actually declined, that 80 percent of the market value in shares was accounted for by wealthier individuals, and that the biggest beneficiaries from the program were the banks, stockbrokers, and lawyers who profited from the transactions.

Three Public Policy Failures: The End

Following Thatcher's third election victory in 1987, her position as Conservative Party leader appeared secure. The victory was generally interpreted to mean that she had overcome the 1986 Westland Affair and the resignations from the cabinet of Michael Heseltine and Leon Brittan. However, unpopular policies in three areas—the poll tax, relations with Europe, and the economy—undermined her position.[133] The poll tax politicized central-local relations to the benefit of the Labour Party,[134] and Thatcher's opposition to additional measures for European integration, including her long-standing opposition to Britain joining the Exchange Rate Mechanism, split the Conservative Party.[135] In addition, in response to rising inflation between 1988 and 1990, the government increased interest rates to an eight-year high. This action contributed to a deep recession in which manufacturing output and gross domestic product fell for five successive quarters.[136] Critics charged that the recession could have been avoided if the government had acted in a timely fashion to lower interest rates and that government policy was in a state of chaos due to the internal conflict between Chancellor of the Exchequer Nigel Lawson and Sir Alan Walters, Thatcher's personal economic advisor.[137] By 1990, the Conservatives trailed the Labour Party by twenty points in the public opinion polls, and the same polls showed that a majority disagreed with Thatcher's stand on many major issues. Increasingly, what has been termed her "active-negative" style came to be interpreted as an attitude of callousness, rigidity, and "not caring."[138] Following the resignation of Nigel Lawson as chancellor of the exchequer in 1989 and Sir Geoffrey Howe as leader of the house in 1990, an increasing number of Conservative MPs became convinced that the party could not win the next election with Margaret Thatcher as its leader. This concern led to her defeat in the 1990 leadership race.

NATURE AND SCOPE OF CHANGE

A proper assessment of the scope of change during the Thatcher era requires the avoidance of both Thatcher's grandiose claims to have changed everything and the position of some opponents that nothing was accomplished except a change of style and rhetoric.[139] It is also important to give due consideration to the pressures for political and policy continuity that existed throughout the 1980s and may have contributed to Thatcher's political demise.[140] In policy areas where change has been apparent, the central issue is the degree to which Britain's economic, social, or political life was permanently transformed. Two issues are central to an understanding of the Thatcher legacy: (1) the degree to which the political and electoral dimension was transformed, including changes in the pattern of political discourse, public opinion, and the manner in which leaders attempt to deal with national political turbulence; and (2) the performance of the economy during the Thatcher years, with special emphasis on the degree to which Britain's economic decline was slowed or reversed.

Change: The Political and Electoral Dimension

The emergence of Thatcherism coincided with a major period of change in British social and political life that resulted from the achievement of post-industrial society, the decline of the industrial workforce, the emergence of postmaterialist political values, and demographic shifts from North to South and from urban areas to small towns. Within the general context of a society in transformation, both Thatcher and her program acted as powerful catalysts for political change. To the extent possible for a leader in a democracy, Thatcher dominated British politics for a decade and had a powerful impact on the political agenda, the style of government, the ideological commitments of the major political parties, and the nation's electoral politics. Aided by the internal contradictions of the welfare state and the emerging intellectual ascendancy of the New Right in much of the Western world, Thatcher redefined the political agenda and reshaped the national political discourse. She successfully discredited collectivist policies and institutions and, employing such measures as the privatization of nationalized enterprises, the sale of council housing, deregulation, and the change in the legal and political status of trade unions, made a return to the collectivist polity impossible. Thatcher's "strong state" and centralist style of government proved extremely popular with the general electorate because it met the psychological needs of citizens anxious about their personal and collective futures.

Thatcher's general strategy for dealing with opposition and controlling the elements of turbulence that were the byproducts of decline was to employ a crude power politics.[141] Her political legacy was, above all, one of agenda deconstruction, deintegrative electoral politics, and social division on the basis of class and race. By 1990, the era of consensus-based politics seemed only a distant memory.

Thatcher's deintegrative electoral strategy had a devastating effect on the political opposition. The old Labour Party constituencies, which were already under pressure from the effects of long-term socioeconomic change, were further divided by contentious issues such as immigration and "union reform" and by the effects of Thatcherite programs like the sale of council housing. Equally damaging, Thatcher's relentless campaign to identify the Labour Party with failed economic management, chaotic industrial relations, and increasing poverty was highly successful. Thatcher's 1987 election victory marked the fifth successive election in which the Labour Party failed to garner 40 percent of the vote, a defeat that forced the Labour leadership to undertake the "great transformation" to a "new model" Labour Party that recognized the essential role of the market, deemphasized public ownership, and abandoned many of the party's other traditional policies.[142] Despite making some electoral gains, the Labour Party lost again in the 1992 election (after Thatcher's resignation), which prompted serious students of British politics to argue that the British political system had become a "predominate-party system" or "democratic one-party state" with one major party (the Conservatives), one minor party (Labour), and one peripheral party (the Liberal Democrats).[143]

Despite Thatcher's dominance of British politics throughout most of the 1980s, by the time of her resignation, the political limits of the Thatcher revolution had become clear. Thatcher's resignation in 1990, which was forced by major defections within the parliamentary party, demonstrated that she had temporarily dominated the Conservative Party but had not converted it to her position on such issues as the poll tax or relations with Europe. It also became clear following her resignation that she had not prepared a successor. In addition, public opinion surveys spanning the 1980s clearly demonstrated that there had been no Thatcherite "cultural revolution" and that on nine out of ten major issues, the electorate had become "less Thatcherite" and more welfare-oriented as the decade progressed.[144] As Andrew Gamble and others have argued, Thatcher helped to discredit the social democratic and collectivist order, but Thatcherism was not sufficiently popular at either the elite or mass level to form the basis of a new national consensus on which successful national projects must be based.[145]

The Economic Record

Thatcherism reversed the economic priorities of previous postwar governments and replaced Keynesianism with a mixture of monetarist, supply-side, and service sector initiatives advocated by a small minority of professional economists. The control of inflation took priority over reducing unemployment, monetary policy was assigned greater importance than fiscal policy, and wage and incomes policies were abandoned for programs designed to liberate market forces.[146] In addition, the Thatcher government accepted dramatically higher rates of unemployment and demonstrated to the rest of Europe that a government could survive electorally despite a doubling of unemployment in its first term (to more than 11%).[147] All this was done in order to achieve future gains in competitiveness and productivity and to arrest economic decline.

Thatcher's economic record remains a topic of intense debate, but it is clear that the achievements fell far short of her claims to have produced an economic revolution. Thatcher's supporters point to the fact that she forced the issue of economic competitiveness to the forefront and cite the following accomplishments: (1) growth in the number of self-employed persons and small firms, (2) the development of new attitudes toward work and achievement, (3) increased productivity and profitability in manufacturing, (4) a reduction of the inflation rate by half compared to the years 1970 through 1979, (5) an increase in employment of 2 million, or 8 percent, between 1979 and 1990, and (6) a reduction of state spending as a share of the gross domestic product.[148] Despite these positive developments, however, the economic record is, at best, mixed. During the Thatcher years, the average annual growth of the GDP was 2.3 percent, which was a slight improvement over the 1.9 percent growth achieved between 1970 and 1979 but well below the performance of the 1960s.[149]

Since the growth that did occur was primarily achieved in the south, one of the legacies of Thatcherism was an increasing regional imbalance, leading to a widening of the north-south divide. In addition, although the Thatcher government assigned top priority to the goal of controlling inflation, when Thatcher left office in 1990, the inflation level of 9.7 percent was only slightly lower than the rate of 10.3 percent she had inherited when she took office in May 1979.[150] Further, unemployment during the 1980s was an average of 6 percentage points higher than in the 1970s.[151] Between 1979 and 1981 alone, the number of unemployed individuals doubled to more than 2 million, and it peaked in 1986, when more than 3.3 million, or 11.1 percent of the workforce, was unemployed. Unemployment dropped after 1986 and stood at 5.7 percent at the time of Thatcher's resignation in 1990, but by the time of the 1992 election, it had returned to more than 11 percent.

Thatcher's critics also argue that a decade of supply-side initiatives did little or nothing to improve Britain's global trading position. During the 1990s, Britain's share of world trade in manufactures stabilized at 8 percent but did not rise.[152] In addition, between 1980 and 1988, investment in manufacturing fell by 30 percent (partly the result of the end of exchange controls in 1979), and there was an increase in import penetration that led to an increasing balance of payments deficit from 1987 on.[153] Even in the area of tradable services, a key element of Thatcher's accumulation strategy, Britain's competitiveness and trade surplus declined after 1986.[154] Considered collectively, the trends of the 1980s appear to be consistent with the overall pattern of economic performance since the 1960s rather than harbingers of an economic miracle. This is not surprising since the economic changes required to enhance a nation's competitiveness require enormously expensive, long-term investments in technology, the infrastructure, and human development. These the Thatcherites did not make, and throughout the 1980s, an increasingly large share of investment capital left Britain in quest of overseas profits. The judgment seems inescapable that Thatcher was far more successful in dealing with British political turbulence than she was in confronting the shortcomings of the nation's economy.

INTERPRETING MARGARET THATCHER AS LEADER

Margaret Thatcher's career illustrates well the opportunities and constraints that confront leaders in the period of political turbulence. Thatcher's opportunity for power came as a result of the disempowerment of ideas, groups, and institutions upon which the postwar Keynesian welfare state depended. These included the Keynesian economic model, the trade union movement, the Labour Party, and the "wet" faction within the Conservative Party, which supported Keynesianism. Specifically, the worsening of British economic performance that occurred after 1970 made possible an attack on the welfare state. As Britain's economic decline accelerated throughout the 1970s, criticisms of Keynesianism as a theory became both increasingly credible and politically rewarding.[155] With the simultaneous loss of 2.8 million jobs in the decades of the 1970s and 1980s, the position of the trade unions was also weakened in both industrial relations and national politics. The decline of the wet faction and the British Labour Party followed specific events. The wets lost control of the Conservative Party following the defeat of the Heath government in the two elections of 1974, and the Labour Party was discredited within the general electorate, possibly permanently, following the failures of the economic policies of the Wilson and Callaghan governments between 1974 and 1979.

Thatcher's rise to power was also aided by the general empowerment of capitalist and private sector interests that occurred in Britain and throughout the Western world. In the decades of the 1970s and 1980s, the number of policy institutes, business interest groups, and professional economists espousing New Right economic principles steadily increased and became an important source of theoretical support for Thatcher's program. Especially important was the increased influence of the British financial sector over government economic policy, which resulted, in part, from the need of the governments of the 1970s to borrow more money from private markets.[156] These institutes and groups contributed to legitimizing monetarism as an alternative to the Keynesian economic model. Thatcher also benefited from changes within the general population that accompanied the movement to a mass consumer society. The change in the production and consumption patterns of many households toward the private sector and away from public goods and services prepared the way for her program of cuts in public spending and privatization.[157]

In the three electoral victories, Thatcher's support was narrowly based among upper-income groups, property owners, employers and the self-employed, and private sector workers and consumers.[158] This Conservative electoral support was reinforced by privatizations, anti–trade union policies, and reductions in public spending, which expanded the influence and role of the private sector. Although Thatcher's share of the vote never exceeded 43.9 percent and declined in each election, her support was far more unified and dependable than that of the opposition, which was fragmented among several parties and susceptible to divisive appeals to such issues as race and law and order. Because of substantial support for third parties, Thatcher was able to achieve an absolute parliamentary majority while receiving only a minority of the national vote.[159]

Once elected, Thatcher exploited the full potential of the Office of the Prime Minister for generating sustained political power and developing coherent policy. In her quest for power, Thatcher was aided by the structure of British politics of the 1980s, including the following factors: the centralized and unitary nature of the constitution; the nondocumentary constitution, in which legislation can alter the system of government (as with local government in the London area); disciplined Conservative Party majorities in Parliament; cabinet domination of the parliamentary party; and the power of the prime minister over appointments and patronage.[160] Simply stated, the British system of government offered few constraints on Thatcher's dogmatic and personal style of government, which ignored traditional conventions of collegiality, bypassed Parliament, and established rule by a political clique. The most important factor in her domination of politics for a decade was the weakness of the opposition. The Labour Party was discredited by its commitment to an antiquated version of socialism, while the third parties in Parliament and the moderates within the Conservative Party were unable to offer a fully articulated, alternative program to Thatcherism.[161] Following the disempowerment of the Keynesian welfare state, the Thatcherites were presented with a great opportunity to remake the national political agenda. Thatcher succeeded in discrediting the previous Keynesian system, but not in converting the British population to the specific policies of her program.

In the final analysis, Thatcher's fall from power in 1990 can be largely attributed to the effects of political turbulence. Britain's membership in the European Community presented the Thatcher government with complex issues having both domestic and foreign policy dimensions. Thatcher's opposition to the expansion of the EC after 1988 ran counter to the beliefs of the overwhelming majority of the Conservative Party that Britain's future was in Europe and that a "one nation" approach to the economy was impossible in the age of global capitalism.[162] Similarly, the poll tax was also a serious miscalculation because it provided Labour Party–controlled local governments with an issue around which to organize opposition to Conservative Party rule. The Conservative Party, which was proud of its tradition as the "party of government," permitted Thatcher a wide latitude in policy making and government management, as long as she was capable of winning elections. When public opinion surveys in 1990 revealed a growing probability of defeat in the upcoming election, the hierarchy of the party acted to remove her. In the end, she was the victim of political turbulence at two levels, facing opposition from future-oriented groups seeking further integration of the United Kingdom into the European Community system and opposition from local-level groups seeking to return to the policies and system of local taxation of the Keynesian welfare state.

NOTES

1. A. G. Champion and A. R. Townshend, *Contemporary Britain: A Geographic Perspective* (New York: Edward Arnold, 1990), p. 14.

2. Ibid., p. 17.

3. See Stephen A. Marglin and Juliet B. Schor, eds., *The Golden Age of Capitalism: Reinterpreting the Postwar Experience* (New York: Oxford University Press, 1991), pp. 39–125.

4. Mark Kesselman and Joel Krieger, eds., *European Politics in Transition* (Lexington, MA: D. C. Heath and Company, 1987), p. 47.

5. See Samuel H. Beer, *Britain Against Itself: The Political Contradictions of Collectivism* (New York: W. W. Norton and Co., 1982).

6. Kesselman and Krieger, pp. 9–13, 44–47.

7. Ian Stone, "The UK Economy," in Frans Somers, ed., *European Economies: A Comparative Study* (London: Pitman Publishing, 1991), p. 174.

8. Kesselman and Krieger, p. 55.

9. Martin Harrop, "The United Kingdom," in Martin Harrop, ed., *Power and Policy in Liberal Democracies* (New York: Cambridge University Press, 1992), p. 71.

10. See Andrew Gamble, *Britain in Decline* (London: MacMillan Press, 1990), pp. 10–40. See also Robert A. Isaak, *European Politics: Political Economy and Policy Making in Western Democracies* (New York: St. Martin's Press, 1980), pp. 99–125.

11. Gamble, p. 25.

12. John Clark and Mary Langan, "Restructuring Welfare: The British Welfare Regime in the 1980s," in Allan Cochane and John Clarke, eds., *Comparing Welfare States: Britain in International Context* (London: Sage Publications, 1993), p. 51.

13. Kesselman and Krieger, pp. 46–47.

14. See Beer, pp. 110–114.

15. Judith Ryder and Harold Silver, *Modern English Society* (London: Methuen and Company, 1977), p. 288.

16. Samuel Beer, *Modern British Politics: Parties and Pressure Groups in the Collectivist Age* (London: Faber and Faber, 1982), pp. 304–317.

17. Ibid., pp. 386–388.

18. Beer, *Britain Against Itself*, pp. 171–172.

19. For a discussion of individual neocorporate structures, see Richard Rose, *Politics in England: Change and Persistence*, 5th ed. (Boston: Scott, Foresman and Company, 1989), pp. 239–241.

20. Beer, *Britain Against Itself*, pp. 4–12.

21. Margaret Weir, "Ideas and Politics: The Acceptance of Keynesianism in Britain and the United States," in Peter A. Hall, ed., *The Political Power of Economic Ideas: Keynesianism across Nations* (Princeton, NJ: Princeton University Press, 1989), pp. 74–75.

22. Peter A. Hall, "The Movement from Keynesianism to Monetarism: Institutional Analysis and British Economic Policy in the 1970s," in Sven Steinmo, Kathleen Thelen, and Frank Longstreth, eds., *Structuring Politics: Historical Institutionalism in Comparative Analysis* (Cambridge, England: Cambridge University Press, 1992), p. 94.

23. For a study of Britain's interaction with the European Community, see Stephen George, *An Awkward Partner* (New York: Oxford University Press, 1990).

24. Harrop, "United Kingdom," p. 74.

25. See James N. Rosenau, *Turbulence in World Politics: A Theory of Change and Continuity* (Princeton, NJ: Princeton University Press, 1990), pp. 7–12.

26. Colin Leys, *Politics in Britain: From Labourism to Thatcherism* (New York: Verso, 1989), p. 72.

27. Kesselman and Krieger, pp. 54–55.

28. Ibid., p. 54.

29. Ibid., p. 55.

30. Beer, *Britain Against Itself*, pp. 23–30.

31. Ibid., pp. 15, 16–19.

32. Ibid., p. 16.

33. Ibid., p. 17.

34. Kesselman and Krieger, pp. 58–59.

35. Ibid., p. 61.

36. Ibid.

37. Peter Jenkins, *Mrs. Thatcher's Revolution: The Ending of the Socialist Era* (Cambridge, MA: Harvard University Press, 1988), p. 82.

38. Ibid.

39. Kenneth Harris, *Thatcher* (London: Weidenfeld and Nicolson, 1988), p. 45.

40. Ibid., p. 42.

41. Hugo Young, *The Iron Lady: A Biography of Margaret Thatcher* (New York: The Noonday Press, 1989), p. 7.

42. Ibid., pp. 14–15.

43. Ibid., p. 31.

44. Jenkins, p. 85.

45. Ibid.; Young, p. 25; John Ranelagh, *Thatcher's People: An Insider's Account of the Politics, the Power and the Personalities* (London: Fontana, 1991), pp. 24–25.

46. Jenkins, p. 3.

47. David Willets, *Modern Conservatism* (New York: Penguin Books, 1992), p. 45.

48. Ibid., p. 43.

49. Ibid., pp. 42–43.

50. Ibid., p. 50.

51. Andrew Beesley, cited in Dennis Kavanagh, *Thatcherism and British Politics: The End of Consensus?* 2nd ed. (New York: Oxford University Press, 1990), p. 107.

52. Ibid., pp. 80–92.

53. Ibid., p. 89.

54. Robert Skidelsky, ed., *Thatcherism* (Cambridge, MA: Basil Blackwell, 1990), p. 15.

55. Kenneth Hoover and Raymond Plant, *Conservative Capitalism in Britain and the United States* (New York: Routledge, 1989), pp. 22–23.

56. Desmond S. King, *The New Right: Politics, Markets and Citizenship* (Chicago: The Dorsey Press, 1987), p. 11.

57. Kavanagh, p. 106.

58. Leonard Tivey and Anthony Wright, eds., *Party Ideology in Britain* (New York: Routledge, 1989), p. 64; Kavanagh, p. 106.

59. Kavanagh, p. 106.

60. Andrew Beesley, cited in Kavanagh, p. 107.

61. Ivor Crewe, "The Thatcher Legacy," in Anthony King et al., *Britain at the Polls 1992* (Chatham, NJ: Chatham House Publishers, 1993), p. 19.

62. Bob Jessop, Kevin Bonnett, Simon Bromley, and Tom Ling, eds., *Thatcherism: A Tale of Two Nations* (New York: Polity Press, 1988), p. 5.

63. Ibid., p. 166.

64. Concerning the lack of a master plan in the early years, see Peter Riddell, *The Thatcher Era and Its Legacy* (Cambridge, MA: Blackwell, 1991), p. 5.

65. See Riddell, pp. 113–114; Jessop, Bonnett, Bromley, and Ling, p. 63.

66. Willets, p. 50.

67. For the best presentation of these issues by a Thatcher supporter, see Nicholas Ridley, *My Style of Government: The Thatcher Years* (London: Fontana, 1992). See also Riddell, pp. 13–126.

68. For a presentation of this view, see Joel Krieger, *Reagan, Thatcher and the Politics of Decline* (New York: Oxford University Press, 1986), pp. 29–30, 189–198.

69. Ray Hudson and Allan M. Williams, *Divided Britain* (New York: Belhaven Press, 1989), p. 16; Jessop, Bonnett, Bromley, and Ling, p. 167.

70. See Hudson and Williams, chapters 2–6.

71. Andrew Gamble, *The Free Economy and the Strong State: The Politics of Thatcherism* (Durham, NC: Duke University Press, 1988), pp. 213–215.

72. For a good discussion of deintegrative issues, see Kesselman and Krieger, pp. 105–112.

73. Kavanagh, p. 106.

74. Kenneth Minogue, cited in Jessop, Bonnett, Bromley, and Ling, p. 39.

75. Jim Bulpitt, cited in ibid., pp. 38–39.

76. Crewe, "The Thatcher Legacy," p. 2.

77. Ibid., p. 3.

78. Ibid., pp. 2–3.

79. Henk Overbeek, *Global Capitalism and National Decline: The Thatcher Decade in Perspective* (Boston: Unwin Hyman, 1990), p. 203.

80. Gamble, *The Free Economy and the Strong State*, p. 233.

81. K. D. Ewing and C. A. Gearty, *Freedom under Thatcher: Civil Liberties in Modern Britain* (Oxford, U.K.: Clarendon Press, 1990), pp. 17–18.

82. Ibid., p. 85.

83. For an interesting discussion by Thatcher of her economic views at the time she assumed office in 1979, see Margaret Thatcher, *The Downing Street Years* (New York: Harper Collins, 1993), pp. 5–15, 38–56.

84. See Gamble, *Britain in Decline*, pp. 143–147.

85. Ibid., p. 152.

86. Ibid., p. 147.

87. Gamble, *The Free Economy and the Strong State*, p. 226.

88. See Ron Martin, "The Economy," in Paul Cloke, ed., *Policy and Change in Thatcher's Britain* (New York: Pergamon Press, 1992), pp. 128–131.

89. For a theoretical discussion of the stages of Thatcherism, see Jessop, Bonnett, Bromley, and Ling, pp. 11–20, 59–67.

90. Concerning the coalition, see Crewe, "The Thatcher Legacy," in Anthony King, pp. 33–35.

91. Jessop, Bonnett, Bromley, and Ling, p. 61.

92. Ibid.

93. Ibid., p. 62.

94. J. Denis Derbyshire and Ian Derbyshire, *Politics in Britain from Callaghan to Thatcher* (Oxford, U.K.: Chambers, 1988), p. 76.

95. Ibid., pp. 83, 87.

96. Leys, p. 106.

97. Ibid., p. 107.

98. Ivor Crewe, "Has the Electorate become Thatcherite?" in Skidelsky, ed., pp. 48–49.

99. Derbyshire and Derbyshire, p. 110.

100. See ibid., pp. 111–116.

101. For an excellent presentation of this thesis, see Philip Norton, "The Conservative Party from Thatcher to Major," in King et al., pp. 38–48.

102. See Patrick Seyd, "Prospects for British Politics in the 1990s," in King et al., pp. 70–100.

103. Derbyshire, p. 170.

104. Leys, p. 123.

105. For an excellent analysis of these factors, see Norton in King, pp. 38–48.

106. Thatcher, pp. 834, 837, 859.

107. Peter Jones, "Evaluation," in Martin Harrop, ed., *Power and Policy in Liberal Democracies* (New York: Cambridge University Press, 1992), p. 241.

108. See Dennis Kavanagh and Anthony Seldon, eds., *The Thatcher Effect: A Decade of Change* (Oxford, U.K.: Clarendon Press, 1989); see also Jenkins.

109. See Ridley, pp. 25, 28.

110. Crewe, "The Thatcher Legacy," p. 3.

111. Ibid.

112. Ibid.

113. Ibid.

114. Cited in Gerald Wistow, "The National Health Service," in David Marsh and R.A.W. Rhodes, eds., *Implementing Thatcherite Policies: Audit of an Era* (Philadelphia: Open University Press, 1992), p. 101.

115. Jonathan Bradshaw, "Social Security," in Marsh and Rhodes, p. 81.

116. Martin, p. 133.

117. R. A. W. Rhodes and David Marsh, "Thatcherism: an Implementation Perspective" in Marsh and Rhodes, p. 10.

118. Martin, p. 126.

119. Riddell, pp. 18–24.

120. John MacInnes, *Thatcherism at Work: Industrial Relations and Economic Change* (Philadelphia: Open Press, 1987), p. 46.

121. Kesselman and Krieger, p. 113.

122. Crewe, "The Thatcher Legacy," p. 5.

123. R. A. W. Rhodes, "Local Government Finance," in Marsh and Rhodes, p. 60. For Thatcher's defense of her position on the community charge, see Thatcher, pp. 642–655.

124. Riddell, p. 115.

125. Crewe, "The Thatcher Legacy," p. 16; Riddell, p. 115.

126. Crewe, "The Thatcher Legacy," p. 17.

127. Christopher Johnson, *The Economy Under Mrs. Thatcher 1979–1990* (London: Penguin Books), pp. 158, 163.

128. Ibid., p. 172.

129. Bob Rowthorn, "Government Spending and Taxation in the Thatcher Era,"

in Jonathan Michie, ed., *The Economic Legacy 1979–1992* (New York: Academic Press, 1992), p. 263.

130. Riddell, p. 152.

131. Crewe, "The Thatcher Legacy," p. 15.

132. Ibid., pp. 15–16.

133. Norton, pp. 39–48.

134. Rhodes, p. 60.

135. Norton, p. 43.

136. David Sanders, "Why the Conservative Party Won—Again," in A. King, p. 177.

137. For a discussion of this thesis, see David Smith, *From Boom to Bust: Trial and Error in British Economic Policy* (New York: Penguin Books, 1992).

138. This concept is attributed to James David Barber, cited in Norton, p. 39,

139. For Thatcher's views on her achievements in the area of economic policy, see Chapter 23, "To Cut and to Please," in Thatcher, pp. 668–688.

140. Patrick Dunleavy, "Prospects for British Politics in the 1990s," in Patrick Dunleavy, Andrew Gamble, and Gillian Peele, eds., *Developments in British Politics 3* (New York: St. Martin's Press, 1990), p. 13.

141. Krieger summarized by Jessop, Bonnett, Bromley, and Ling, p. 39.

142. Seyd, pp. 70–78.

143. Anthony King, "The Implications of One-Party Government," in King et al., p. 224.

144. Cited by Norton, pp. 32–33.

145. See Gamble, *The Free Economy and the Strong State*, pp. 208–231.

146. See Peter M. Jackson, "Thatcherism: Implementation Perspective," in Marsh and Rhodes, pp. 11–15.

147. Crewe, "The Thatcher Legacy," p. 12.

148. Martin, pp. 136–149.

149. Ibid., pp. 139–140.

150. Jonathan Michie and Frank Wilkinson, "Inflation Policy and the Restructuring of Labour Markets," in Jonathan Michie, ed., *The Economic Legacy* (London: Academic Press, 1992), p. 195.

151. Johnson, p. 245.

152. Jackson, p. 23.

153. See Ken Coutts and Wynne Godley, "Does Britain's Balance of Payments Matter Any More?" in Michie, pp. 60–67.

154. Martin, p. 144.

155. Hall, pp. 90–113.

156. Ibid., p. 100.

157. Stephen Edgell and Vic Duke, *A Measure of Thatcherism: A Sociology of Britain* (London: Harper Collins Academic, 1991), pp. 21–45, 217–221.

158. Ibid., pp. 217–219.

159. David Beetham, "Political Theory and British Politics," in Patrick Dunleavy, Andrew Gamble, Ian Holliday, and Gillian Peele, eds., *Developments in British Politics 4* (London: The MacMillan Press, 1993), p. 364.

160. F. F. Ridley, "That Happened to the Constitution under Mrs. Thatcher?" in

Bill Jones and Lynton Robins, eds., *Two Decades in British Politics* (New York: Manchester University Press, 1992), pp. 123–125.

161. For an insider's view of the wets' failure, see Ian Gilmour, *Dancing with Dogma: Britain under Thatcherism* (New York: Simon and Schuster, 1993), pp. 36–53.

162. Ibid., pp. 324–326.

Helmut Kohl and the German Reunification Project

THE NATIONAL POLITICAL-ECONOMIC CONTEXT

The German Question in Long-Term Perspective

Since its inception in 1949, the Federal Republic of Germany has established an impressive record of political stability and economic achievement. The Federal Republic is, however, the product of a tumultuous and complex history. Major studies done in the aftermath of World War II have described the history of the German people as one of political extremes, divergent forces, and even deviations from the main lines of European political and cultural development.[1] Four historical factors were especially important in the political development of the German people, without reference to which German politics in the nineteenth and twentieth centuries cannot be understood. First, Germany was the last major European state to achieve political unification. Despite the fact that Germans shared a distinct linguistic and cultural identity for almost two thousand years, a single state with a strong central authority was not established in the area of present-day Germany until 1871. German politics of the last two centuries has been dominated by what has been called the "National Question," the quest to establish a national state and define its territory and population. Second, the quest for national unity was greatly complicated by Germany's geographic location and structure. Situated at the center of Europe, Germany was for centuries a strategic battleground for foreign and indigenous groups seeking to establish political or military supremacy. The nearly endless civil strife, religious wars, and foreign invasions have fostered perceptions of victimization among Germans and contributed to the growth of a defensive and xenophobic nationalism.

The third historical factor concerned the manner in which Germany achieved unified statehood. When political unification was finally achieved in 1871, the process was dominated by the ruling political elites of Brandenburg-Prussia. Prussia's political culture and leadership groups were more antidemocratic than their counterparts in other German states.[2] Brandenburg-Prussia became synonymous with bureaucratic absolutism, the militarization of society, and an aggressive foreign policy, which led to wars with neighboring states. Despite a liberal and federal facade, the unified state that was created in 1871 superimposed the major features of Prussia on the entire country. Finally, the process of industrialization in Germany was both late and rapid. These two facts had several important economic and social consequences for the nation's future development. In order to speed industrialization, German state elites became deeply involved in economic planning, and especially in aiding selected industrial sectors like steel and railroads. The high concentration of economic power in these industries and the close association between industries and banks helped Germany become the dominant economic power in Europe by 1914. Equally important, the rapid industrial process created a huge social upheaval as a largely peasant population was recruited to the rigors of industrial life in little more than a generation.[3] In response, the population of "peasant workers" became radicalized, with many turning to the socialist movement to achieve better working conditions and increased political rights.[4] In short, German development prior to World War I was characterized by successful economic modernization but incomplete political modernization.[5]

Recent studies stress that Germany was not alone in its experience with late industrialization and domestic political conflict, and it is impossible to identify any ideal or "healthy" pattern of state development.[6] Certainly, it cannot be demonstrated that any limited set of factors led inevitably to specific events such as World War I, Nazi ascendancy, or the Holocaust. The four conditions were, however, important long- and medium-term factors in shaping the historic development of both Germany's domestic political relationships and its relations with other states. The German drive to create a unified state had profound effects on neighboring countries. Between 1864 and 1870, the Prussian military fought wars with Denmark, Austria-Hungary, and France, which resulted in territorial gains for Germany. After 1871, Europe was confronted with a powerful and unified German state with greatly increased capabilities. The German pursuit of national unity, exercise of power, and quest for a commensurate role in world politics ultimately impacted every state in Europe.[7] The German Question became a major and permanent concern: what would be the military and political effects of a sovereign, unified German state, and was a strong Germany compatible with peace in Europe? In 1914, Germany was a major player in the process of crisis and escalation that led to World War I. The issue of culpability for the war has been fiercely debated by historians since that time, but in Article 231 of the Treaty of Versailles, the victorious powers forced Germany and its allies to accept sole blame for the war. In the aftermath of World War I, the victorious European states, France in particular, sought to resolve the German Question by placing severe limitations on the size of Germany's military and by weakening the nation economically through war reparations and other means.

In the twentieth century, Germany experienced prolonged periods of political instability punctuated by a series of radical regime changes. Despite impressive economic achievements, Imperial Germany (1871–1918) was unable to resolve deeply-rooted regional rivalries and socioeconomic conflicts. The Imperial German system ended with military defeat in World War I and the abdication of the Kaiser Wilhelm II in November 1918. The political vacuum left by its collapse was filled by a left-of-center coalition which established the Weimar Republic. The Weimar Republic was a parliamentary-democratic regime with a federal structure and a cabinet system in which the chancellor and his cabinet were responsible to the popularly elected legislature. Although its failure was by no means inevitable, the Weimar Republic was confronted by a number of serious obstacles, including the following: identification with the military defeat in World War I, the burden of war reparations and the harsh terms of the Treaty of Versailles, a lack of public support, and the violent opposition of radical revolutionary movements on both the left and right wing. The fledgling German democracy collapsed in the wake of the world depression of 1929–1930 and the political crisis that followed. The demise of the Weimar Republic and the subsequent imposition of a totalitarian regime traumatized the nation and left in their wake a legacy of concern that German political culture or national character might in some way be antithetical or incompatible with democracy.

On January 30, 1933, Adolf Hitler became the Chancellor of Germany as a result of a cabinet reshuffling, and the era of the Third Reich began. His supporters moved quickly to establish the Nazi dictatorship, ruthlessly suppressing political opponents. During their twelve years in power, the Nazis sought to impose an artificial unity on Germany through the imposition of Nazi ideology on all segments of the population.[8] Nazi foreign policy, which sought to unite by force all German-speaking groups into a "Greater German State" and to reorder Europe according to Nazi racial theories, was responsible for precipitating World War II. Between 1939 and 1945, the Nazis waged aggressive war against much of Europe and committed crimes against humanity in the Holocaust, in which between 4.5 and 6 million Jewish, Slavic, and Gypsy victims perished. The Nazi era ended in 1945 with the total defeat of Germany and the death of Adolf Hitler.

In the aftermath of World War II, the German Question reemerged with renewed intensity, and fear of German power rose to an all-time high. Germany became an occupied nation with separate zones of occupation administered by the four victorious Allied powers, the United States, Britain, France, and the Soviet Union. By 1947, it became clear that the Cold War rivalry between the West and the Soviet Union would prevent a comprehensive peace treaty and the early reestablishment of German sovereignty. The continued four-power occupation also reflected the fact that the victors could not agree on a solution to the German Question, that is, on how to control German power in the future. Both the Western Allies and the Soviet Union sought to enlist German resources for their respective military and political alliances. In 1949, Germany was divided into two rival states, the democratic-parliamentary regime of the Federal Republic of Germany, supported by the Western Allies, and the Stalinist German Democratic Republic, sponsored by the USSR.

The Short-Term Perspective: Divided Germany, 1949–1990

The two Germanys created in 1949 were more than frontline states in the Cold War; they were created as conscious attempts to develop new forms of state and society that would be radically different from those of the immediate Nazi past.[9] Their records of development also became experiments or tests of the relative merits of the competing democratic-capitalist and communist models of society.[10] Each state subsequently became a showpiece of successful economic and political development for its respective bloc. During this period, the concern for German power declined, at least among the allies of the two Germanys, because each state became integrated into rival military alliances, political structures, and economic organizations.

In the decade between 1948 and 1958, the United States and its allies supported the economic and political reconstruction of West Germany through the establishment of a separate West German state (the Federal Republic of Germany, or Bonn Republic), West German membership in the European Coal and Steel Community (ECSC) and European Economic Community (EEC), West German rearmament, and the nation's membership in the North Atlantic Treaty Organization (NATO). German power was to be "tamed" by penetrating and imbedding the Federal Republic in the multilateral political and economic institutions of the Western Alliance.[11] Under the American-sponsored Marshall Plan of 1947, West Germany was made eligible for economic aid on an equal basis with other states, but the program's objective was also to harness the Federal Republic to the causes of European recovery, European security, and Western European economic integration.[12] Similarly, French support for the Schuman Plan and the European Coal and Steel Community in 1951–1952 was intended to place German coal, steel, coke, and iron resources under a European supranational authority and also to guarantee France privileged access to those resources for its own program of modernization.[13] By the time of German reunification in 1990, the Federal Republic of Germany was integrated into a Western institutional complex that included the European Community/European Union, NATO and the Western European Union, the Conference on Security and Cooperation in Europe (CSCE), the Organization of Economic Cooperation and Development (OECD), the Group of Seven (G-7), and the General Agreement on Tariffs and Trade (GATT). This institutional network served to prevent the isolation of Germany, reinforce democratic values, facilitate Germany's participation in the dominant economic system of the world, and remove foreign and security policy from the sole jurisdiction of the West German state.

For its part, the German Democratic Republic (GDR) was a member of the Soviet bloc throughout the postwar period. Soviet support for a communist state in eastern Germany occurred in response to the creation of the Federal Republic by the Western Allies, and subsequent aid was designed to give the GDR an international status equal to that of the Federal Republic. In the 1950s, the GDR became an integral part of the Warsaw Treaty military alliance and the Council of Mutual Economic Assistance. As a result the East German state assumed the essential characteristics of a neo-Stalinist regime—one-man rule, communist party (SED)–dominance of the government and other symbolic parties; a centrally planned economy; a state security apparatus (the STASI or State Security police), complete with a network of informants; forced political conformity; and controls on contacts with West Germans and other foreigners. East German leaders used Cold War hostilities to justify the building of a "surveillance state" and gain increased aid and support from the USSR.[14] They remained committed to an orthodox communist political, social, and economic system until the last year of the regime. The building of the Berlin Wall permitted the temporary consolidation of the regime between 1961 and the late 1980s, and triumphant claims by East Germany's leaders to have achieved "real socialism" hid the GDR's political and economic vulnerabilities, but only for a time.[15] The East German neo-Stalinists could not survive the political reforms that swept Eastern Europe after the 1985 accession to power of Mikhail Gorbachev in the USSR and the subsequent Soviet decision to withdraw from Eastern Europe.

Development of the Federal Republic: Democracy and Prosperity Consolidated. In its first four decades of existence, the Federal Republic of Germany's greatest achievement was the establishment of a stable democratic regime. Despite criticisms that German political institutions displayed a "democratic deficit" because they failed to conform to the Anglo-American model, a distinctively German pattern of political democracy emerged.[16] The process of democratization included several different dimensions, which were mutually reinforcing. These included the development of a democratic constitution, the evolution of the party system, the transformation of the political culture, and changed behavior at both the elite and mass levels.[17]

The Basic Law of 1949, a constitution intended as temporary until the end of the division of Germany, established the rule of law and gave every German citizen fundamental human rights and civil liberties. The Basic Law established a federal republic with eleven *Länder,* or states (actually, ten Länder plus the city of Berlin) and a parliamentary system in which political authority issued from the control of the bicameral Federal Parliament (Bundestag—lower house, and Bundesrat—upper house) by democratically elected political parties.[18] The party or coalition of parties having the majority in the Bundestag selects the chancellor, the German equivalent of prime minister, who serves as head of government. The political party system also played an important role in the consolidation of democracy. In the early years of the Federal Republic, the number of parties in the Bundestag was reduced to three, with two large parties—the Christian Democratic Union/Christian Social Union (the CDU's Bavarian affiliate) and the Social Democratic Party—and the smaller, Free Democratic Party. They assumed the characteristics of catchall, "people's parties" appealing to broad electorates. The parties' ideological positions and programs placed them between the moderate center-right and center-left of the political spectrum, with the Free Democrats occupying the political center. By the 1960s, German parties had successfully demonstrated the ability to mobilize the electorate, provide for the alternation of power, and govern responsibly. Democratization was also aided by steadily improving social and economic conditions and the process of generational change. Each successive decade revealed a growing acceptance of democratic politics and an increased commitment to democratic values, especially among those younger Germans who reached political maturity in the postwar era.

Postwar Economic Development. The recovery and growth of the postwar West German economy has been aptly called an "economic miracle." In June 1948, even before the establishment of the West German state, German administrators implemented currency, price, and regulatory reforms. In one stroke, these reforms "legitimated the laws of supply and demand and subverted the economic controls that had grown up since the 1930s and been continued after 1945."[19] Throughout the postwar period, West German economic policy was guided by the concept of the social market economy, which sought to incorporate traditional Catholic concerns for social justice into the capitalist framework that was created after 1948. As implemented, German policy always assigned primacy to the maintenance of a competitive and vibrant market system. The tax laws, concern for currency stability, and predictable nature of government policies were all beneficial to business. Despite initial heavy dependence on American foreign aid, the German economic revival accelerated throughout the 1950s and 1960s. The year 1950 marked the beginning of a period of twenty-four years of nearly continuous economic growth, which was interrupted only by the brief recession of 1966–1967.[20] Between 1948 and 1965, the West German gross national product grew by an average of 6.7 percent per year, and by 1960, industrial production had risen to two and a half times the level of 1950.[21] By the 1960s, German economic prosperity had proven a decisive factor in both the success of the democratic system of government and the rise of the Federal Republic to the position of economic coleader of the European Community.

German economic growth slowed considerably in the early 1980s, as structural weaknesses (e.g., high labor costs, labor market inflexibility, and extensive government regulations) contributed to the decline of Germany's international economic competitiveness. The period of the economic miracle came to an end as growth rates averaged only about half those of the 1950s and 1960s, and the problem of unemployment (above 9% in 1988) proved to be particularly resistant to solution. However, Germany's economic performance did improve after 1983, and at the time of reunification in 1990, Germany was generally recognized as the world's third strongest capitalist economy (behind the United States and Japan).

TURBULENCE: THE CHALLENGE OF REUNIFICATION

The union of the two Germanys was an event of momentous historical significance for Germany, Europe, and the world. Reunification marked the end of the Cold War, the division of Europe, and a crisis period of more than seventy-five years' duration in the European state system. As a recent work argued, "The current restructuring of Europe can be understood as the settlement in Europe of World War II, which itself was part of a European civil war beginning in 1914 and ending only in 1990."[22] German reunification was immediately recognized as a contribution to the extension of market capitalism, the spread of democracy, and the possible development of a "New World Order," to which the single German state would provide important support. German reunification was a critical part of what amounted to the political restructuring of the European continent. The accession of the former German Democratic Republic to the Federal Republic of Germany, and, thus, to NATO and the European Community, along with the Soviet Union's pledge to withdraw all troops from German soil by 1994, contributed to the demise of the Warsaw Treaty military alliance and the end of the Soviet-sponsored economic organization in Europe, the Council of Mutual Economic Assistance. In addition, reunification produced a powerful new German state with a population of 79 million, which seemed destined to dominate the European Community. This reality, in turn, generated a powerful new force for increased political integration in Western Europe, as other Western European states sought to safely channel the growing influence of Germany within the larger framework of the European Community and, later, the European Union.[23]

Despite the profound international and domestic ramifications, once begun, the reunification process was accomplished quickly and with relative ease. Less than eleven months elapsed from the opening of the Berlin Wall on November 9, 1989, to the official establishment of a single German state, on October 3, 1990. One month later, on December 2, 1990, the first all-German national election since 1932 was held. The speed of German reunification was attributable to three factors: (1) the absence of any serious international opposition, and especially the absence of opposition from the Soviet Union, Britain, France, or the United States;[24] (2) the skill and energy with which the government of the Federal Republic pursued the unification project; and (3) the short-term intensity of German nationalism that prevailed in 1989–1990 in eastern Germany and, to a lesser extent, western Germany.[25]

Excluding the Soviet decision to undertake a strategic withdrawal from Eastern Europe, German nationalism was the most important factor in the events of 1989–1990.[26] The reunification process was driven by the determination of millions of East Germans to escape the political and economic constraints of the GDR and, later in the process, by a belated consensus in the western Länder that the Federal Republic should seize the opportunity for political union before possible upheavals in the Soviet Union produced a change in Soviet policy. In the GDR, the peaceful demonstrations of 1989, which initially had demanded only reform and the democratization of the political system, gave way to an ever-growing exodus to the Federal Republic. More than a half million workers, mostly young, skilled laborers and professionals, "voted with their feet" and fled to the West between November 1989 and March 1990. Millions of other East Germans took trips to West Germany and were able to compare for themselves the conditions in the two halves of the country.[27] East German mass behavior demonstrated what one source has called a "profound estrangement"[28] from the government of the GDR, which ultimately developed into a rejection of its legitimacy and a demand for unification with the Federal Republic. West German attitudes toward reunification had traditionally been ambiguous and mixed, with significant generational differences. Following decisive steps by the Kohl government in spring 1990, however, well over 60 percent of West Germans endorsed the goal of reunification, which they associated with peace, greater European security, and increasing respect for the Federal Republic globally.[29]

The process of reunification was not without its opponents and critics. In the Federal Republic, some sources in the West German government, the Bundesbank, and groups in the private sector warned of potential difficulties in consolidating the reunification project. Economists cited the possible inflationary effects on the German economy, conservatives expressed anxiety about a possible communist influence, and businesspersons and pundits questioned the industriousness and trainability of workers from the GDR.[30] In addition, a wide range of single issues were cited, ranging from the question of ownership of private property in the East to possible adverse foreign reactions to reunification. Of course, it is always important to keep in mind that in the period immediately following the opening of the Berlin Wall, no one in the Kohl government anticipated an early reunification. In the East, the leaders of the civic groups and political organizations, which had made possible the "Peaceful Revolution" of 1989, also opposed rapid reunification. Unlike their supporters, they hoped that a reformed GDR would survive and preserve those elements of the socialist experiment that had proved socially valuable. At a minimum, these dissidents expected a prolonged national debate on those elements of socialism that deserved to be incorporated into the new German state; however, by the spring of 1990, events had passed them by.

Reunification impacted every dimension of German politics and caused a sudden and dramatic increase in political turbulence. The following conditions from the model of political turbulence can be directly attributed to the reunification process:

1. a dramatic, year-long increase in activity (November 1989–December 1990) by the West German government—involving shuttle diplomacy, negotiations with the GDR, presentations to the EC, intracoalition bargaining, and discussions with the domestic political opposition;

2. the development of contentious new political issues—the outcome of the need to determine the timing, legal conditions, and political terms of reunification;

3. a proliferation of actors—the result of groups in both Eastern and Western Germany organizing to defend their interests during the reunification process;

4. the articulation of diverse political objectives—a result of the inclusion of 16.5 million new citizens with different life experiences and political expectations;

5. a dramatic increase in the demands for government services—an outcome of the inclusion of the economically and socially less developed territories of the former GDR;

6. increased complexity in the institutional structure of the German state—the result of the inclusion of five new Länder and various political agencies of the former GDR;

7. increased physical and spatial mobility of the population—the product of efforts by new citizens and immigrants to exploit regional economic differences;

8. new patterns of political conflict—a manifestation of the pursuit of social and economic equality by eastern Länder, local governments, and interest groups;

9. the expression of new political styles, including acts of violence against immigrants and guest workers—a manifestation of economic frustration and estrangement from authority;

10. a general increase in partisan political activity—a result of the efforts of western political parties and interest groups to extend their recruiting and mobilizing efforts to the eastern Länder;

11. frequent policy reversals by the government in Bonn and those of various Länder—a consequence of the worsening economic performance in the eastern Länder and the subsequent political reaction in the western Länder;

12. a sharp increase in public anxiety—the result of Westerners' concerns for the

economic costs of reunification and Easterners' resentment at what they perceived to be their status as second-class citizens.

Most of these conditions had manifested by mid-1991, when the full economic consequences of reunification became clear.

Despite the fact that German political patterns had displayed considerable continuity throughout the postwar period, reunification forced major changes. Viewed from a political perspective, the accession of East Germany meant the inclusion of a population with an "autonomous political life," which included different and uncertain voting patterns, a legacy of secret police informants, a confused neo-Nazi element, and political attitudes on single issues, such as abortion, that differed from those of the old Federal Republic.[31] In the economic sphere, the absorption of the weak eastern economy resulted in the existence of a "dual or split economy" within the unified state. This greatly complicated the task of economic management, as the need for massive economic aid to the East threatened to undermine the traditional objectives of fiscal and monetary policy and to reduce international competitiveness. In the important public policy areas of health, social welfare, and employment, reunification and exposure to the competition of market capitalism undermined the "security culture" that had existed in the GDR. Its collapse revealed the degree to which Easterners had been dependent on state-sponsored services and subsidies. After reunification, the tasks of social maintenance and integration required the development of special, costly public policies necessitating additional taxation and government borrowing. These, in turn, created widespread resentment among Westerners, who would be required to pay. By the end of 1992, studies and public opinion surveys had documented a growing "mental division" or "inner wall" that separated Easterners and Westerners.[32]

The problems inherent in reunification were magnified by the timing of the event. The costs of funding the unification project served to aggravate the structural crisis in the German economy that had existed since the mid-1980s and predated unification.[33] Reunification also coincided with the implementation within the European Community of the internal market program of the Single European Act. This development produced fears in Germany that the achievement of a single, internal market might lead to "social dumping": the movement of industrial and financial capital from the more developed areas of the EC, of which West Germany was a part, to the less developed areas. Such a strategy would clearly disadvantage Germany, and the new fears about the economic consequences of reunification reinforced these earlier concerns. In addition, the next stage of EC integration—the signing of the Treaty on European Union in 1992—produced new and frequently conflicting demands by member states for additional German financial contributions and interest rate sacrifices in the interests of building the Continental economy.

Finally, reunification was accompanied by new and unprecedented demands for German resources from the international community. The demise of the Soviet empire was accompanied by a general expectation that Germany would play a leading role in the reconstruction of Eastern Europe, perhaps similar to the role played by the United States through the Marshall Plan in postwar Western Europe. This expectation was underscored by the articulation of the U.S. policy of "New Atlanticism" by the Bush administration which called on Germany to become a "partner in leadership" with the United States.[34] The simultaneous calls for leadership of the European Community, leadership in rebuilding Eastern Europe, and leadership in the defense of Western Europe produced fears in the Federal Republic that its resources might be insufficient for these tasks and that policy overstretch and a domestic political backlash might result. The enormous economic challenge of reunification only added to these fears.

The success of the reunification project ultimately depended on the ability to transform the East German economy. This task actually involved two transformations: (1) the movement from state socialism to market capitalism, and (2) the modernization of the East's obsolete and largely noncompetitive economy.[35] Early assessments of the economic conditions in the five eastern Länder, as well as estimates of the costs of modernization, proved excessively optimistic. By 1991, major deficiencies in the East German economy had been identified, including outdated technology and capital stock, a low level of industrial specialization, lagging investment, low labor productivity compared to West Germany, and infrastructural and environmental problems that were major impediments to attracting private investment.[36] Economic performance in the East declined further following the achievement of German Economic and Monetary Union (GEMU) in July 1990. GEMU extended the institutions of market capitalism to the East and established the Deutsch mark as the single national currency. The state of affairs in the East necessitated huge transfers of public funds, which increased in each successive fiscal year. A major tax increase and additional government borrowing were required to fund these transfers, and these became the most contentious issues of the entire unification process.

THE LEADER AND HIS GROUP: HELMUT KOHL AND THE CHRISTIAN DEMOCRATIC UNION

Helmut Kohl, the man who was to lead the Federal Republic through the reunification process, was born near the Rhine river port of Ludwigshaven in the present-day Rhineland-Palatinate state. Kohl's family belonged to the Roman Catholic, conservative, petit bourgeois segment of the middle class. His father, who was a midlevel civil servant in the local tax office, won promotion for bravery to the rank of officer in World War I.[37] Although a Catholic, Kohl's father was a supporter of the right-wing German National

People's Party (DNVP) in the interwar period rather than of the more traditional Catholic Center Party.[38] Kohl's family stressed the values of hard
work, frugality, self-discipline, duty, and opposition to socialism. As Helmut
Kohl observed after becoming chancellor, "my inability to be a socialist came
to me with my mother's milk."[39] Kohl's fervent belief in the Roman Catholic
faith and strong sense of national duty also originated in his youth.

Although a member of the first postwar generation, the age cohort too
young to be called to active military service in World War II, as a child Kohl
nonetheless experienced the full horror of war. Before his forced evacuation
to the Bavarian countryside, Kohl survived more than a hundred bombings
of the Ludwigshaven area, including one in which his older brother was
killed.[40] Like other German leaders of his generation, Kohl also experienced
the shock of defeat and foreign occupation, the complete disillusionment
with the criminal Nazi regime, the economic deprivation of the early postwar
period, and the complete political and economic dependence on the occupation authorities in the immediate aftermath of World War II. Most sources
acknowledge that Kohl's traumatic childhood was a major contributing factor to his extreme caution, pragmatism, emphasis on personal loyalty, and
unswerving support for democracy and capitalism.

Helmut Kohl's initial involvement in democratic politics occurred during
the era of the "CDU State" (1949–1966), the Cold War years in which Chancellor Konrad Adenauer and his party, the Christian Democratic Union,
dominated German politics. In the seventeen uninterrupted years in which
the Christian Democratic Union and its allies governed, a conservative national project was established which, with minor modifications, remained the
program of the center-right up to the time of German reunification. Central
to the CDU program were five major policies for German recovery and
development: (1) support for the Atlantic Alliance and friendship with the
United States, (2) friendship and cooperation with France, (3) support for
European integration, (4) support for a vibrant market economy, and (5)
adherence to the principles of the social market economy in social policy
matters. For Kohl, as for nearly all center-right politicians, these policies
became honored principles, which were validated over time by Germany's
growing national strength and affluence. At every stage of his political career,
Kohl reaffirmed his support for these policies and openly acknowledged his
intellectual debt to Adenauer and other founders of the CDU.

Kohl's entry into politics and his lifetime affiliation with the CDU began
early in the postwar period. In 1947, Kohl founded a youth chapter of the
CDU in Ludwigshaven, and he joined the party the next year.[41] As a student
working his way through Frankfurt am Main University, Kohl remained
active in local CDU activities and was elected to the Ludwigshaven City
Council. Following graduation from Frankfurt, Kohl attended Heidelberg
University, where he studied history. In 1958, he received his doctorate for
a study that analyzed the development of postwar West German political

parties.[42] In many respects, Kohl's early adulthood was typical of that of many middle-class university students, but his achievements in the affairs of the CDU were not. At age twenty-three, Kohl was elected to the leadership of the Rhineland-Palatinate state party; by age thirty, he was the youngest member of the Rhineland-Palatinate state legislature; at thirty-three, the youngest state floor leader; at thirty-nine, the youngest state minister-president (the equivalent of governor of an American state); at forty-three, the youngest chairman of the CDU; and at fifty-two, West Germany's youngest chancellor.[43] These accomplishments are generally attributed to Kohl's hard work and attention to detail at the grassroots level rather than to charisma, vision, policy expertise, or accomplishments outside politics. Observers regularly refer to Kohl's "matchless instinct," "mastery of politics," ability to recognize by name thousands of CDU functionaries, skillful use of patronage, and the fact that "the party is his life."[44] Kohl's career has been more that of a political survivor and party "team leader" than that of a statesman or dominating national figure of the Adenauer type.

Kohl's rise to the leadership of the CDU coincided with a period of major transition in the German party system, which saw the end of the CDU's political dominance. In 1961, the CDU lost its absolute majority in the Bundestag; from 1966 to 1969, the CDU was forced to share power in a coalition government with its main rival, the Social Democratic Party (SPD); and in 1969, it found itself out of power for the first time since 1949. The loss of power occurred when the CDU's former coalition ally, the Free Democratic Party (FDP), deserted to join in a coalition with the opposition SPD. The CDU remained out of power for thirteen years, until 1982. After competing unsuccessfully for the party's leadership in 1971, Kohl replaced Rainer Barzel as party leader in 1973, following the party's loss in the 1972 general election. At the time of his elevation to party leader, Kohl was the successful minister-president of the Rhineland-Palatinate, a post he held from 1969 to 1976. As a typical provincial career politician, Kohl had strong regional backing but was totally lacking in experience in the national legislative arena of the Bundestag. As his party's leader, Kohl was the designated candidate for chancellor in the 1976 election. Although the CDU's performance improved and it actually received a higher percentage of the popular vote than the SPD, the CDU was unable to regain power because the small Free Democratic Party remained committed to its coalition with the Social Democrats.[45] Following the election, Kohl did not relinquish his post as party leader but instead used his growing influence over party patronage and appointments to gain the additional position of CDU parliamentary leader (leader of the opposition) in the Bundestag. In this capacity, he gained indispensable legislative experience and public exposure at the national level.

In the period from 1976 to 1980, Kohl was involved in a prolonged struggle for leadership of the center-right coalition. Kohl's rival was Franz-Josef Strauss, the Minister-President of Bavaria and leader of the Christian Social

Union (CSU). Although primarily a power struggle, the conflict also took on personal and ideological dimensions and precipitated the most serious crisis in the CDU/CSU coalition since the 1950s. Strauss sought to move the coalition to the right by reemphasizing its free-market and anticommunist principles and to achieve electoral victory over the Social Democrats through a greater polarization between the parties of the center-right and center-left.[46] Strauss rejected the position that the Free Democrats could be lured away from their coalition with the Social Democrats if the CDU embraced moderate policies. In contrast, Kohl campaigned for the support of the moderate wing of the coalition and sought to occupy the political middle ground.[47] He argued that the strategy of the CDU/CSU should be to win back the Free Democrats by accepting domestic reforms favored by the FDP and endorsing the FDP/SPD policy of Ostpolitik, which sought to improve relations with the Soviet Union and the states of Eastern Europe. In the initial stages of the conflict, Kohl's support declined and Strauss was selected as the candidate for chancellor in the 1980 election. Following the CDU's disappointing showing in that election and the opposition's success at depicting Strauss as a political extremist, Kohl reemerged as the undisputed leader of the center-right coalition.

After 1981, political conditions were right for a return to power by the CDU/CSU, and events confirmed the validity of Kohl's overall strategy. Between 1980 and 1982, a number of international and domestic problems, including a major recession, contributed to the weakening and, finally, the demise of the SPD/FDP coalition. In September 1982, the FDP withdrew from its coalition with the Social Democrats, and on October 1, 1982, Helmut Kohl won a constructive vote of no confidence to become the first CDU chancellor since 1969. After waiting six months to allow the FDP time to solidify its electoral support, Kohl led the CDU/CSU–FDP coalition to victory in the March 1983 election. The coalition won reelection in 1987.

The CDU's electoral victory in 1983 was accompanied by widespread speculation that Kohl would initiate a major policy shift to the right similar to that undertaken by Prime Minister Margaret Thatcher in Great Britain and, to a lesser extent, by President Ronald Reagan in the United States. Such expectations were fueled by the CDU's political slogans during the campaign, which called for *"Die Wende,"* a major change, or turnaround. In practice, Kohl's program fell far short of a New Right economic or social revolution, and he remained committed to the general principles of the social market economy. The Kohl government did, however, take an approach toward the domestic economic recession that was similar to that of other conservative governments: deficit spending was avoided, long-term budgetary restraint was promoted, and social welfare benefits were adjusted to fall within the limits of federal and state budgets.[48] The Kohl government benefited from the general improvement in both the European and world economies as well as from increased domestic demand after 1986, but economic performance in the 1980s continued to lag far behind that of the 1960s and 1970s. The problem of unemployment proved especially intractable, remaining above 8 percent until 1989.

Between 1982 and 1989, the Kohl government also experienced a series of political crises, including scandals, embarrassing resignations, strikes by the metal workers' union for a thirty-five–hour work week, protests against the deployment of U.S. intermediate-range nuclear missiles on German soil, and continued infighting between various political factions of the governing coalitions.[49] These crises were frequently accompanied by sharp declines in Kohl's standing in public opinion polls which, in turn, led to frequent prediction of his political demise. Such predictions proved premature, however, and by the end of the 1980s Kohl had served as chancellor longer than any other postwar figure except Konrad Adenauer.

In retrospect, it seems clear that Kohl's career left him well placed to respond in a forceful and effective way to the collapse of the German Democratic Republic in 1989–1990. Despite his personal penchant for caution and restrained response to the initial events of 1989, Kohl had embraced the goal of reunification and the establishment of a democratic and capitalist Germany during his entire career. As he made clear in a 1990 interview, "The dream, not just for me, but for a whole generation, was to obtain German unity and European unity."[50] Attitudes acquired since adolescence prepared him to act decisively once it became clear that the German Democratic Republic had lost its political legitimacy. Kohl's performance as chancellor also proved to be a factor of critical importance. Despite the renewal of Cold War tensions that followed the Soviet invasion of Afghanistan and the election of Ronald Reagan as president of the United States, the Kohl government continued to pursue a dual policy of military and political cooperation with the Western allies at the same time that it sought to improve relations with the Soviet Union and the German Democratic Republic. In the complex environment of the 1980s, German support for NATO modernization and missile deployment promoted good relations with Washington, while Germany's commitment to increased European integration assured the continuation of the Franco-German special relationship.[51] At the same time, West Germany's continued support of Ostpolitik produced an improvement in relations with the Soviet Union and East Germany. Consequently, at the time when the reunification process began Kohl was a respected world leader who had excellent working relationships with the leaders of all four victorious powers of World War II. Kohl's close personal relationship with Soviet leader Mikhail Gorbachev proved to be especially important because as late as 1990, "the road to German reunification still passed through Moscow."

Kohl's background also determined his general approach to the reunification process. For Kohl, who was a life-long supporter of the ideals of parliamentary democracy and social market capitalism, reunification demanded the extension of West German institutions and practices to eastern

Germany, not the coexistence of institutional forms or the development of some new political "middle way." In addition, as a practical politician who was not an economist, Kohl assigned primary emphasis to the short-term political factors of reunification, especially the diplomatic, public relations and electoral dimensions. Within a year of the fall of the Berlin Wall, it was clear that Kohl had underestimated the long-term social and economic problems that would result from the merger of the two Germanys.

The CDU/CSU–FDP Coalition

Throughout his tenure as chancellor, Helmut Kohl has headed a coalition government composed of the Christian Democratic Union/Christian Social Union and the Free Democratic Party. As with any public policy, the successful implementation of the reunification project required the development of policies capable of gaining the support of the various factions of the coalition. In the critical period between mid-1989 and December 1990, all significant segments of the center-right coalition supported Kohl, although of course this consensus did not apply to opposition parties. Kohl successfully drew on decades of national solidarity rhetoric, emphasized the moral duty to help citizens of the East, and equated support for Easterners with support for democracy, human rights, and the market economy.[52] Especially important was the backing of Foreign Minister Hans-Dietrich Genscher, leader of the Free Democrats and vice-chancellor. Genscher held the post of foreign minister continuously from 1974 to 1992, when he retired, and was an internationally respected expert in the field. "Genscherism" was synonymous with the policy of working to improve relations with the Soviet bloc and with support for European integration. Genscher played an important role in the shuttle diplomacy designed to ease the fears of German reunification in foreign states.

THE REUNIFICATION PROJECT

The Kohl government's policy toward German reunification unfolded in three stages. In the first stage, which extended from July to November 1989, the government responded to the initial events in East Germany that documented the GDR's loss of legitimacy and the inability or unwillingness of communist party elites to undertake decisive action to preserve the regime. This stage, which is often referred to as a "peaceful revolution," included the exodus of tens of thousands of East Germans to the West through Hungary and Czechoslovakia after those states had opened their borders, as well as the dramatic opening of the Berlin Wall on November 9. The Kohl government's main policy response in this stage was the modest "Ten-Point Plan," which called for the creation of common, "confederative structures" but had a political impact far beyond that which had been expected.

In the second stage, lasting from December 1989 to December 1990, the opportunity for political union became clear and the Kohl government responded with bold initiatives. These included the so-called "two-plus-four talks" for diplomatic negotiations with the four victorious states of World War II, negotiations with the European Community on the inclusion of eastern Germany in the EC, and the two major agreements between the Federal Republic and the GDR that accomplished reunification—the First State Treaty, creating German Economic and Monetary Union (GEMU), and the Second State Treaty, which accomplished the full political accession of the East to the Federal Republic. This stage ended with the all-German national election of December 1990, the first since 1932, in which Kohl's CDU/CSU–FDP coalition won reelection in what amounted to a national referendum on the reunification project. By successfully mobilizing electoral support in both halves of Germany, the Kohl government gained the opportunity to pursue the consolidation of the reunification project.

The third stage involved the period from December 1990 to November 1994, comprising the initial three and a half years of the postreunification period. During this stage, the Kohl government was confronted with the full economic and social consequences of reunification. It soon became apparent that the problems associated with reunification had been both deliberately understated and poorly understood. These problems created a complex series of policy trade-offs in which all available policy options carried high political costs. These trade-offs ranged from general issues, such as whether to pay for the costs of reunification by taxing or borrowing, to very specific issues, such as selecting the capital city of the unified state.

Stage One: July 1989–November 1989

The sudden and unexpected collapse of the GDR occurred at the end of a complex chain of events that began in 1985 but escalated sharply in the first months of 1989. Confronted with Gorbachev's program of reforms, the leadership of the GDR proved incapable of change and found itself increasingly isolated within the Soviet bloc. As one source argued, in 1989 the GDR became the victim of "falling dominoes in Eastern Europe."[53] In April, the opposition movement, Solidarity, was legalized in Poland; in May, the Hungarian government opened its border with Austria; and in September, Czechoslovakia permitted East Germans occupying the West German embassy in Prague to leave for the West. By traveling to these neighboring states, East German citizens were able to escape to the West for the first time since the building of the Berlin Wall in 1961. The scope of the exodus increased week by week for the next six months until it reached more than two thousand persons a day. In the face of these defections, the GDR leadership vacillated between a number of ineffective policies, its indecision made worse by the personal absence of communist party (SED) leader Erich Honecker due to illness. Belated efforts to prevent travel outside the GDR provoked mass demonstrations in several East German cities.

Official STASI reports on the flight blamed resentment at living conditions, and specifically, dissatisfaction with consumer products, inadequate service in shops, deficient medical care, travel restrictions, unsatisfactory working conditions, and low wages.[54] This critique was partially valid because the existence of the GDR had always depended on individual East Germans making daily compromises in the form of outward support for the regime in exchange for material benefits.[55] It soon became clear, however, that two more fundamental forces were at work: first, in the changing East German society, the neo-Stalinist regime had suffered a widespread and irreversible loss of legitimacy among all segments of the population, and, second, the GDR was not viable in 1989–1990 without the forceful intervention of the Soviet Union, and that support was not forthcoming.[56]

The political leadership of the Federal Republic, like that of the GDR, was totally unprepared for the speed and intensity of events in East Germany in 1989. For more than a decade, the reunification issue had been absent from the public agenda in a practical sense because the union of the two Germanys was not considered a practical political possibility in the near future. The initial West German response to the events of the spring and summer reflected two different concerns, a humanitarian impulse to help East Germans arriving in the Federal Republic and anxiety that the exodus might adversely impact existing agreements with the GDR. In August and September 1989, both Helmut Kohl and Foreign Minister Genscher publicly urged Hungary to keep open its borders, and by the third week of September, more than 40,000 young East Germans had left the GDR via Hungary. At the same time, however, Kohl's foreign policy advisor, Horst Teltschik, warned that premature talk of the demise of the GDR or of reunification would arouse fears among Germany's neighbors.[57] At this stage, the Kohl government still embraced the traditional policy of encouraging reform and liberalization in the GDR without confronting the issue of reunification.[58]

In October and November, the political crisis in the GDR deepened. By early October, a formal (but illegal) opposition movement, New Forum, had come into existence; major demonstrations for democratic reforms and freedom of travel had occurred in several cities; and it had become clear during Mikhail Gorbachev's visit to East Germany on October 6–7 that the Soviet Union would not intervene to save the Honecker regime from domestic reformers.[59] By the time the GDR celebrated its fortieth anniversary on October 7, more than 100,000 former citizens, mostly younger skilled workers and professionals, had already left the country. Eleven days later, Erich Honecker was forced to resign as leader of the communist party (SED) and was replaced by Egon Krenz. The removal of Honecker only served to embolden the opposition and increase the number of people willing to openly demonstrate against the regime. In the first week of November, Krenz announced a package of reforms intended to preserve the regime, which included a general right to travel abroad. The announcement of this policy led to the peaceful breaching of the Berlin Wall on November 9 and the subsequent opening of the entire East German border. These events constituted a genuine "revolutionary moment" in the history of postwar Germany,[60] which was driven by the pent-up desire of ordinary citizens from both halves of the country for change, reform, and unity.[61] Incredibly, 9 million persons crossed the frontier in the first week after the opening of the Berlin Wall.[62] East Germans who visited the Federal Republic for the first time returned home but increasingly came to demand reunification.

The events of November increased pressure on the Kohl government for a forceful public response and compelled it to fundamentally rethink the basic relationship between the two Germanys.[63] Prior to this time, Foreign Minister Genscher and others had been more visible in addressing the issue of the flight from the GDR, but now Helmut Kohl took the initiative, which he was not to surrender again until after the 1990 national election. On November 28, without clearing the text with Genscher or other leaders of the FDP, Kohl presented his Ten-Point Plan in a speech before the Bundestag. The plan has been aptly described as "a carefully calibrated opening gambit . . . well designed to capture domestic endorsements before tackling the forbidding international obstacles."[64] It was also intended to restore stability to an increasingly volatile situation and give direction to the national debate on the future of the two Germanys. Using terms first suggested by GDR leader Krenz in a telephone conversation on October 27, Kohl called for closer relations between the two states through the creation of a "contractual (treaty) community" or "confederative arrangement" which would constitute the initial steps toward a "federation or federal order."[65] In a deliberately vague reference to a future unified state, Kohl noted the following: "Nobody knows today how a unified Germany will look in the end. But I am certain that unity will come if the German people want it."[66] Kohl also pledged additional economic aid contingent on the continuation of political and economic reforms in the GDR and specifically endorsed the demand of East German demonstrators for free elections. The entire project was to occur within the context of the European peace system, including European and Atlantic cooperation, East-West disarmament, and the Conference on Security and Cooperation in Europe.[67] Taken as a whole, the plan addressed the concerns of East Germans seeking the continuation of reforms in the GDR, the demands of those Easterners and Westerners seeking some blueprint for reunification, and the fears of foreign states concerned about the German Question and, specifically, the future course of action of a united Germany.

Given the growing public support for reunification in both halves of Germany, Kohl's Ten-Point Plan was a moderate and cautious response. Certainly, at this stage, elite expectations regarding reunification lagged behind those of the general population. Kohl's speech, however, received a positive and enthusiastic response in both halves of Germany, primarily because it indicated a change in thinking from acceptance of the division of Germany to the pursuit of reunification.[68] It became a catalyst for subsequent actions and placed Kohl at the forefront of the debate on reunification.

Stage Two: December 1989–December 1990

After the opening of the Berlin Wall, rapidly changing conditions in the GDR and the emergence of new attitudes in both the Federal Republic and the international community produced an acceleration of the reunification process. These new factors gave the Kohl government the opportunity to push forward the timetable for reunification and determine the specific terms under which the process would proceed. The challenge at this stage was to adjust West Germany's strategy to the rapidly changing conditions and co-ordinate actions and policies at the domestic and international levels to achieve the desired result—a reunification process dominated by the Federal Republic.

Conditions in the GDR. By the end of 1989, a political culture of protest had spread throughout the GDR which increasingly undermined the regime and culminated in a popular demand for reunification.[69] The size and scope of the demonstrations grew throughout the "revolutionary autumn," as fear of the regime declined. On December 3, Egon Krenz was forced out as leader of the GDR after only forty-five days in office and was replaced by Hans Modrow, the reform-minded party leader of Dresden. Also in December, the first meeting of the Round Table occurred, in which the SED renounced its monopoly on power and engaged in consultations with opposition groups seeking reform of the regime. This organization functioned for a time as a kind of interim government and set the date for the first free parliamentary elections, which were ultimately held in March 1990.[70] After the fall of the Berlin Wall, however, the time for reform of the regime had passed. Large numbers of Easterners continued to go to West Germany in search of a better life, and this flight, combined with the exposure to West German goods, contributed to the collapse of the East German economy. Simply stated, the GDR was incapable of winning an economic competition with the Federal Republic. In January and February, demonstrators in the streets increasingly called for reunification, not reform of the GDR, and in February, public opinion surveys revealed that 75 percent of East Germans now favored re-unification.[71] In the face of the mounting domestic crisis, opposition groups like New Forum, which favored only reform of the socialist system, proved unable to convince their fellow citizens to support a "socialist alternative" or "third way." In the March 1990 election, both the SED (which was re-named the Party of Democratic Socialism for the election) and the civil opposition groups favoring only reform of the socialist system (organized in the electoral alliance Bündnis 90) were overwhelmed by parties having West

German affiliates and favoring reunification. The biggest winner in the election was the East German Christian Democratic Union and its alliance partners, which were organized in the Alliance for Germany. The election removed the final obstacles in the GDR to a reunification process dictated by the Federal Republic.

Conditions in the Federal Republic. Like their counterparts in the GDR, most citizens in the Federal Republic were unprepared for the events surrounding the fall of the Berlin Wall. Public opinion surveys as late as 1988 revealed that only 3 percent of those polled expected reunification in the near future; in this context, the surprise opening of the Berlin Wall was initially greeted with euphoria.[72] By January 1990, however, there was growing concern about the size of the exodus from the GDR. Between November 9 and December 31, 1989, a total of 116,000 East Germans left for the West, and this number was increased by an additional 145,000 refugees between January 1 and March 31, 1990.[73] The influx taxed West German social services and administrative structures and created anxiety about the long-term economic ramifications. At the governmental level, there was also growing concern about several developments. In December and January, demonstrators sacked the offices of the STASI in Berlin, raising questions about the maintenance of public order in the GDR, and by January, basic services in health and other areas seemed near collapse.[74] In combination, these events raised questions about the ability of the Modrow government to carry out reforms, even if it genuinely desired to do so, which in itself was questionable. In addition, at the level of domestic politics, the opposition Social Democratic Party and other critics on the left had begun to criticize the intent and direction of Kohl's policy on the GDR. These criticisms intensified throughout the spring and clearly indicated an end to the brief consensus that had followed the presentation of the Ten-Point Plan. Finally, there was fear that a fundamental change in the policy of the Soviet Union toward the GDR might occur if Mikhail Gorbachev were replaced as leader of the Soviet Union. At a February 1 meeting with Hans Modrow in Moscow, Gorbachev had indicated acceptance in principle of German reunification provided the united German state were neutral.[75] Although neutrality was unacceptable to Kohl, it was feared that subsequent Soviet leaders might oppose any change of status in the GDR.

The weakening of the regime in the GDR convinced the Kohl government to undertake an assertive policy of no compromise in its dealings with the Modrow government. By mid-January, the goal of establishing closer relations through confederative structures was abandoned in favor of one aimed at denying the Modrow government any political and economic support that might strengthen its position. Kohl now believed that Modrow was obstructing major reforms and was so weak that he had become "no more than a footnote in history."[76] Challenging the legitimacy of the Modrow government, Kohl made it clear that free elections and sweeping economic reforms were preconditions for increased cooperation and major economic aid. Discussions on the future of Germany would, therefore, have to wait for free elections in March. During Modrow's official visit to Bonn on February 13, the Kohl government rejected outright East German requests for 15 billion Deutsch marks, which Modrow and the Round Table government considered necessary to stave off economic collapse. At the same time, the Christian Democratic Union in West Germany increased its financial and moral support to the Christian Democratic Party in the GDR, which had broken from the SED-controlled bloc of parties in January. As the election approached, Kohl made six campaign appearances in the GDR on behalf of the CDU and its two alliance partners, which made up the Alliance for Germany.[77] (West Germany's two other major parties, the Social Democrats and the Free Democrats, also supported their East German affiliates.) West German money, leadership, and electoral expertise were decisive factors in the victory of the prounification parties. Despite heavy criticism from opposition parties and left-wing critics, Kohl was now convinced that reunification could be carried out on West German terms.

Attitudes in the International Community. The prospects of a reunited Germany resurrected the German Question in Europe and involved the four victorious powers of World War II in the reunification process. At the beginning of 1990, the Soviet Union still had 360,000 troops stationed in the GDR, all four states had special rights in Berlin, and the two Germanys remained members of rival military alliances. Reunification would, therefore, require the approval of all three Western allies and the Soviet Union, and each would have to surrender all special rights if Germany were to regain full sovereignty at the time of reunification. The German Question was also of vital interest to the neighboring state of Poland, which had been a victim of Nazi aggression and sought guarantees of its existing borders (the Oder-Niesse line). For the Kohl government, the reunification project also had an international dimension, which required the development of a diplomatic strategy capable of garnering international support for its project.

The Kohl government demonstrated early in the process its sensitivity to economic, political, and security issues raised by the prospects of a united Germany. Following the presentation of the Ten-Point Plan, the Kohl government initiated a vigorous round of shuttle diplomacy in Western Europe, the Soviet Union, and North America to emphasize the Federal Republic's commitment to European integration and European security.[78] Undoubtedly, its most potent argument was its record for constructive and positive policies since 1949. Among the Western allies, the United States gave full and enthusiastic support from the outset, and American-German unity on the issue was probably sufficient to overcome the initial British and French reservations.[79] Beyond this, however, the Kohl government addressed French concerns by giving full support to the EC's single-market program and the proposals for increased economic and political integration that were ultimately adopted in the Maastricht Treaty. Thus, Germany was to remain committed to a "deeper European Community," and the subsequent acceptance of the East German Länder into the EC (April 28, 1990) served to "widen" the organization. French policy slowly evolved toward acceptance of the German position, and Britain's more serious reservations were untenable once the Soviet Union had accepted the principle of reunification.[80]

The Kohl government's approach to the Soviet Union was based on the assumption that the initial Soviet position of opposition to reunification was a weak one and could not be sustained. The regime in the GDR was not viable in the long run, the Warsaw Treaty Organization was on the verge of breakup, and Soviet economic weakness made the potential of aid from West Germany an important factor.[81] By January 1990, the Soviets had accepted the concept of reunification in principle but demanded in return German neutrality and disarmament. Rejecting these conditions, the Kohl government maintained that the unified German state must be free to establish its own alliance commitments. In its continuing approach to the Soviet Union, the Kohl government emphasized the following points: (1) NATO was no longer the enemy of the Soviet Union, (2) a stable and unified Germany would contribute to European stability, (3) the Helsinki Accords (to which the USSR was a signatory) guaranteed the sovereign equality of nations and provided for self-determination under United Nations (UN) rules, and (4) Germany was prepared to guarantee existing European borders (after a troublesome delay, both Germanys confirmed the existing Polish borders on June 21).[82] The position of the Kohl government grew even stronger after the victories of the prounification parties in the 1990 elections in the GDR. During a personal meeting with Kohl in the Soviet Union on July 15, Mikhail Gorbachev finally accepted German reunification and NATO membership in exchange for the following military and political concessions by Germany: (1) a planned reduction in German force levels to 370,000 and a prohibition on nuclear, biological, and chemical weapons; (2) a prohibition against the extension of NATO military structures to East Germany until after the withdrawal of Soviet forces; (3) a 1994 deadline for the withdrawal of all Soviet troops from East Germany, which was to be mostly paid for by the Federal Republic; and (4) German guarantees of all existing European borders.[83]

In a formal sense, the four victors of World War II negotiated the conditions of German reunification within a framework that became known as the "two-plus-four talks" (involving the two Germanys plus the United States, the United Kingdom, France, and the Soviet Union). Originally suggested by the United States and immediately endorsed by Foreign Minister Genscher, the mechanism was formally agreed to at a meeting of NATO and Warsaw Pact countries in Ottawa, Canada, on February 12, 1990. The two-plus-four talks continued throughout the spring and summer and formally ended on September 12 with the signing by all six states of the "Treaty on the Final Settlement with Respect to Germany," which endorsed reunification. The acceptance of the two-plus-four mechanism proved to be of great significance. It recognized the right of the two Germanys to consider reunification, precluded any four-power discussions without their participation, and made German reunification a central item on the East-West agenda.[84]

MOBILIZING FOR POWER: THE UNION OF THE TWO GERMANYS

The formal institutions that united the two Germanys, the First and Second State Treaties, were negotiated, signed, and implemented between February and October 1990. The legal steps to reunification were completed on October 3, Unification Day, when the five eastern Länder joined the Federal Republic of Germany and the GDR ceased to exist. Early reunification was made possible by the election in March of a legitimate government committed to such reunification; this was the coalition government headed by the CDU-East and its leader, Lothar de Mazière. In an outcome widely viewed as a personal victory for Helmut Kohl, the CDU won 40.8 percent of the vote, compared to 21.8 percent for the Social Democrats and only 16.3 percent for the Party of Democratic Socialism (the former SED).[85] The timing and conditions of the State Treaties became the topic of intense political debate within the Federal Republic. Despite the strong position of the Kohl government at this point, the treaties were the products of hard bargaining within the CDU coalition, as well as with the rival SPD and the governments of the western Länder.[86]

The First State Treaty

German Economic and Monetary Union, which was established by the First State Treaty, proved to be the most contentious single issue of the reunification process. Negotiations between the two Germanys began in February and were driven by the continuous movement of East Germans to the Federal Republic at a rate of more than 2,000 per day. On February 7, Kohl formally asked the East German government for negotiations on economic union, and the Federal Republic established a special cabinet committee on German unity in the same month.[87] As Kohl later acknowledged, the decision to pursue economic union was a political one and was intended as a practical solution to the economic collapse of the GDR and the resulting mass flight: "If the German mark does not come to the people of Leipzig, the people from Leipzig will come to the German mark."[88] In its campaign in East Germany in March, the CDU stressed the themes of ending "socialist experimentation" and bringing about "affluence for all" and early reunification.[89] In a personal campaign appearance on March 13, Kohl pledged an exchange rate of one Deutsch mark (DM) to one East mark (for savings up to 4,000 East marks), an extremely favorable rate for the East Germans. Although nearly a month of delay followed the election, the decisive nature of the CDU's victory created an unstoppable dynamic for GEMU. West German experts dominated the various committees that were established to implement the treaty, and in a decisive showdown on May 3, the Kohl government rejected a series of conditions demanded by the East Germans and the opposition Social Democrats in the Federal Republic.[90] The treaty was signed by the East and West German governments on May 18 and came into effect on July 1.

The First State Treaty was a decisive step in the reunification process and represented the most important initiative since the Ten-Point Plan of November 1989. In the words of one observer, the GDR became a "shadow of a state," which was deprived of its control of taxes, the money supply, economic and social policies and without representation in the government of the Federal Republic.[91] Officially entitled the State Treaty on Economic, Monetary, and Social Union, the agreement extended the entire legal and institutional framework of market capitalism to the GDR and covered the following areas: (1) currency union—adoption of the West German mark in the GDR; (2) the role of the Bundesbank (West Germany's central bank) as a common institution; (3) trade—the end of restrictions between the Germanys; (4) acceptance of European Community rules by the GDR; (5) restructuring of GDR economic enterprises; (6) labor laws; (7) regulations for environmental protection; (8) agricultural regulations; (9) social insurance; and (10) budgetary law.[92] The treaty thus established a single market before the final achievement of political union.

By late March, the terms of the impending state treaty became the topic of an intense domestic political debate. The critics, who included economic experts, opposition West German politicians, and some East Germans, found ample grounds for criticism. Economists in the West German government and the Bundesbank stressed that the planned treaty represented an "inversion of conventional economic thinking" in which monetary union is usually the final stage of a long process of economic reform and convergence, and not the initial step.[93] Following Kohl's statements favoring parity conversion (a one-to-one exchange rate), Bundesbank President Karl Otto Pohl also argued for a two-to-one rate instead, citing the dangers of inflation in West Germany and the likelihood of bankruptcies and unemployment in East Germany under parity conversion. The cabinet supported Kohl, however, and Kohl partly negated the Bundesbank's influence by appointing Pohl as head of a committee to oversee the implementation of economic unification.[94] Oskar Lafontaine, the SPD's chancellor candidate for the upcoming December election, attacked Kohl for putting forth a "gross deception" regarding the future costs of economic union and called for a slower, more gradual approach.[95] Although Lafontaine's observations ultimately proved correct, Kohl was able to counter them in the short run by pledging, as he had in 1989, that no additional taxes would be required of West Germans beyond the cost of the already established Fund for German Unity. He also made several minor concessions to the SPD to divide Lafontaine and the party's moderates.[96] The treaty was subsequently ratified by both the Bundestag and Bundesrat (in which the SPD had a majority).

The Second State Treaty

Political union required the development of a second treaty, the Treaty on the Restoration of the State Unity of Germany. Negotiations were rendered contentious by ideological differences between East and West, divisions within the coalition government of the GDR, Western interference in GDR party politics, and political considerations resulting from the impending election scheduled for December.[97] The Basic Law (the German constitution) provided for two alternative routes to reunification: (1) Article 146 required a formal treaty between two sovereign states and the probable drafting of a new constitution, while (2) Article 23 required only the dissolution of the GDR and the accession of the five eastern Länder to the Federal Republic. Kohl favored accession as the shortest route and one that assured the retention of the Basic Law and most West German institutions; however, the Left in the GDR and the Social Democrats in the Federal Republic favored a slower reunification which the SPD hoped would help Oskar Lafontaine to win the December 1990 election.[98]

The Kohl government proceeded on the basis of Article 23, and Bonn's chief negotiator, Wolfgang Schäuble, set the tone of the negotiations in his address to the GDR's delegation at the first session on July 6:

This is the accession of the GDR to the FRG and not the reverse. . . . We have a good Basic Law that is proven. We want to do everything for you. You are cordially welcome. We do not want to trample coldly on your wishes and interests. But this is not the unification of two equal states.[99]

The prospects for successful negotiations improved following the commitment by the Kohl government and the West German Länder on May 14 of DM 115 billion (the Fund for German Unity), to pay for reunification, and the announcement on August 19 that the first all-German elections would be held on December 2.[100] Negotiations continued throughout July and August, despite defections from the GDR coalition and last-minute demands by the SPD in the West. The treaty was finally signed by both governments on August 31, and the GDR ceased to exist on October 2, 1990.

In the end, the five new Länder, which were reconstituted in May from the former GDR Administrative districts, acceded to the Federal Republic of Germany. The 1,000 pages of treaty text provided for the extension of West Germany's constitutional order to all of Germany, as well as the integration of East German institutions into those of the Federal Republic. Important exceptions were articulated area by area, and a two-year period was provided for some disputed constitutional issues, such as the legal status of abortion. It was clear, however, that Kohl had prevailed in imposing his conception of reunification on the other parties.

The All-German Election, December 2, 1990

In a practical sense, the national election of December was the closing act of the reunification drama. The issue of reunification dominated all other concerns, and the election was viewed throughout Germany as a referendum on the Kohl government's handling of the unity process. The political momentum that was to carry Helmut Kohl and the CDU to victory began to build in June 1990 when Kohl's standing in the polls improved markedly. By September 1990, Kohl and the CDU had moved ahead of Lafontaine and the SPD in major public opinion surveys for the first time since September 1987.[101] These results clearly indicated growing approval of Kohl's conception of reunification, as well as the fact that Lafontaine's largely negative campaign to exploit social fears was losing its effect. Viewed as the "architect of reunification," Kohl personally moved ahead of his challenger in the polls by 20 percent in November.[102] Kohl's approval rating was the highest in East Germany; in the October 1990 state elections in the five new Länder, the CDU received the highest total of votes in four of the five contests, losing to the SPD only in Brandenburg. In the all-German election in December, the CDU/CSU captured 43.8 percent of the national votes, the Free Democrats received 11 percent, and the Social Democrats gained only 33.5 percent, their lowest total since the 1950s.[103] The CDU/CSU–FDP coalition consequently became the first legitimate government for all of Germany since 1932 and won the right to undertake efforts to consolidate the reunification process.

STAGE THREE, IMPLEMENTATION: CONSOLIDATING THE REUNIFICATION PROJECT

Within months of the 1990 election, the complexity of the economic, social, and political problems associated with reunification became apparent. Reunification had brought together two very different industrial societies, increased the population of the Federal Republic by 25 percent (from 63 to 79 million), and increased its territory by 24 percent.[104] Viewed from an economic perspective, the inequality between the eastern and western Länder created a nation with a dual economy. In addition, the inclusion of five new Länder and the reconstituted Land of Berlin introduced new disparities in size, population, and economic development into the federal system. Most important, reunification combined two populations with different and, in some cases, unrealistic expectations regarding the timing and agenda of the reunification process. Between 1991 and early 1993, Germany experienced a transition crisis, which included a national economic downturn (later officially declared a recession), growing concern for higher taxes and public indebtedness, and the continuation of the East-West cultural divide.[105] The crisis was the result of the interaction of a number of factors, which included the following: (1) the weak state of the eastern economy, (2) the influence of market forces, (3) the negative effects of earlier policies (instituted in 1990), (4) limitations on the usefulness of transferring institutions from western to eastern Germany, (5) unrealistic promises by political leaders regarding the cost of reunification, (6) the existence of structural weaknesses in the economy of the Federal Republic that predated reunification, and (7) the effects of the international and European recessions.

For East Germans, the revolutionary phase of reunification did not end with the formal union of the two German states. In the new Länder, as in other postcommunist states, the transition to market capitalism brought the breakdown and destruction of economic, political, and social relationships that had developed under communism.[106] Since the transition to capitalism was more rapid and extensive in the former GDR than anywhere else in Eastern Europe, institutions and practices from western Germany could not immediately replace them. A population accustomed to provision and subsidy by a paternalistic state suddenly experienced unemployment, real prices, and competition; the result was widespread anxiety, fear, and frustration. Revelations of mass complicity with the former STASI and scandals involving East German politicians further lowered morale. Most important, as it became clear that social and economic equality for the two parts of Germany would not be achieved quickly, Easterners became increasingly resentful of what they perceived as their second-class citizenship. For West Germans, the problems of reunification built on earlier concerns about structural weaknesses in the German economy, which surfaced in the early 1980s. Most West Germans initially assumed that reunification would require only the extension of western institutions to the East and that major changes would be confined to the area of the former GDR. As the true cost of reunification was understood and huge transfers of funds were required to subsidize the new Länder, Westerners also incurred heavy adjustment costs in the form of higher taxes, a larger public debt, and higher interest rates. West Germans concerned with the maintenance of national affluence and competitiveness grew increasingly fearful that these adjustment costs would delay needed modernization and structural changes in the national economy. Resentment also grew toward Easterners when it appeared that they were the recipients of special benefits and subsidies.

For the Kohl government, the reunification issue was transformed from one that had produced an electoral realignment in its favor to one that placed it on the defensive and challenged its ability to lead. The economic problems that surfaced after 1990 made a mockery of Chancellor Kohl's claim that no one would be made worse off economically by reunification and that no additional taxes would be required to pay for it. Certainly, the medium- and long-term prognosis for both the new Länder and the Federal Republic of Germany as a whole remained good, and few individuals questioned the historic value of reunification as a contribution to the end of the division of Europe. However, as the costs of union became visible in the first three years of the postreunification period, popular attention shifted from the long-term benefits to the short-term costs and troublesome single issues such as the legal status of abortion and the disposition of STASI files. The problems raised by reunification defied easy solution because they were numerous, complex, and interrelated.[107] The consolidation of the reunification project involved complicated trade-offs between such values as equity and efficiency, short-term and long-term interests, private and public activities, and eastern German versus western German interests.[108] For example, the rapid increase in the wages of Easterners to satisfy short-term demands complicated long-term efforts to attract outside investment, while increased transfers of public funds to transform the eastern economy inevitably made less aid available to poorer areas in the original Länder. In the face of these complicated trade-offs, the Kohl government acted much less decisively in dealing with the social and economic problems of 1991–1993 than it had in dealing with the diplomatic and political challenges of 1990. Public opinion polls demonstrated a corresponding decline of public confidence in the government, and criticisms of Kohl returned to the levels of 1987.

The Eastern Economy

The central task confronting the Kohl government was the revitalization and transformation of the eastern economy. In his optimistic assessments of the costs of reunification in 1990, Kohl had assumed that the introduction of economic and monetary union (July 1990) would produce an "economic miracle" of growth and expansion similar to that experienced by West Germany after 1948.[109] Contrary to such expectations, following GEMU the five eastern Länder experienced what the OECD called "the virtual collapse of production and employment."[110] The collapse included the following elements: industrial output in the second half of 1990 fell by 50 percent from the year before; by 1991, 30 percent of the labor force experienced short-term unemployment; and only 25 percent of industrial firms proved economically viable in the new market environment.[111] Between 1989 and 1992, employment in agriculture in the East declined by 70 percent, employment in manufacturing declined by 60 percent, and employment in mining and energy production fell by 39 percent.[112] Overall, 3 million jobs (34 percent of the total) were lost during this period. The majority of job losses followed the privatization of previously state-owned enterprises by the Treuhandanstalt (the Trust Agency, created in 1990) which had sold 78 percent of such enterprises and liquidated 17 percent more by July 1993.[113]

The breakdown of the eastern economy was the result of a number of unanticipated factors. Above all, the breakdown reflected the adverse effects of forty years of poor management, neglect of the infrastructure, and aging capital stock in the GDR. The majority of eastern firms were simply not competitive in the contemporary world economy. In addition, the breakdown reflected the economic effects of Kohl's policy of a one-to-one conversion at the time of GEMU's introduction in 1990. Although it was a sound political decision and signaled West Germany's intention to accelerate the reunification process, parity conversion represented a "drastic overvaluation of the East mark," which overvalued eastern wages and prices and denied the new Länder the competitive benefits of a lower level of exchange.[114] West German unions also contributed to the pressure for higher wages. In 1990, they extended their organizing activities to the new Länder and subsequently demanded wage parity between eastern and western workers.[115] After a series of strikes and prolonged negotiations, a planned phase-in of parity was announced.

Further, private investment in the GDR lagged far behind the initial, optimistic predictions that reunification could be financed in large part by the privatization of formerly state-owned firms. Outside investors were deterred by a number of risks and obstacles including possible legal claims by previous owners whose property had been confiscated by Nazi or Communist authorities and the poor condition of the infrastructure. As a result, with its task of privatization nearing completion in 1994, the Treuhandanstalt reported a deficit of DM 300 billion.[116]

The Impact on Western Germany

In the most difficult period, from 1991 to the end of 1993, the eastern population was sustained by the transfer of public funds from the West. By 1993, the cost of funding the reunification project had reached DM 180 billion a year (excluding the debt of the Treuhandanstalt), about half of the total tax revenues, and it was anticipated that this amount would be required annually for at least an additional five years.[117] The consolidation of reunification placed heavy burdens on West German taxpayers. According to Bundesbank estimates, the net contribution of western taxes was DM 107 billion in 1991, DM 128 billion in 1992, and DM 135 billion in 1993.[118] In addition, reunification contributed to a large increase in the total public debt, from DM 1.05 trillion in 1990 to DM 1.51 trillion in 1993 (estimated to reach DM 1.73 trillion by the end of 1994). This made servicing the debt the second most expensive item in the budget.[119] The debt problem was made worse by the refusal of the Kohl government to acknowledge the need for new taxes until mid-1991, when social security contributions were increased by 1.5

percent and a 7.5 percent surcharge was placed on income and corporate taxes (from mid-1991 to 1992).[120] Other tax increases occurred in 1992. Kohl's reluctance to seek new taxes was apparently the result both of a desire to uphold his 1990 pledge that no additional taxes would be required and a genuine belief that German taxes were already among the highest in the world and constituted a drag on competitiveness. In what became known in political circles as the "tax lie," Kohl attempted to justify the 1991 increases as payment to the Soviet Union for the withdrawal of its troops from Eastern Europe and as Germany's contribution to the Persian Gulf War.[121] Following the increases, Kohl's standing in the polls dropped further.

Financing reunification was also harmful to the West German economy in other ways. The huge transfers to the East that resulted from parity conversion in 1990 and from subsequent federal aid packages fueled inflation, which reached 4.1 percent in 1991. To contain inflation, and as a result of heavy government borrowing on private financial markets, interest rates remained high well into 1993, when the first modest declines occurred. The combination of tax increases, high public debt, and high interest rates resulted in a decline in the rate of growth in western Germany from 3.6 percent in 1991 to .8 percent in 1992. In 1993, the GDP for both parts of Germany contracted by over 1 percent. In June 1993, 2.2 million workers were unemployed in western Germany (7.8%) and 1.1 million workers were unemployed in the former GDR (15.1%).[122] Unemployment peaked in January 1994, when 4.03 million workers (10.5% of the national workforce) were out of work, a postwar record. For those with jobs in western Germany, wages fell an average of 1 percent in real terms between 1993 and 1994. For the West German population, which prized the maintenance of economic affluence and stability above all else, this was a time of great anxiety and frustration.

As would be expected, the high costs of consolidation took a heavy political toll on Helmut Kohl and his coalition. Public opinion polls showed a near-continuous decline in Kohl's standing from 1991 on, and the CDU suffered electoral defeats in both eastern and western Germany. In March 1993, the CDU lost local elections in Hesse, and in September, it also lost elections in the city-state of Hamburg, receiving only 25.4 percent of the vote. The voters in Hamburg also demonstrated their discontent by giving unprecedented support to smaller, protest parties. In December, the CDU lost again in the state election in Brandenburg, the first such election in an eastern Land since reunification. In March 1994, the CDU also lost to the Social Democrats in the Land of Lower Saxony, receiving only 36.5 percent of the vote. The contest in Lower Saxony was important because it was the first of nineteen elections for state parliament, local council, and the national parliament to be held in 1994 (the fate of Kohl and the CDU/CSU–FDP coalition was decided in the Bundestag election of October 16).[123]

Despite these electoral setbacks, there were also indications that the worst of the economic recession was over and that the Kohl government had established a possible basis for successful consolidation. During 1993, the government took steps to confront more effectively the problem of financing the transformation of eastern Germany. In the autumn of 1992, Kohl proposed a "Solidarity Pact," a formula for funding reunification at approximately $60 to $70 billion a year for ten years.[124] Although a modest fiscal compromise, it called for reductions in social spending to offset the reunification costs and a "solidarity surcharge" of 7.5 percent on 1995 corporate and personal income taxes.[125] These measures were intended to offset public sector borrowing. To satisfy the interests of the western Länder, the pact also provided increased revenues for those states. In July 1993, the Kohl government also confronted the problem of right-wing violence against foreigners. Police measures against neo-Nazi violence were increased, and violent acts subsequently declined. In addition, on July 1, an initial, restrictive asylum law took effect to slow the influx of foreigners, which had reached a level of nearly 400,000 a year.[126] Although highly controversial at the political party level, the measure proved popular with the general electorate.

In early 1994, a number of short-term factors combined to improve Kohl's standing in the polls and suggest that the "Kohl era" in German politics might not end in the October election. Once again, the rival Social Democratic Party was divided and lacked a proven leader. Reversing a year-long trend, polls in early June showed Kohl ahead of his personal rival, Rudolf Scharping, by 13 percent.[127] For his part, Kohl retained unchallenged control over the center-right coalition. He won an important political victory in May, when his personal choice for the office, Roman Herzog, was elected president of Germany, and in the election in June for the European Parliament, the CDU alliance defeated the Social Democrats, 40 to 33 percent. In combination, these events indicated a reversal in Kohl's personal political fortunes. In addition, there was a general feeling that the worst of the recession was over, and confidence in the economy seemed to be returning. Economic indicators demonstrated modest but steady improvement in the first three months of 1994, and government sources were able to predict a 1994 economic growth rate of 1.5 percent for all of Germany. Most important, the prevailing political dialogue indicated a growing public realization that the consolidation phase of reunification would require ten to twenty years at a minimum and might take a generation or longer. In this context, Kohl's campaign sought to depict him as the experienced, proven "steward" who was most able to direct the next stage of the consolidation process.

As was generally predicted toward the end of the campaign, Helmut Kohl's center-right coalition won the October 1994 election, enabling him to continue in the post of chancellor, which he had held for twelve years. The CDU/CSU received 41.5 percent of the vote, down 2.3 percent from 1990, while the Social Democrats received 36.4 percent, 2.9 percent higher than in 1990. Kohl's coalition partner, the Free Democratic Party, won

6.9 percent, while the Party of Democrat Socialism won thirty seats, with 4.4 percent of the vote (and four victories in Berlin constituencies). The decisive factors in Kohl's victory appeared to be the relative inexperience of his SPD rival for chancellor and the reluctance of western German voters to opt for another major change. The election left the CDU/CSU–FDP coalition with a slim ten-vote majority in the Bundestag, and the outcome testified to considerable popular dissatisfaction with the results of reunification in both parts of Germany. Most important, the results of the election testified to the continuing political and cultural divide in Germany, with Kohl's coalition winning in the majority of western states but losing in four of the five eastern Länder.

NATURE AND SCOPE OF CHANGE

Recent studies have argued that more happened in the ten months following the fall of the Berlin Wall than usually occurs in ten years[128] and, moreover, that Germany changed more between 1989 and 1993 than it had in the previous four decades.[129] Both observations correctly point out the extensive changes that occurred in the wake of the events of 1990, as well as the changes resulting from the ongoing effort at consolidation of the reunification project. Four years into consolidation, a tentative evaluation of these changes would require an extensive, book-length survey, which is beyond the scope of this chapter. From the perspective of Helmut Kohl as leader, however, it is useful to make a few observations. First, viewed from an international perspective, German reunification was an event of great significance, which contributed to the end of the Cold War, the end of the division of Europe, and to the demise of the communist/neo-Stalinist order in Europe. Reunification also contributed to the spread of democracy and market capitalism and to popular self-determination.[130] In the end, 16.5 million former citizens of the GDR, who had demonstrated their consent through immigration, peaceful protests, and the ballot box, acceded to the liberal-democratic order of the Federal Republic. For the Atlantic Alliance, the European Community and German Christian Democracy, this was the optimal outcome of the forty-five–year competition of the Cold War. Regardless of the problems that surfaced after the union of the two Germanys, this outcome fully justified the Kohl government's determination to seize the historic opportunity of 1989–1990 before new factors intervened.

The failed coup against Mikhail Gorbachev of August 1991, as well as the recent growing strength of Russian nationalists, testify to the wisdom of this decision, and indeed, it is hard to imagine how the reunification project could have been carried out more quickly or skillfully. In their dealings with the four victors of World War II, Kohl and his government fully exploited Germany's postwar record of constructive and responsible international relations; in its relations with the GDR, in which West Germany had a preponderance of power, the Kohl government acted decisively to be certain that reunification was accomplished on its terms.[131] It is also to the credit of the Kohl government that the accession process was carried out without any significant acts of violence or diplomatic ultimatums and in accordance with the rules of the EC, the United Nations, and the two-plus-four framework.

Second, viewed from the perspective of German diplomacy, reunification and the various agreements that accompanied it represented "the German answer to the German Question."[132] The German answer was really a "European answer," that reunification should occur within the context of continued membership in the European Community/European Union, NATO, and the Conference on Security and Cooperation in Europe. Instead of being a threat to peace, unified Germany would contribute to peace and stability in eastern and central Europe as well as to the increasing integration of the Continent. The Kohl government underscored this commitment by supporting the Maastricht Treaty and economic aid to the Commonwealth of Independent States, signing the German-Soviet Friendship Treaty (1990), and guaranteeing all existing borders in Eastern Europe. Germany was the major beneficiary of the events that transformed Europe after 1985, and it emerged with greatly enhanced power capabilities.[133] The message of reunification that the Kohl government sought to communicate was that these new capabilities would continue to be mediated through Germany's democratic political culture and its established commitment to multilateral cooperation.[134]

Finally, reunification is certain to transform German domestic politics as Easterners and Westerners struggle to consolidate the unification process over the next one to two decades. Many changes have already occurred. Since 1990, the reunification issue has dominated the political agenda, taxes and public borrowing have increased, the inclusion of new parties from eastern Germany has widened the political spectrum, and the federal system has been made more complex by the inclusion of the new Länder. The need for massive subsidies has also threatened the position and benefits of major political groups, including western taxpayers; the western Länder, which compete for tax revenues; trade unions, which are concerned with the protection of wage scales and benefit packages; and the established political parties, which seek to preserve their share of the vote in the new circumstances. Despite the continuity of postwar political patterns, reunification is certain to compel adjustments in the relationship between the central government and the Länder, the social welfare system, the scope of government intervention in the economy, and the degree of commitment to the concept of the social market economy. At present, the exact parameters of these changes cannot be precisely determined, but it is clear that they will occur within the context of the Basic Law, a stable and democratic political culture, and a party system dominated by centrist parties with a proven record of responsibility and effectiveness.

NOTES

1. For these theories, see Freidrich Meinecke, *The German Catastrophe* (Boston: Beacon Press, 1967); Louis L. Snyder, *Basic History of Modern Germany* (New York: D. Van Nostrand Company, 1957); and A. J. P. Taylor, *The Course of German History: A Survey of the Development of Germany since 1815* (New York: Capricorn Books, 1962).

2. Dietrich Rueschemeyer, Evelyne Huber Stephens, and John D. Stephens, *Capitalist Development and Democracy* (Chicago: University of Chicago Press, 1992), pp. 106-109.

3. Mark Kesselman and Joel Krieger, ed., *European Politics in Transition* (Lexington, MA: D.C. Heath and Co., 1987), p. 238.

4. Ibid., p. 238.

5. Richard Tilly, "Germany," in Richard Sylla and Gianni Toniolo, eds., *Patterns of European Industrialization: The Nineteenth Century* (New York: Routledge, 1991), p. 175.

6. Mary Fulbrook, *Germany: 1918–1990; The Divided Nation* (London: Fontana Press, 1991), p. 5.

7. See Dirk Verheyen and Christian Søe, eds., *The Germans and Their Neighbors* (Boulder, CO: Westview Press, 1993), pp. 1–9; and David Calleo, *The German Problem Reconsidered: Germany and the World Order, 1870 to the Present* (Cambridge, England: Cambridge University Press, 1980), pp. 9–25.

8. See Fulbrook, pp. 66–96; and David Childs, *Germany in the Twentieth Century* (New York: Icon Editions, 1991), pp. 61–85.

9. Mary Fulbrook, *The Two Germanies, 1945–1990: Problems of Interpretation* (London: Macmillan, 1992), pp. 2–3.

10. Ibid., p. 89.

11. Peter Katzenstein, "Taming of Power: German Unification 1989–1990," in Meredith Woo-Cumings and Michael Loriaux, eds., *Past as Prelude: History in the Making of a New World Order* (Boulder, CO: Westview Press, 1993), pp. 70–73.

12. Michael J. Hogan, *The Marshall Plan: America, Britain, and the Reconstruction of Western Europe, 1947–1952* (Cambridge, England: Cambridge University Press, 1989), p. 430.

13. See Michael Loriaux, "The Riddle of the Rhine: France, Germany, and the Geopolitics of European Integration, 1919–1992," in Woo-Cumings and Loriaux, pp. 83–110, esp. pp. 96–99.

14. Arthur M. Handhardt, Jr., "The Collapse of the German Democratic Republic and Its Unification with the Federal Republic of Germany, 1989–90," in Michael G. Huelshoff, Andrei S. Markovits, and Simon Reich, eds., *From Bundesrepublik to Deutschland: German Politics after Unification* (Ann Arbor: The University of Michigan Press, 1993), p. 208.

15. Henry Ashby Turner, Jr., *The Two Germanies since 1945* (New Haven, CT: Yale University Press, 1987), p. 177.

16. Steven Muller, "Democracy in Germany," *Daedalus: Journal of the American Academy of Arts and Sciences,* Winter 1994, p. 38.

17. See Jutta A. Helm, "The Study of Germany in Comparative Politics," in Huelshoff, Markovits, Reich, pp. 11–29.

18. Gordon Smith, *Democracy in Western Germany: Parties and Politics in the Federal Republic,* 3rd ed. (Aldershot, U.K: Dartmouth, 1990), pp. 47–48.

19. Peter J. Katzenstein, *Policy and Politics in West Germany: The Growth of a Semisovereign State* (Philadelphia: Temple University Press, 1987), p. 87.

20. Richard L. Carson, *Comparative Economic Systems. Part 3: Capitalist Alternatives* (New York: M. E. Sharpe, 1990), p. 680.

21. Kesselman and Krieger, p. 47; W. R. Smyser, *The German Economy: Colossus at the Crossroads,* 2nd ed. (New York: St. Martin's Press, 1993), p. 16.

22. Meredith Woo-Cumings, "Introduction," in Woo-Cumings and Loriaux, p. 1.

23. Elizabeth Pond, "Germany in the New Europe," *Foreign Affairs,* 71(2) (1992): 114–130.

24. H. G. Peter Wallach and Ronald A. Francisco, *United Germany: The Past, Politics, Prospects* (Westport, CT: Praeger, 1992), p. 73.

25. Katzenstein, "Taming of Power," p. 60.

26. Ibid., p. 60.

27. Henry Ashby Turner, Jr., *Germany from Partition to Reunification* (New Haven, CT: Yale University Press, 1992), p. 242.

28. Ibid., p. 259.

29. Peter H. Merkl, *German Unification in the European Context* (University Park, PA: The Pennsylvania State University Press, 1993), pp. 139–140.

30. Wallach and Francisco, pp. 62–67.

31. Merkl, p. 396.

32. Thomas Kielinger and Max Otte, "Germany: The Pressured Power," *Foreign Policy* 91 (1993): 47.

33. Ibid., p. 45.

34. Jonathan Story, "Europe's Future: Western Union or Common Home?" in Colin Crouch and David Marquand, eds., *The Politics of 1992: Beyond the Single European Market* (Cambridge, MA: Basil Blackwell, 1990), p. 57.

35. Stephen Padgett, "The New German Economy," in Gordon Smith, William E. Paterson, Peter H. Merkl, and Stephen Padgett, eds., *Developments in German Politics* (Durham, NC: Duke University Press, 1992), p. 187.

36. Merkl, pp. 234–236.

37. Childs, p. 283.

38. Ibid.

39. *New York Times,* July 1, 1990, p. 4.

40. Ibid.

41. Ibid.

42. Childs, p. 283.

43. *New York Times,* July 1, 1990, p. 4.

44. Ibid.

45. For a discussion of this election, see Ian Derbyshire, *Politics in West Germany from Schmidt to Kohl* (Cambridge, U.K.: Chambers, 1987), pp. 19–26.

46. Ibid., pp. 20–23.

47. Ibid., pp. 20–22.

48. Gerhart Hoffmeister and Frederic C. Tubach, *Germany: 2000 Years from the Nazi Era to German Unification,* vol. 3 (New York: Continuum, 1992), pp. 227–228.

49. John W. Young, *Cold War Europe 1945–1989: A Political History* (New York: Edward Arnold, 1991), pp. 76–77.

50. *Time Magazine,* June 25, 1990, p. 38.

51. Derbyshire, pp. 120–122.

52. Konrad H. Jarausch, *The Rush to German Unity* (New York: Oxford University Press, 1994), p. 28.

53. Merkl, p. 69.

54. Cited by Jarausch, pp. 23–24.

55. Fulbrook, *The Two Germanies,* p. 75; Dirk Philipsen, *We Were the People: Voices from East Germany's Revolutionary Autumn of 1989* (Durham, NC: Duke University Press, 1993), pp. 29–30.

56. Fulbrook, *The Two Germanies,* pp. 81–83.

57. Michael G. Huelshoff and Arthur M. Handhardt, Jr., "Steps Toward Union: The Collapse of the GDR and the Unification of Germany," in M. Donald Hancock and Helga A. Welsh, eds., *German Unification: Process and Outcomes* (Boulder, CO: Westview Press, 1994), pp. 78–79.

58. Ibid., p. 79.

59. Ibid., p. 80.

60. Philipsen, p. 22.

61. Wallach and Francisco, p. 2.

62. Jarausch, p. 65.

63. Ibid.

64. Merkl, p. 127.

65. Ibid., p. 124.

66. Jarausch, p. 68.

67. Merkl, p. 124.

68. Jarausch, p. 68.

69. For a discussion of this point, see Hanhardt, pp. 207–233.

70. Wallach and Francisco, pp. 46, 48.

71. Merkl, p. 130.

72. Michael Balfour, *Germany: The Tides of Power* (New York: Routledge, 1992), p. 233.

73. Denis L. Bark and David R. Gress, *A History of West Germany.* Vol. 2, *Democracy and Its Discontents 1963–1991,* 2nd ed. (Cambridge: Blackwell, 1993), p. 711; Balfour, p. 235.

74. Bark and Gress, pp. 710, 714.

75. Ibid., p. 714.

76. Elizabeth Pond, *Beyond the Wall: Germany's Road to Unification* (Washington, DC: The Brookings Institution, 1993), p. 192.

77. Wallach and Francisco, p. 50.

78. Ibid., p. 70.

79. Paterson and Smith, "German Unity," in Smith, Paterson, Merkl, and Padgett, p. 16.

80. Ibid., p. 17.

81. Ibid., p. 18.

82. Concerning the Helsinki Accords, see Wallach and Francisco, p. 70.

83. Pond, pp. 221–223.

84. Bark and Gress, pp. 721–722.

85. Paterson and Smith, p. 31.

86. Jarausch, p. 148.

87. Bark and Gress, p. 717.

88. Cited by ibid., p. 718.

89. Wallach and Francisco, pp. 53–54.

90. Merkl, p. 199.

91. Ibid., pp. 202–203.

92. Ibid., p. 200, and Padgett, pp. 187–193.

93. Padgett, pp. 187, 193.

94. Huelshoff and Hanhardt, p. 85.

95. Jarausch, p. 145.

96. Ibid., p. 147.

97. Ibid., p. 171.

98. Arthur M. Hanhardt, p. 227.

99. Cited in Jarausch, p. 170.

100. Wallach and Francisco, p. 74.

101. Merkl, p. 155.

102. Ibid., p. 156.

103. Gordon Smith, "The New Party System," in Smith, Paterson, Merkl, and Padgett, pp. 87–88.

104. Stephan Eisel, "The Politics of a United Germany," *Daedalus: Journal of the American Academy of Arts and Sciences,* Winter 1994, p. 154.

105. For the dynamics of this crisis, see Jurgen Kocka, "Crisis of Unification: How Germany Changes," *Daedalus: Journal of the American Academy of Arts and Sciences,* Winter 1994, pp. 173–192.

106. Ibid., p. 174.

107. For a discussion of this point, see Ullrich Heilemann and Reimut Jochimsen, *Christmas in July? The Political Economy of German Unification Reconsidered* (Washington, DC: The Brookings Institution, 1993), pp. 18–20.

108. Ibid., p. 53.

109. Padgett, pp. 188–189.

110. Cited in ibid., p. 193.

111. Ibid., p. 193.

112. Kocka, p. 181.

113. Ibid., p. 180.

114. Padgett, p. 192; Heilemann and Jochimsen, p. 11.

115. For a discussion of this point, see Christopher Flockton and Josef Esser, "Labour Market Problems and Labour Market Policy," in Smith, Paterson, Merkl, and Padgett, eds., pp. 281–300.

116. "Model Vision: A Survey of Germany," *Economist,* May 21, 1994, p. 27.

117. Ibid., p. 6.

118. Cited in Eisel, p. 160.

119. Model Vision, p. 7.

120. Michael Kreile, "The Political Economy of the New Germany," in Paul B. Stares, ed., *The New Germany and the New Europe* (Washington, DC: The Brookings Institution, 1992), p. 82.

121. Catherine McArdle Kelleher, "The New Germany: An Overview," in Stares, pp. 32–33.

122. Kurt J. Lauk, "Germany at the Crossroads: On the Efficiency of the German

Economy," *Daedalus: Journal of the American Academy of Arts and Sciences*, Winter 1994, p. 59.

123. For a discussion of these elections, see "A Long Year in German Politics," *Economist*, June 8, 1994, pp. 47–48.

124. Eisel, p. 160.

125. See the *Economist*, March 6–12, 1993, pp. 13, 51–52; March 20–26, 1993, pp. 19–20; June 5–11, 1993, pp. 48, 53.

126. Klaus J. Bade, "Immigration and Social Peace in United Germany," *Daedalus: Journal of the American Academy of Arts and Sciences*, Winter 1994, p. 91; the *Economist*, May 14–20, 1994, p. 5.

127. Forsa Poll, cited in the *New York Times*, June 23, 1994, p. 6.

128. Timothy Garton Ash, *In Europe's Name: Germany and the Divided Continent* (New York: Random House, 1993), p. 343.

129. Kocka, p. 173.

130. Jarausch, pp. 197–200.

131. Concerning its dealings with the four victors, see Jarusch, p. 201; Wallach and Francisco, pp. 2, 22–23.

132. Ash, p. 357.

133. Wolfram F. Hanrieder, *The New Germany and the New Europe*, Working Paper 2.10, Center for German and European Studies (University of California at Berkeley, November 1992), p. 3.

134. For a discussion of these influences on German foreign policy, see Beverly Crawford, *German Foreign Policy after the Cold War: The Decision to Recognize Croatia*, Working Paper 2.21, *Center for German and European Studies* (University of California at Berkeley, August 1993), pp. 5–6.

Lech Walesa and the Emergence of Postcommunist Poland

THE NATIONAL POLITICAL-ECONOMIC CONTEXT

Poland stands today as a monument to the human desire for freedom. From 1772 to 1989, with the exception of some twenty interwar years (November 1918–September 1939), Poland struggled to assert its place in the world as a sovereign independent state.[1]

For over 800 years (966–1772), Poland had been a major player in central European politics, but beginning with the late eighteenth century, it fell into a period of decline. In 1772, three neighboring states (Russia, Prussia, and Austria) capitalized on this weakness and carried out the so-called "First Partition of Poland." The shock of this act caused a resurgence in Polish national sentiment, but it came too late. Despite the passage of a constitution on May 3, 1791 (the second modern state constitution in the world, after the United States), a "Second Partition," this time by Russia and Prussia only, subsequently took place (1793). Tadeusz Kosciuszko, a Polish officer who fought in the American Revolution, led a national insurrection in 1794, but the weight of the armies of Prussia, Russia, and Austria crushed the uprising. This allowed the victorious states to perform the final "Third Partition" (October 24, 1795), thus eliminating Poland from the map for 122 years. Two more great national insurrections, the "November Uprising" (1830–1831) and the "January Uprising" (1863–1864) joined the "Kosciuszko Uprising" (1794) as quixotic-appearing attempts to regain national independence.[2] These struggles did, however, nurture the political struggle, which bore fruit in the successful reassertion of sovereignty in November 1918, when all three partitioning powers collapsed as a result of World War I. Freedom, however, was not long-lived, for twenty years later, the allied Nazi-Germans and the Soviet-Russians, in the beginning act of World War II in Europe, partitioned Poland for the fourth time.

The Soviet Union was forced to switch sides, however, when the Nazis invaded the USSR on June 22, 1941. The USSR was, nevertheless, able to keep the spoils of the period of the Nazi-Soviet Pact and gather most of Central Europe under Communist control when she emerged victorious, along with the Western Allies, in 1945. However, the inheritance of 800 years of independence, the three insurrections, and the twenty years of interwar freedom had their effects, for Poland was certainly the most turbulent of the Soviet satellites during the Soviet Empire's existence. For as long as eight years after the 1944 entrance of Soviet forces onto indisputedly Polish ethnic territory, there was armed resistance to the imposition of Communist rule. Then, in 1956, 1968, 1970, 1976, 1980–1981, and 1988, there were major anti-regime demonstrations during which security forces and the population clashed. By early 1989, the Communist government of Poland realized it could no longer rule and began talking with the opposition in the so-called "round table" discussions, and on April 7 of that year, an agreement was reached which began the process of decommunizing the country. Thus, in summer 1989, after a partially free election and a number of political perturbations, Tadeusz Mazowiecki became the first noncommunist prime minister in the Soviet bloc and Poland moved into the postcommunist phase of its development.

Two Polish politicians were movers and shakers of the 1980s who caused this to happen. One was General of the Army Wojciech Jaruzelski, a graduate of the Soviet General Staff officers' college and First Secretary of the Polish United Workers Party (*Polska Zjednoczona Partia Robotnicza* or *PZPR*)—the Communist Party of Poland, and Lech Walesa, an electrician in the Gdansk "Lenin" Shipyard who was of peasant background and served as the leader of the Solidarity (*Solidarnosc*) movement. By the end of the decade, the high Communist official was preparing for retirement while the worker was preparing to be President of the Republic.

NATIONAL TURBULENCE

National Turbulence before the 1980s

At the beginning of modern times, the Polish-Lithuanian Commonwealth (a joint venture of Polish and Lithuanian-Rus' nobles, in which the Polish element eventually gained the upper hand) was the largest state in Europe. However, due to its decline, partitions, and over 120 years of subjugation, Poland emerged from captivity in 1918 as a much weakened state. Many groups, especially Lithuanians, Ukrainians, and Belarus'ians, that had more or less willingly taken part in the old multiethnic Commonwealth resisted incorporation into the newly resurrected country. Thus, the desire to achieve the borders of 1772 (the borders before the First Partition) was thwarted after November 1918. Nonetheless, a very large and predominantly Polish (but still multinational) state emerged in the early post–World War I period. However, two of the partitioning powers (Austria no longer being a major force)—Russia, under the guise of the Soviet Union, and the truncated Weimar (and subsequently Nazi) Germany—were dissatisfied. The Soviets bore a particularly strong grudge against the Poles because at the "Battle on the Vistula River" in August 1920, their armed forces were defeated by the Polish Army just when they had hoped that their "War Communism" would be successful in carrying the Bolshevik Revolution into the heart of Europe. This defeat of the Communists and the subsequent "Riga Peace Treaty" with the Soviet Russians, plus the weakness of Germany until the middle 1930s, allowed a breathing space for Poland.

As rapidly as possible, the main politician of the interwar period and the greatest hero of the struggle for independence, Jozef Pilsudski, tried to reconstruct and strengthen the state. However, neither the Soviet Union (whose one-time foreign Minister, Vyacheslav Molotov, had once referred to Poland as "the monstrous bastard of the Peace of Versailles") nor Adolf Hitler (who called Poland "a ridiculous state") wanted the country to exist.[3] Thus on September 1, 1939, eight days after the signing of a Nazi-Soviet peace and friendship pact (August 23, 1939), the so-called Molotov-Ribbentrop Pact, the Germans attacked Poland and World War II began. On September 17, 1939, acting according to secret provisions of the pact, the Soviets invaded from the east and, by October 5, 1939, Poland had been totally overrun and divided in two.

The nightmare of Soviet occupation in eastern Poland was matched by that of the Nazi occupation in the western part. Both sides wished to eliminate Poland forever, and tens of thousands of specifically targeted intellectuals were liquidated on both sides of the dividing line. The Germans uprooted and drove into a new rump administrative district (the *General-Gouvernement*) the Polish population from former Polish territories, which were directly annexed to the expanded German Reich. Meanwhile, the Soviets incorporated portions of eastern Poland into the Soviet Republics of Ukraine, Belarus and, later, Lithuania. The majority of the Polish ethnic inhabitants of these new Soviet territories were deported to Soviet Central Asia and Siberia.[4] Some 2.5 million men, women, and children were exiled, and by the end of World War II in 1945, it is estimated that less than 500,000 remained alive. Of a particularly egregious nature were the murders of approximately 25,700 officers, government officials, and border guards in the spring of 1940 by the Soviet Security Forces (NKVD) after they had been captured in September 1939 and had proven resistant to Sovietization. These multiple mass murders, commonly known as the "Katyn Forest Massacre" (referring to a wooded area near Smolensk in western Russia, where 5,000 bodies were eventually found), also include mass graves in Kharkiv, Ukraine, near Tver, Russia, and at other sites.[5]

The influence of the Katyn Forest tragedy on post-war Polish politics cannot be underestimated. The Polish Communist regime and the Soviets blamed the affair on the Germans, while knowledgeable people both inside Poland and outside the country understood who was really responsible. The Soviets finally admitted responsibility shortly before the collapse of the USSR.

On June 22, 1941, the Nazis invaded the Soviet Union and armored columns drove deeply into the western parts of the USSR, but by 1944, the Germans were in headlong retreat. The USSR was by now an ally of Great Britain and the United States, and the question of what to do about Poland became a major issue. Although the war began over Poland, although the Soviets got their half of that country by reason of an alliance with Hitler, although several hundred thousand Poles were arrayed on both the eastern and western fronts, and although Poland's total contribution to the war, in percentage of capacity to fight, was greater than anyone else's, as was the percentage of loss of both lives and property, the Western Allies were not prepared to defy the Soviet leader, Joseph Stalin, on behalf of Poland.[6] Eventually, in February 1944 at Yalta, the Soviets were authorized to establish a "friendly" government, which ignored the Polish government-in-exile that had been established in London. The Soviets rather freely interpreted the meaning of "anti-Nazi" and "democratic" when they allowed a puppet group of pro-Soviet leftists and Communists to proclaim a provisional government near the city of Lublin on July 22, 1944.[7] Noncommunists were declared to be pro-Nazi and undemocratic! The period of the "People's Republic of Poland" had begun, although this exact title was adopted somewhat later.

This time period, from July 1944 to February 1990 (when the Polish communist party dissolved itself), was an era of forty-five years of Communist experimentation. At the end of World War II, Poland was prostrate and her interwar territories were truncated, with nearly half the country permanently annexed by the Soviet Union and the land added to the Soviet Republics of Lithuania, Belarus, and Ukraine, where it remains today. Poland was partially compensated in the West by the acquisition of land formerly controlled by Germany east of the Oder and Western Niesse (Nysa) Rivers; nevertheless, this piece of territory is less than the land lost to the USSR. Upwards of 25 percent of Poland's prewar population had been lost to changing borders, massacre, concentration camps, deportations, famine, and disease. However, despite the human tragedy, the state emerged in a more coherent form. First, the national question was largely settled: Ukrainians were generally now beyond the eastern frontier, either by deportation, forced dispersal, or the shift of borders; Germans, with rare exceptions, had been driven out, while the formerly large Jewish population had been decimated by the Nazis (with perhaps 3.5 million Jews falling victim of German racial policies), to not more than 5,000 today. Thus, Poland is today ethnically nearly 100 percent Polish. Second, the size and shape of the country was now more or less quadrilateral and compact. Third, industrialization possibilities were increased by accession of the whole of the Upper Silesian coal and steel basin while lower Silesia offered better agricultural land. Fourth, access to the sea was enlarged by receipt of the Pomeranian coast on the Baltic, while Gdansk (Danzig) at the mouth of the Vistula returned definitively to the Polish state and Szczecin (Stettin), at the mouth of the Oder River (in fact, beyond the Oder-Niesse line), came under Polish control.

The forty-five years of the existence of the People's Republic (*Polska Rzeczpospolita Ludowa*, or *PRL*) can be divided into five time periods: the first period, 1944–1947, that of the consolidation of power, when the Communists eliminated opponents with direct Soviet assistance; the second, 1948–1956, the period of Stalinist-type rule; the third, 1956–1970, the era of Wladyslaw Gomulka as Party leader; the fourth, 1970–1980, marked by the new communism of Edward Gierek; and, the fifth, 1980–1990, the period of struggle for power between the Communist forces, led by General Wojciech Jaruzelski, and the democratic forces of Solidarity, headed by Lech Walesa.

In the first period, the Polish [communist] Workers Party ran an internal purge of all who were not perfectly aligned with the leadership's pro-Soviet policy. In 1948, the party forcibly absorbed the Polish Socialist Party to form the Polish United Workers' Party (PZPR).[8] In the meantime, all opposition to the line of the "People's" regime was ruthlessly exterminated, while two groups, which were euphemistically called political parties (the Peasant and Democratic *strona*) were purged of any oppositionists and allowed to exist in order to assist and help the communist party without in any sense being an opposition.

In the next period, 1947–1956, the night of oppressive Stalinist communism darkened the whole country. The most savage repressions occurred during this period, and government and society were wrenched into a local copy of the Soviet model.[9] However, the death of Stalin in March 1953 caused a slackening of pressure, and nationalist elements, even within the PZPR, began to pressure for a more "Polish" system. Finally, in 1956, a "national" Communist, Wladyslaw Gomulka, came to power. At first being perceived as some kind of a democratic nationalist, Gomulka quickly disabused the population of this notion, and he ruled as a convinced Communist, with an iron hand. Nevertheless, there was limited freedom to travel and to have contact with the West and, with a conservative and cautious approach to economic development, there was relative peace and economic stability within the country. Gomulka proved too conservative for the population, however, and he was forced from power in 1970, after workers demonstrated against him and he ordered security forces to fire on them.[10]

Edward Gierek, the new First Secretary of the PZPR, declared that he did not agree with Gomulka's use of force against the workers and called upon the same workers to support him and his plan to double the national productive capacity within a decade by building a "Second Poland." He promised that Poland would reproduce the Japanese economic miracle in Central Europe. The West, enamored by Gierek's openness and flexibility, began to pump billions of dollars into the Polish economy in the form of loans.[11] This all proved useless, however, as most of the funds were squandered through poor planning, corruption, and inefficiency. The situation of the country started getting worse rather than better, and in 1976 and 1980 the workers again demonstrated against Communist control.[12] It is at this latter time that Lech Walesa came into the public spotlight; but first, let us look at the old system and the man who tried to preserve it during its last ten years of existence, Wojciech Jaruzelski.

National Turbulence in the 1980s

The now retired President of Poland, former Prime Minister, former First Secretary of the Polish United Workers Party, former Minister of Defense, former head of the Committee of National Salvation (the martial law council), and General of the Army (Retired) Wojciech Jaruzelski was born in the eastern part of interwar Poland in 1923. His upbringing was "deeply anti-Russian and anti-Soviet," as both his grandfathers had fought the Russians.[13] He was sixteen years old when Nazi Germany attacked Poland, and he and his relatively affluent family fled to Lithuania. "We were convinced that we would return home soon, that an English-French offensive would enable the Polish army to go on fighting against the Germans. It was not to happen."[14]

Instead, in 1940, as the Soviets consolidated power in eastern Poland and took over the Baltic countries, the young Jaruzelski was shipped to Siberia and made to submit to forced labor for three years. It was there that his eyes were damaged, so that to this day, he must wear tinted glasses.[15]

In 1943, Jaruzelski was recruited into the Kosciuszko Division, a Soviet-officered, Polish army unit on the Eastern Front of World War II, with which he fought on the Baltic coastland in Poland until the end of the war.[16] Despite the rather negative introduction to Russia and the USSR, Jaruzelski found an opportunity in the new Polish People's Army and in the training he received in Soviet officer schools. He joined the Polish communist party in 1947.[17] He came to believe the USSR was a "great Ally," and since the world was divided into two camps (the Communist Eastern camp and the Western Democratic one) he threw his lot in with the Soviets who controlled Poland.[18]

Wojciech Jaruzelski first rose to international prominence in 1968, under Wladyslaw Gomulka when, as a professional officer who had served since 1960 as head of the military department of the PZPR's Central Committee, he became Minister of National Defense.[19] In December 1970, when Gomulka ordered security forces to shoot at workers, it was said that he by-passed Jaruzelski in giving the order, thus, now General of the Army Jaruzelski was not tainted with that crime, and under the new Gierek regime he retained his post and even became a deputy member of the PZPR Polit-buro (the Political Bureau—the highest policy-making body of the com-munist party).[20] By 1978, Jaruzelski was a full voting member of the Politburo.

General Jaruzelski came through the collapse of the Gierek regime, too. In fact, while retaining his post as Minister of Defense, he also became Prime Minister on February 9, 1981, in the midst of the Solidarity crisis. Beyond that, he became First Secretary of the PZPR in October 1981.[21]

Using his three offices (Minister of Defense, Prime Minister, and First Secretary) for maximum leverage, on December 13, 1981, he declared Martial Law in order to eliminate the Solidarity movement from the political playing field.[22] Why General Jaruzelski declared Martial Law at that particular mo-ment is a matter of some controversy, but suffice it to say, he justified it as a move to prevent an armed Soviet intervention in Poland to preserve so-cialism, as was done to Czechoslovakia in 1968 in order to crush "socialism with a Human Face" there. Jaruzelski's main argument was the prevention of the bloodshed that most certainly would have occurred had Soviet troops invaded.[23] To be sure, upon his retirement in March 1993, General Jaruzelski expressed his regrets about having ordered Martial Law.[24]

All this being said, what was the general preserving and aiding in the 1980s? Certainly, and minimally, he was trying to keep in power those Poles who found themselves on the wrong side of the East-West divide in Europe, hav-ing, for reasons of conviction, careerism, or some combination thereof (or even in the hope of ameliorating Soviet domination of Poland), joined the pro-Soviet forces. The people who scrambled to the top of this ruling elite formed what is called the *Nomenklatura*. The Nomenklatura consisted (and still consists, in regions where Communist parties remain in control) of those people in important, powerful positions within the state and party apparatus. These are the people who really ruled in Soviet-type systems.[25] They, along with their families, friends, and hangers-on, amounted to some 2 million people of the 35 million population of Poland in the 1980s. These people saw no reason to change things. There was no point since they already had access to whatever they needed, and power to boot. Unfortunately for them, how-ever, the old system was breaking down and new, powerful political forces were emerging.

Features of the Old System

Communism's great claim to moral and philosophical superiority is based on its *weltanschauung*. Marxist-Leninists state that they understand the past (humans have traversed the epochs of primitive communalism, slavery, and feudalism), the present (the existence of Capitalism and its antithesis, Socialism), and the future (the cooperative era of full-scale communism). Their job is to ease the human race out of oppressive, capitalistic individualism and competition into the superior system of cooperative socialism and then on to full equality in communism.

This position is taken as a morally superior one since it is based on a "scientific" understanding of the human situation, which is governed by laws of development fully understood only by communists. Opponents to this stand are by definition ignorant or evil because they either are not intelligent enough to understand the truth or, for evil reasons, they will not accept it. Further, Marxist-Leninists claimed to have discovered the only correct methods (based on the Soviet model), for carrying out the transition from capitalism to socialism and, eventually, communism.[26]

The justification for communist seizures of power throughout the world was that only the communists could comprehend the contemporary world—all noncommunists, by definition, could or would not—and only communists could lead the human race into a happy future. Having justly gained power, the communists proceeded to organize society as they saw fit. The principal activities were the elimination of all opposition and the rapid industrialization of the country. The elimination of enemies is a well-known tactic, which has been employed by all dictatorships from time immemorial and, especially, by modern totalitarian regimes, and generally through more or less the same means. The two specialties of the Soviet model were: (1) the depth of secret police penetration into society, which was on a scale not hitherto seen (perhaps the STASI of the German Democratic Republic obtained the greatest success, with upwards to one in four of the adult population somehow attached to the security apparatus) and (2) the enormous extent of the slave labor camps under Stalinism and the multimillion death rates due to direct killings or individuals being worked to death.

In Poland, the Polish United Workers' Party wore the mantle of communist orthodoxy and used the Security Service (SB) to repress opposition. The proper organization of society and industrialization (the mobilization and modernization theme) could only be handled by the Communists, who had a monopoly on truth and were able to call upon the experience of the great Soviet Union.

Socialism, by definition, is a cooperative, collective system of social and economic development. The Soviet model, as used in Poland and other Communist Party–ruled states, had the following features:

1. it was totalitarian—power was the exclusive property of a single political party which claimed all power as a right and duty;

2. it involved state socialism—the state apparatus was the principal actor (under control of the Communist Party) in all activities;

3. the autonomy of politics, society, and economics was explicitly rejected;

4. the state apparatus encompassed an area many times larger than that of Western governments;

5. the executive, legislative and judicial powers of the state were fused under the single control of the party;

6. the market mechanism was absent in economic activities;

7. liberal democracy was rejected as leading to "tailism" (following the masses), whereas the Communists were to "lead" the masses;

8. the rule of law was replaced by rule of the party;

9. the economic system was totally planned and directed by the state; this was the "Command" economic system;

10. a Communist Party–ruled country claimed to be a state of a higher order because state ownership of the means of production, the command planning system, and the leading role of the Communist Party prevented the conflict that occurs in private-property capitalism.[27]

Most noncommunist analysts of Soviet-type systems say that the state socialist system collapsed precisely because of these features, not because these principles were poorly understood or incorrectly applied.

Time after time (1956, 1970, 1976, 1980–1981, and 1988) in Poland, the error of "putting all one's eggs in the same basket," concentrating power in one institution, which consequently had to take the blame for everything, brought the ire of the populace down on the state party apparatus. After all, the state (along with its party controllers), was responsible for everything— employment, production, the distribution of all commodities, plus the setting of prices of all goods for sale. State socialism was a gigantic bureaucracy responsible for everything and on which everything depended. Since the Party was superior to law and claimed the right and duty of supervising and controlling everything, it was clear where the blame lay for all the system's shortcomings. When it became clear that the Party could not deliver on its promises, and even more clear that party members were being unjustly benefited by their place in the system, the system itself lost all support, even among "honest" Communists:

State Socialism [had] severely impaired its adaptive capacity. By rejecting a market environment, state socialism put the full burden of economic management on the party-state. As a result, any revealed conflict related to dissatisfaction with economic performance [became] a direct challenge to the state and consequently to the political order . . . [State socialism's] capacity for survival has been strongly dependent on the ideological zeal of its supporters and its ability to repress contending views.[28]

Three other factors for the failure of communism in Poland must be mentioned here which may not be fully apparent from this discussion. First, the involuntary imposition of a Soviet-type system on Poland by the twentieth-century version of one of the partitioning powers, that is, Soviet Russia, already made that system suspect, and those citizens who supported that system were seen as traitors to the national cause. Second, members of the PZPR were able to gain access to the limited goods and services produced by the system more easily than the general population. Thus, the estimated 2 million people who directly benefited (the nomenklatura-related individuals who were known as "the owners of People's Poland") were in disrepute, as they had lost moral authority.

Third, there was the failure of communism outside Poland. Lech Walesa and the Solidarity forces came to power precisely at the time when the collapse of Soviet-type state socialism, in general, became apparent. The last two attempts at reform in Poland, that of Edward Gierek in the 1970s, where his group indiscriminately allocated investment funds and granted wage increases but was unable to increase supplies of consumer goods, and that of General Jaruzelski in the 1980s, which attempted reform by an out-and-out military dictatorship, both failed.[29] Beyond that, the entire of the Soviet bloc plus the independent communist states of Yugoslavia and Albania fell apart. Only the Asian communist states of the People's Republic of China, the Democratic People's Republic of Korea (North Korea), Vietnam, Laos, and the isolated Latin American nation of Cuba, remain. Thus, the Polish dissident movement, when it came to power in fall 1989, found itself having the unenviable task of trying to reverse over fifty years of economic ruin and mismanagement (the six years of World War II, 1939–1945, plus forty-five years of communism).

The Legacy of the Old System

What then was on hand was massive heavy industry, which unfortunately had five negative features. First, industry itself, as constructed on the Soviet model, was already obsolete vis-à-vis world standards on the day each component came on-line. Second, Poland's industries in the postwar period were all geared to serve the USSR first, the Soviet bloc second, Poland third, and the world market last of all. Third, industrial production was inefficient, as was transportation and distribution. Fourth, the workers were generally apathetic—they were used to following orders and initiative had been frowned on. (They expected the state to take care of their needs; one did little oneself.) Fifth, the result of the "damn the torpedoes, full-speed ahead" school of economic development of the communists, also known as the (Soviet) "storming" method, left Poland with some of the worst industrial pollution in the world, especially in the southwest corner (Silesia), where winds also bring in pollutants from similar industrial areas in the former German Democratic Republic and the Czech Republic.

POLITICAL PROFILE OF LECH WALESA AND HIS GROUP

A basic tenet of Marxism-Leninism, the philosophical foundation of twentieth-century communism, is that the industrial workers (called the "proletarians") form the core of the working class and are the only ones capable of carrying out revolutionary change. The proletarians create the colossal wealth of capitalist society by producing its goods, from raw materials to finished products, and only they, as the core of the working class, have the capacity to understand the dynamics of capitalism, overthrow the private owners of the means of production (that is, the capitalists), and create a new, classless, communist society. That most of the leaders of communism, including Karl Marx, Frederick Engels, and Vladimir Ilych Ulyanov (Lenin), were not proletarians is passed over in silence. Because of this philosophical idea, the leaders of communist-ruled states always pretended to be proworker and it produced in them a healthy fear of the proletariat. In this way, they continually tried to keep the workers under tight control. This fear proved to be correct in the case of Lech Walesa.

Lech Walesa was born on September 29, 1943, in the village of Popow, in north central Poland, into the family of a small farmer. At that time, the area was under German occupation, and Lech's father, Boleslaw, was taken away in 1944 to work at forced labor. A few weeks after his return in 1945, he died from physical injuries and malnutrition. Walesa's mother later married a younger brother of his father. In total, there were seven children in the family. Respect for elders, a strong Roman Catholic influence, daily morning and evening prayers, and hard work was how he was brought up. After seven years of primary education, the young Lech was directed to study agricultural machinery at a local vocational school. He finished formal study in 1961 and went to work as an electrician on a state-owned farm. After serving for several years in the army, he joined the massive movement of poor Polish peasants from the countryside to urban industry, and in 1967, he landed a job as an electrician in the Gdansk "Lenin" Shipyard. He married and fathered eight children between 1970 and 1985.

December 1970 was a major turning point for Lech Walesa. Until that time, he had been an unremarkable individual who traveled a path followed by many. The March 1968 university student demonstrations against Wladyslaw Gomulka had passed over him without a trace, as he felt this was a problem for the intellectuals.[30] However, on December 12, 1970, the Communist regime decreed steep increases in the prices of basic foodstuffs. The suddenness of this action in the immediate pre-Christmas season shocked Polish workers, and many went into the streets in spontaneous protest. A week of violent demonstrations in the three main Baltic seaport cities of Poland (Gdansk, Gdynia, and Szczecin) resulted in several hundred deaths when the armed forces fired on the workers.[31] Walesa was drawn into the protest movement on December 15 when he accompanied a group of workers to a discussion with the shipyard managers. In subsequent public marches and attacks on the *Militsia* (police), Walesa attempted to play a moderating role, but without success. He was elected to the shipyard strike committee and, after four workers were shot dead by the police, he was arrested. He was released when Gomulka fell from power on the following Sunday and Edward Gierek took over. In the hope that Gierek would improve the situation, Walesa supported him, but in April 1976, after it had become clear that Gierek's communism yielded results no better than anyone else's, Walesa became active again and was subsequently fired from his job.

In June 1976, two manufacturing areas went out on strike, the huge Ursus tractor plant west of Warsaw and several factories in the city of Radom, south of Warsaw. The government struck back using security forces and the loss of jobs as weapons. At this point, a second major turning point in Walesa's career took place.

In 1956, proletarians had rioted in Poznan due to poor living conditions, but they were shot down. Intellectuals and students held back. However, Stalinist party officials were forced from power in favor of Gomulka. In 1968, the real oppressive nature of Gomulka's national communism had become apparent to all, and the heavy hand of the party on national culture caused an outburst of university student frustration in March of that year; however, this time, the workers held back.[32] In 1970, the workers demonstrated and died while the students and intellectuals again failed to take part. The year 1976, however, resulted in something new. The regime's policy of oppressing dissident workers caused the formation of a number of support groups to help the now jobless, and perhaps homeless, hungry workers. The principal group of this kind was Komitet Obrony Robotnikow or Committee for Defense of Workers (KOR). This group and others like it—such as movement for Defense of Human Rights, Students for a Democratic Society, and the Peasants' Self-Defense Association—plus large-scale underground press activity led to a coalition of workers, students, and intellectuals that the Gierek regime was unable to, or felt it was not prudent to, repress.[33] These groups formed Walesa's main support foundation in the Solidarity years.

Lech Walesa went through several years of being unable to find steady work, living in an apartment with two small rooms and suffering harassment and arrests. However, he slowly became recognized as a leader of the growing dissident movement. In 1980, beginning in February, strikes started breaking out all over the country, and by August, the Gdansk "Lenin" Shipyard stopped working. Walesa again joined in organizing the strike. Other factories soon joined in the protest in solidarity with fellow workers, and on August 31, 1980, the regime signed an agreement of understanding with the workers. For the next sixteen months, Walesa stood at the head of an ever-growing "Independent Self-Governing Labor Union 'Solidarity' (*NSZZ Solidarnosc*). The regime was in turmoil, but the Soviet Union, under Leonid Brezhnev, attempted to put some backbone into the ruling Communist Party by threatening a Warsaw Pact invasion, as had happened to Czechoslovakia, in similar circumstances, in 1968. During these months, members of KOR and other groups worked closely with Walesa to keep the Communists from getting control of Solidarity. Walesa received worldwide recognition as the first leader of an independent proletarian trade union to rise in a Communist state. This was an earthshaking occurrence for the Soviet bloc, and it had to be ended. In the meantime, several successors to Edward Gierek proved unsuccessful in containing Solidarity, so General Jaruzelski proclaimed Martial Law on December 13, 1981.[34] Lech Walesa, members of KOR and other support groups, and leaders of Solidarity numbering several thousands were interned in military-controlled camps.[35] A WRON (Military Council for Nation Salvation) was formed to rule the country. For the next several years, Jaruzelski pursued a policy of "normalization" while ignoring Solidarity. In 1983, Walesa received the Nobel Peace Prize for his nonviolent methods of protest.

Two things occurred that allowed a return of Lech Walesa and the Solidarity movement. The first was a change in Soviet leadership with the death of Leonid Brezhnev and the subsequent short terms in office as General Secretary of the Central Committee of the Communist Party of the Soviet Union of Yuri Andropov and Konstantin Chernenko (both died quickly), which culminated in Mikhail Gorbachev coming to power in March 1985. Gorbachev's policies of *perestroika* (restructuring), *glasnost* (openness), and *Novoye Myshlenie* (New Thinking) cut the ground out from under the Polish military regime. Second, Poland proved ungovernable without at least some consent of the people. Thus, in early 1989, Round Table talks began between Solidarity and the regime. By late Spring, it was decided to reinstitute a two-house legislature (the Senate, the upper-house of the legislature, had been eliminated in 1947 as part of Communist "reforms") and renew the office of President of the Republic (an office also reformed away, in 1952). In the elections that followed, members of the lower house, the Sejm (a body resembling the U.S. House of Representatives), were elected according to a prearranged plan whereby a certain percentage of seats in the legislature were set aside for each group running. The newly reconstituted Senate was open to free election. A Solidarity coalition won ninety-nine out of the one hundred Senate seats, while in the Sejm, the PZPR was outmaneuvered when two former puppet groups, the Democratic and Peasant Parties (*strona*) cut their strings with the Communists and joined with Solidarity to form a parliamentary majority. Suddenly, there was the possibility of the first noncommunist government in the Soviet bloc. Not being sure of the reaction of the USSR, the slogan, "Our premier, your president" was followed, and the noncommunist Tadeusz Mazowiecki became Prime Minister. Later, the Communist Wojciech Jaruzelski became President, by a margin of one in a vote of both houses of the newly elected legislature (at that time, the houses of the Polish legislature together decided who would be president rather than selecting him or her by vote of the general population, as in the United States.)[36]

A change made in the Polish national constitution in 1990, however, allowed for direct popular election of the President of the Republic, and early elections were called. On November 25, 1990, Walesa received 40 percent of the popular vote in a field of six candidates, and in the second round (December 9), in a runoff between the two highest vote getters, he won a majority. On December 22, 1990, he was sworn in as the first democratically and popularly elected president in Polish history.[37]

THE NEW PROGRAM—THE GRAND DREAM AND BITTER REALITY

The program of the Solidarity movement and its allies was mainly negative, involving opposition to Communist control. The plan was to end censorship in the media and arts, do away with the PZPR monopoly in the economy, force the PZPR to yield some political power, prevent further church-state clashes (to end pressure on the Roman Catholic Church), eliminate Soviet domestic and foreign policy influences as far as possible, and in general, let people have more say in their own lives. This program, which allowed for a Communist facade to appease the Soviet Union while creating internal and domestic freedom, was more successful than Solidarity members ever dreamed, for today censorship is gone, the party has disappeared, and the Soviet Union has self-destructed.

It is sometimes said, "Be careful lest your wishes [or dreams or prayers] come true," and in this regard, Solidarity found itself in an awkward situation—in power. Solidarity was always a single-goal coalition of diverse elements, from extreme nationalists on one side to noncommunist leftists on the other, and from fervent religious believers to noncommunist atheists. Once the enemy, the Communist regime, was gone, the coalition fell apart.

All sides recognized that Poland must make extremely rapid strides in order to catch up with the West. These strides included a rapid democratization of society, marketization of the economy, pluralization of the political system, and quick moves toward joining the European and the world economic systems—in short, rapid movement into the community of the liberal-democratic market economies of the technologically advanced states that constitute the Western world.

In the area of democratization, the new government quickly eliminated the censorship department of government, which formerly controlled all media, arts, and public performances. The monopoly on distribution of printed matter represented by the *Ruch* corporation was also done away with. The ownership of newspapers and periodicals was turned over to private hands, while the postal interception of foreign printed matter was ended. In a major departure from former Communist practice, all citizens not under court orders to the contrary are now free to apply for and receive passports and, consequently, to travel wherever they wish. Extraordinary reviews of past repressive court sentences have, *ex post facto,* righted many of the wrongs of the previous regime (unfortunately, in many cases, posthumously) and measures formerly applied for limiting religious activities were repealed. The former secret police system has been revamped into a small unit for protection of the state, while the regular police are called just that, *police,* instead of *Militia,* which was a social control department that also had political crimes as part of its purview. In general, today Polish citizens now have all the rights of West Europeans, and with their passports they can travel anywhere in Western Europe without visas. This democratization is clearly the greatest achievement of the Polish Republic, which now no longer carries the name "People's."

In the area of political pluralism, however, the results are much worse. When the PZPR dissolved itself, there was some fear that it would be replaced by a new Solidarity-church coalition. In retrospect, that fear is laughable because anarchy appears to be the actual result. Currently, there are twenty-nine political parties represented in the national legislature, from the Confederation for Polish Independence (KPN) on the right to the Social Democrats (a spin-off of the PZPR) on the left; there is even a "Party of the Friends of Beer." There have been four governments since Mazowiecki's first, noncommunist regime in August 1989. There is a general disability to formulate legislative programs or pass credible budgets. Beyond that, a new noncommunist constitution is a major bone of contention, with only an abbreviated (*Maly*) constitution having been passed as of this writing (fall 1994).

As a possible remedy for this near-anarchy, there have been suggestions of attempting a French Gaullist solution by strengthening the office of the president. However, a power struggle between the president and legislature has prevented this from happening. Further, there are those who view Walesa as untrustworthy and a false democrat.[38]

A market economy was instituted in Poland as of January 1, 1990, when the "shock therapy" of Economic Minister Leszek Balcerowicz was put into effect. In the fall of 1989, hyperinflation wiped out nearly all the savings of the Polish population; only those who were clever enough to get their hands on foreign/hard currency or buy fixed property (factories, land, and housing) were saved. At the beginning of 1990, with World Bank backing, Poland went over to convertible currency in one jump. It became possible to suddenly convert any amount of the local Polish currency (the zloty) into any hard money at a rate that floated, initially, around 10,000 zloties to 1 U.S. dollar. Immediately after that, the market in general was freed up; anyone could buy and sell freely. Foreign investment is now encouraged, although investors are hesitant due to constantly changing rules, and state enterprises are available for purchase. The private import and export of goods, which was formerly a state monopoly, also became possible.[39]

The results of the shock therapy have been somewhat mixed, to say the least. A multiyear slide in production and per capita income, which had already started in the 1970s, continues or, perhaps, has bottomed out. It is thought that the Poles will not reach the levels of income of some of the poorer European states, such as Portugal or Greece, until well into the twenty-first century. Inflation continues, with over 20,000 zloties to 1 U.S. dollar the current rate. Unemployment is still high, and production has not recovered to some 1970s levels. The state sector of the economy is still large, with no takers for the large, inefficient industrial units of the Communist era. The government's budget is constantly in deficit, and the small, inefficient farmers are feeling the pressure of foreign competition, which could put them out of business.[40]

"Taking the Road to Europe" (and the world) is a common theme in Poland today. It refers to opening the country to West Europe and joining, not only the European economic community and NATO, but also the world trading system as a full partner.

Under communism, the country was tied to the USSR and the other communist states. Trade was based on annual, bilateral trade agreements and nearly anything of worth could be bartered or sold to other communist states. Communism has never been known to produce high-quality goods at the world standard, with the exception of some military hardware. Now, Poland is attempting to trade with the major players—North America, Japan, and the European Union. In order to do so, Poland has had to submit to World Bank and International Monetary Fund directives—much to the dislike of nationalists. Along these lines, Poland has negotiated an "Associate State" agreement with the European Free Trade Association (EFTA). EFTA itself has signed an agreement with the European Union (EU), also known as the "the Fifteen" West European states, to form a European Economic Area free trade zone. Poland has hopes of joining the EU sometime after the turn of the century and, if possible, the European-North American military alliance, NATO, as well.[41]

MOBILIZING FOR POWER

In contradistinction to the leaders of noncommunist countries discussed in this volume, Lech Walesa did not, and does not, have either a specific continuous political backing or even a positive political program (we discuss the political program in the next section).

In 1980, the initial aim, which was thought to be immediately achievable, was pressuring the Communists to give up some political power. At a closed meeting addressed by a Solidarity activist in fall 1981, the speaker stated that the communist party would be allowed to maintain limited control of Poland's international affairs because of the Soviet threat. The USSR had emplaced in its western-most territories, that is, directly adjacent to Poland's eastern frontier, a huge armed force and beyond that, to the west of Poland in the German Democratic Republic, there were twenty Soviet occupation divisions being held at the first level of preparedness. Moreover, 50,000 Soviet personnel were based in Poland itself, where they manned supply lines and several air and naval bases. The 1956 failure of the West to come to the aid of anti-Communist rebels in Hungary showed that it was unprepared to support Poland when and if push came to shove. Thus, the speaker indicated that the Communist Party in Poland still had a role to play—that of a shield and buffer between the Polish people and the Soviets—and, therefore, Solidarity actually wanted, and insisted on, the maintenance of the PZPR. Within the country, however, Solidarity, *de facto,* would take control, though indirectly. Officially, the movement would declare itself a nonpolitical trade union, but in fact, it would handle the domestic affairs of the country.

Solidarity was always a disparate coalition of anti-Communist forces, and its main aim was pressuring the Communists to give up some power. Other than this *anti*thrust, it had no positive program at all.

Even after its period of suspension and dissolution (December 1981–spring 1989), the "program" of Solidarity remained the same. Everyone was surprised when the party-state regime gave up significant power in the round-table talks of spring 1989, the election of June 1989 resulted in a noncommunist premier, the Soviets did not react, when the PZPR dissolved itself in February 1980, and the Soviet Union finally collapsed in December 1991. It took everyone's breath away; no one conceived of taking full political power as could be thought of, and as was done, by leaders in Great Britain, Germany, and India. Here was a totally unplanned and unforeseen outcome. Once the dust had settled, the fragility of "Solidarity" was manifested. The various political forces that had combined together in the *anti*program allowed, and even forced, Lech Walesa to be the spear-point. The movement fell into political infighting, and Solidarity ceased to function as a unified force. While Solidarity had its single enemy, its members could focus their hatred on that enemy. Now, however, the real struggle for power began.

Unfortunately, when Lech Walesa turned to see who was backing him after the Communists had left the political arena, he found few people behind him. Walesa always hoped to be above partisan politics and he never tried either to affiliate with any of the specific political parties that came into existence nor to form one. The closest he has come to that is the formation of a "Non-Party Bloc for the Support of Reform" (*Bezpartny Blok Wspierania Reform,* or *BBWR*), a type of political grouping. This formation failed miserably in the elections of September 1993. Oddly enough, this action has been given an honorable place in Polish history, for the "George Washington" of the resurrected interwar Poland, Jozef Pilsudski, did the same thing with his Non-Party Bloc for Cooperation with the Government (*Bezpartny*

Blok Wspolpracy z Rzadem, also abbreviated *BBWR*). However, this does not necessarily reflect well on Walesa because while in power, Pilsudski, despite being a revolutionary hero, was also a paternalistic authoritarian (he died in 1935).[42]

Consequently, while Walesa may have mobilized the masses to gain power, it was a real surprise when power was, in fact, gained in the absence of a positive program.

IMPLEMENTING THE NEW PROGRAM—THE POLITICAL DIMENSION

There was little of an explicit program in Poland in the 1980s, other than getting the corrupted and bankrupt Communists to give up power (and even then, not all of it). When communism disappeared as a force in Central and Eastern Europe, members of the defunct parties, if they wanted to continue political activity, went to join other parties or formed new ones of their own. Those few former (so-called "repainted") Communists who wished to maintain a socialistic and left-wing orientation formed several socialist, leftist, and democratic parties. No political party of any kind publicly came forward with a nondemocratic program. Thus, the immediate "political program," which came on almost by itself, was accepted by all; only the speed and extent of change came under contention.

The following events occurred within two years of the collapse of communism:

1. Censorship of media and performance was eliminated.
2. The *militsia* was transformed into a normal, nonpolitical police force.
3. Communist party property, which was often illegally acquired even according to the rules of "People's" Poland, was taken over or sold. The national communist party headquarters in Warsaw, for example, was turned into a commercial office building.
4. The officer corps of the armed forces was purged, mainly by retirements, and nonpolitical officers were advanced to command positions.
5. The security forces were eliminated and only a small state protection agency was retained.
6. Archives and files of the party were taken over by the State Archive system, and some of these and other closed records were opened to researchers.
7. State property began to be sold off as the state withdrew from direct economic activities.
8. Political appointees without actual skills were removed from state enterprises that were still in public hands.
9. The state monopoly on printing and distribution was eliminated.

10. Borders were opened and now Polish citizens could freely travel without difficulty and Westerners could enter without visas.

11. The domestic currency, the zloty, became a freely convertible one, exchangeable without state interference with any other currency.

12. The state monopoly on foreign trade was ended.

13. Prices were allowed to rise to their world market levels.

14. State food subsidies were, in general, removed.

15. All state subsidies are in the process of being phased out wherever feasible.

16. Competition both domestic and foreign is now allowed in all areas.

17. The state monopoly on education has been eliminated.

18. Pressures on religious institutions have been done away with.

19. Confiscated property is being returned to the original owners or their heirs.

20. In general, Poland has turned toward becoming like any other democratic state of Europe.

Poland is simply reverting to democracy and the market system, from which it was separated for fifty years. All political parties agree to this general approach, so no single one can claim it as its program.

NATURE AND SCOPE OF CHANGE

That political parties agree in general to the nature and scope of political and economic change in Poland does not mean that they agree on specifics. For example, the shock of the January 1, 1990, caused by the change of the zloty to a convertible currency was not at that time appreciated by everyone as correct. Who was able to, and did, purchase state property is of great controversy. The issue of what to do with the former security apparatus records, especially those dealing with the people who cooperated with these agencies, caused the failure of one of the postcommunist governments and may cause other difficulties in the future.

With these types of specifics constantly in mind, we may nevertheless state that Poland has undergone wrenching change since spring 1989. The whole political system has turned topsy-turvy. The monopoly party is gone, and nearly thirty new ones have emerged. The currency has gone from controlled to free. Formerly condemned private enterprise is now openly encouraged. The rules of how to get things done (by whom and by what means) are all new. Poland is open to the world with travel and export and import now free. Incomes are now based, to some extent, on ability, where who you know and membership in the party were formerly decisive. Incomes have taken the greatest hit, with state employee salaries rapidly losing their purchasing power, while private entrepreneurs are doing well.

The fact of the matter is that only some of the middle-aged people and perhaps all the young but few of the older citizens have adapted to the change. Obviously, there is some nostalgia for the former order of things, as found in the results of the September 1993 parliamentary elections, in which two parties run by repainted Communists—the Polish Peasants Party and the Democratic Left Alliance—won a large percentage of the vote and, in coalition with several other groups, were able to form a government.[43] This new government has slowed the pace of change and will maintain or restore some of what the Communists had yielded in exchange for political support, including a stronger social safety net and a continuation of state ownership and intervention in the economic arena.

Thus, at the time of this writing, Poland is in a state of flux, but it is certain there will be no turning back to the former single-party situation.

INTERPRETING LECH WALESA AS LEADER

Lech Walesa, as the leader of the now defunct Solidarity movement and the present President of the Republic of Poland, faces many critical challenges. Zbigniew Brzezinski (National Security Advisor to President Jimmy Carter, as well as a scholar and former faculty member at Columbia University), who is currently at the Center for Strategic and International Studies in Washington, D.C., has outlined the problems that Walesa faces:

1. creation of a new democratic constitution;
2. changing the electoral law from the current proportional representation method, which encourages factionalism, to a single member per district representation;
3. preparing and carrying through a thorough and just review of all the crimes and criminals of the Communist regime;
4. preventing the uncontrolled use of Communist secret police documents for political ends;
5. increasing the tempo of economic change, and thus converting the country into a fully free-market economy;
6. putting to good use the funds made available by foreign agencies in order to develop Poland.

Brzezinski further states:

[Because of] the propensity of Poles to form factions and to engage in arguments ... I support a constitution for Poland which provides for a presidential system having a certain similarity to the French one of 1958. ... In short Poland requires great changes similar to those of France in 1958. The genius of de Gaulle depended on the creation of a modern political system which made an allowance for the creative abilities of the French. ... If this is done then Poland could stand as an honorable member of the European Community and a very attractive country for foreign investment. ... Today Poland is, geopolitically speaking, in the best situation it ever has been in the last 300 years. If this is so, it is necessary for Poles to take advantage of this historic moment to build a strong, modern and democratic state.[44]

Lech Walesa, the former members of his fractured coalition, and the Polish people stand at a historic crossroad. Walesa was successful in mobilizing, not only masses of the common people, but also intellectuals in the struggle to overthrow communism. However, perhaps having been blinded by political ambition, he appears to have reached too far. He is the president of the Polish Republic, but since he now has no specific political base—Solidarity is in tatters—and no particular program, it seems he no longer can be the caliber of leader he once was in Poland. Unfortunately, however, no single person or political party has risen to take his place, and Poland, thus, remains in crisis.

NOTES

1. See Piotr Wandycz, *The Price of Freedom: A History of East Central Europe* (London and New York: Routledge, 1992).

2. See relevant sections of *Maly Slownik Historii Polski* [Small dictionary of Polish history] (Warsaw, latest edition).

3. Norman Davies, *God's Playground: A History of Poland: Vol. 2, 1795 to the Present* (New York: Columbia University Press, 1982), p. 393.

4. M. K. Dziewanowski, *Poland in the Twentieth Century* (New York: Columbia University Press, 1977), pp. 112–117.

5. J. K. Zawodny, *Death in the Forest: The Story of the Katyn Forest Massacre* (Notre Dame, IN: University of Notre Dame Press, 1962; reprint, 1972). See also Paul J. Best, "Caliber 7.65" (unpublished 8-page report, 1990).

6. Dziewanowski, pp. 142–144.

7. Ibid., pp. 126–129.

8. Jan B. de Weydenthal, *The Communists of Poland: An Outline History* (Stanford, CA: Hoover Institution Press, 1978), pp. 50–56.

9. See Marian Rybicki, ed., *Sejm Ustawodawczy Rzeczypospolitej Polskiej: 1947–1952* [The constitutional legislature of the Polish republic] (Warsaw: Polish Academy of Sciences, 1977). Rybicki, without apparently wishing to do so, reveals just how democracy was crushed in the Polish legislature. See also the film, *Przesluchanie* [The Interrogation] (directed by Ryszard Bugajski, starring Krystyna Janda, a 1990 Cannes Film Festival winner), for a graphic portrayal of this period.

10. See Nicholas Bethell, *Gomulka: His Poland, His Communism* (Middlesex, U.K.: Pelican Books, 1972).

11. M. K. Dziewanowski, *The Communist Party of Poland*, 2nd ed. (Cambridge, MA: Harvard University Press, 1976), pp. 323–331.

12. Maurice Simon and Roger Kanet, eds., *Background to Crisis: Policy and Politics in Gierek's Poland* (Boulder, CO: Westview Press, 1981), pp. 405–414.

13. John Darnton, "Jaruzelski Is Now Sorry He Ordered Martial Law," *New York Times*, March 4, 1993, p. 12.

14. John Borrell, "Poland: The Man Who Did His Duty," *Time*, October 1, 1990, p. 63.

15. Ibid.; Darnton.

16. Stephanie Kraft, "Poland's Mystery Man," *New Haven Advocate*, November 12, 1990, p. 14.

17. de Weydenthal, p. 180.

18. Darnton.

19. de Weydenthal, p. 135.

20. Ibid., p. 145.

21. Nicholas G. Andrews, *Poland 1980–1981: Solidarity versus the Party* (Washington, DC: National Defense University Press, 1985), p. 279.

22. Ibid., pp. 285–293.

23. See Wojciech Jaruzelski's *Stan Wojenny, dlaczego?* [Martial law, why?] (Warsaw: Polska Oficyna Wydawnicza "BGW," 1992), his official apologia for the martial law period.

24. David Unger, "Editorial Notebook: General Jaruzelski Regrets," *New York Times*, March 5, 1993, editorial page.

25. See Michael Voslensky, *Nomenklatura: Anatomy of the Soviet Ruling Class* (London: The Bodley Head Publishing Co., 1984), for details about how this system works.

26. John Clark and Aaron Wildavsky, *The Moral Collapse of Communism: Poland as a Cautionary Tale* (San Francisco, CA: Institute for Contemporary Studies Press, 1990), chapter 1.

27. Bartlomiej Kaminski, *The Collapse of State Socialism: The Case of Poland* (Princeton, NJ: Princeton University Press, 1991), pp. 3–21.

28. Ibid., pp. 24–25.

29. Ibid., p. 35.

30. Andrzej Ajnenkiel et al., *Prezydenci Polski* [Presidents of Poland] (Warsaw: Sejm Publishing House, 1991), pp. 188–202.

31. Bethell, p. 277.

32. Paul J. Best, "Poland—1968: Domestic Politics and Intra-Party Struggle," *Connecticut Review* 6(2) (1973): 87–98.

33. Andrews, p. 21.

34. See Jaruzelski.

35. Wojciech Jaruzelski, "Jaruzelski Declares Martial Law—December 15, 1981," in Gale Stokes, ed., *From Stalinism to Pluralism: A Documentary History of East Europe since 1945* (New York: Oxford University Press, 1991), pp. 214–215.

36. Tadeusz Mazowiecki, "A Solidarity Government Takes Power—August 24, 1989," in Stokes, pp. 240–242.

37. Ajnenkiel et al., pp. 201–203.

38. See Jacek Kurski and Piotr Semka, *Lewy Czerwcowy* [The Crooks of June] (Warsaw: Editions Spokania, n.d. [1992]), in which the authors accuse Walesa of being mixed up with members of the previous regime, and Jaroslaw Kurski, *Lech Walesa: Democrat or Dictator* (Boulder, CO: Westview Press, 1993), which deals with just what the title says.

39. The World Bank, *Poland: Economic Management for a New Era: A World Bank Country Study* (Washington, DC: The World Bank, 1990), p. 117.

40. For an optimistic view of the Polish economy, see "Conversion," *World Peace*

Report, 8 (9) (June 1992): p. 2-3. For a pessimistic view, see "Review of Periodical Literature—Aftershocks," *Polish Studies Newsletter,* June 1992, p. 2.

41. "The European Community: Altered States," *Economist,* July 11, 1992, p. 27.

42. Adam Michnik, "Czy Lech Walesa jest Jozefem Pilsudskim" [Is Lech Walesa a Jozef Pilsudski?] *Nowy dziennik* [New Daily] (New York), June 19–20, 1993, p. 3.

43. Jane Perlez. "New Polish Leaders try to Ease West's Fears," *New York Times,* September 26, 1993, p. 11.

44. Zbigniew Brzezinski, "Swieto i dzien Powszedni" [A holiday and a normal day], *Przeglad Polski* [New York—*Nowy dziennik*], July 2, 1992, pp. 3–4.

Mikhail Gorbachev, Boris Yeltsin, and the Democratization of Russia

THE POLITICAL-ECONOMIC CONTEXT FOR CHANGE IN RUSSIA

Let us suppose that in November of the year 2017, on the hundredth anniversary of the Great Bolshevik Revolution, the neocommunist government of the restored Russian People's Republic decided to arrest Mikhail Gorbachev and Boris Yeltsin and put them on trial for causing the collapse of the World's first Marxist-Leninist state, the Soviet Union. Aleksandr Stakhanov, marshal of the Russian People's armed forces and the present leader of the country, had discovered the reason for this collapse in his rereading of Marx and Lenin: the people's enemies would undermine a communist state by using either unwitting fools or conscious evil-doers. The proponents of the new political philosophy of Marxism-Leninism-Stakhanovism now seek to prove that Gorbachev and Yeltsin were conscious tools of rival Eurasian powers and that, although seeming to be in opposition to each other, they had acted in concert to overthrow the first workers' state in Eurasia.

Although the two men were quite old (each aged eighty-six), and although each was ill but recovering, Gorbachev from a stroke (they found him in a rehabilitation hospital for the aged in his home area of Stavropol near the Caucasus Mountains in Southern Russia), and Yeltsin from alcoholism (he was in a hospital in the Ekaterinburg region of the Ural Mountains), nevertheless, they were hauled to Moscow for a trial on three-dimensional television, to be broadcast live on the republic's satellite hookups.

Despite its otherwise repressive nature, Premier Stakhanov had not applied the full rigors of censorship in the restored state. In any case, Stakhanov thought he did not need to censor the broadcast because these doddering old idiots would surely make fools of themselves and prove his contention that the collapse of the first people's state was caused by the conscious efforts of its enemies. Thus, all the fifteen years of blood and sweat needed to restore the state, including the loss of Perm and Irkutsk to tactical nuclear weapons, was not the fault of the neocommunist party or its predecessor, the Communist Party of the Soviet Union, but of Russia's Eurasian enemies, who had plotted Russia's downfall.

Gorbachev and Yeltsin, despite their known previous enmity, decide to work together, not only to preserve their present miserable existence but also to defend their past actions. Just how could the pair justify what had happened to the second global superpower at the end of the twentieth century? What had caused a totalitarian regime to turn toward liberal democracy? How could they explain to the country's citizens what had gone wrong?

Both Boris Yeltsin and Mikhail Gorbachev were born in the same year, both were raised and educated during the Stalinist regime in the Soviet Union, both were old enough to understand and feel the rigors of World War II, and both were proud of the Soviet Union's power and prestige and the fact that it shouldered itself into the first rank of power in the postwar era. The Soviet Union held one of the five permanent seats in the United Nations Security Council, and it wielded one of the five vetoes available to the permanent members. The Soviet Union had to be taken into account in global politics anywhere on the planet, as it was one of only two states capable of projecting its power worldwide. Its high statistical achievements in industry indicated that its "command economy" was one of the two general possibilities for development of any country (the other being the free-market system of the West). One could not be certain, however, until the end of the 1980s and the beginning of the 1990s, that the twenty-first century would not be the century of totalitarianism, highly centralized government, command economy, and the dominance of the Communist Party. The outcome of the great Cold War, which began definitively in 1945, had by no means been certain.

In fact, both Yeltsin and Gorbachev were products of the Communist Party of the Soviet Union. Mikhail Gorbachev became leader (general secretary) of the party in 1985 and had called Boris Yeltsin to Moscow to assist him in the great task of furthering the Soviet state and global communism. Gorbachev had believed in his mission almost to the very end, but Yeltsin had gone his own way a few years earlier.

Mikhail Sergeyevich Gorbachev was born on March 2, 1931, in the village of Privolnoe in the Red Guard (Krasnogvardeiskii) district of Stavropol province (in the southern part of European Russia, just north of the Caucasian mountains). The area was mainly agricultural and his family was of peasant background, his father, Sergei, being a collective farm tractor driver and his mother, Maria Panteleyevna, a farm worker. His village was occupied by the Germans in World War II for six months (August 1942–January 1943).[1] He was witness, as a youth, to the dislocations of the collectivization of agriculture, but his region was spared the mass deaths (due to starvation) that occurred in other areas of USSR.[2] He also could not fail to know of the deportation of his non-Russian neighbors (Karachai, Kalmyks, Meskhetians, Chechens, Ingush, Kabardins, Balkars, and Tatars) from his and neighboring areas after they were accused of collaborating with the Germans.[3]

At the age of eighteen, he was awarded the Order of the Red Banner of Labor for working as a machine tractor station driver during part of the growing season, and when he finished his secondary education in local schools in 1950, he received a silver medal. Gorbachev then managed to gain admission to the most prestigious higher educational institution of the Soviet Union, Moscow State University, and its law faculty.[4] He completed the five-year program in 1955 and later took a correspondence degree in agronomy (1967) at the Stavropol Agricultural Institute. He also met and married his wife, Raisa Maksimovna Titorenko (born 1932), in Moscow, where she was studying sociology. (Later, she completed a Candidate of Sciences degree with a dissertation about life on collective farms in the Stavropol region.)

Gorbachev's career was spent in work within the party apparatus. Having had a father who was a party member, he joined the Young Pioneers, which later became the Communist Youth League (*Komsomol*), and at a relatively early age, he became a full member of the Communist Party of the Soviet Union and an activist in university youth affairs. He returned to Stavropol for the next twenty-two years (1955–1978), where he rose through the regional party apparatus, initially taking charge of the local Komsomol and later, from March 1962, working in the regional party administrative structure, where he rose to first secretary of the Stavropol Province (*Krai*), the functional equivalent of the chief executive of a U.S. state or Canadian province.[5] In March 1971, at the Twenty-fourth Party Congress, Mikhail Gorbachev became one of the approximately 600 members of the Central Committee of the Communist Party of the Soviet Union, the titular highest party standing committee (in fact, power lay in the fifteen-member Political Bureau, or Politburo).[6] In the meantime, Gorbachev had attended the twenty-second CPSU congress in October 1961 and had already been noticed by party leaders Fedor Kulakov (responsible for agriculture) and Mikhail Suslov (responsible for ideology). Both these men had roots in the Stavropol area, and they became his patrons. Kulakov died in 1978, and Gorbachev, at the age of forty-seven (young for Soviet leaders at that time), took over Kulakov's position and moved to Moscow as a "secretary" of the Central Committee. In order to make Gorbachev's position clear as of 1978, and to indicate how he was positioned in the Soviet power structure, we must make a short diversion to explain how the Soviet Union actually functioned as opposed to how the Soviets said it worked.

Merle Fainsod, the father of post–World War II U.S. Sovietology, explained in 1953, and again in 1967 (in the second edition of his famed book, *How Russia Is Ruled*), in his chapter "Constitutional Myths and Political Realities" that the formal structure of the USSR was a myth, as real power was found in the party alone. Formally, the USSR was a constitutional federation of its republics. Political subdivisions below the republic and the republics themselves were governed by elected assemblies called "Soviets" (councils), while the national "Supreme Soviet" was a bicameral, parliamentary-type legislature; that is, that the legislature was supreme and the other two branches of government, executive and judicial, were subordinate to it. The facts of the matter were quite different. The "elected" members of any level of Soviet came from lists having one candidate per post. Seventy-five percent of these candidates were, in general, Communist Party members, and thus subject to party discipline, while 25 percent were trusted nonparty members. Voting at all levels was unanimous in the Soviets to show the unshakable unity of party and people. *De facto,* the Soviets were rubber stamps to make legal, in terms of written law, the party's policy. The supervision of the Soviets and the government bureaucracy was handled by full-time party workers who were in the (parallel to the government) party apparatus.[7] Moreover, the term *Central Committee* actually had two meanings in the USSR. It meant the large committee of 600 or so party leaders that met twice a year for discussion (Gorbachev being a member since 1970) and the party's (parallel to the government) central bureaucratic apparatus, which was housed in buildings in downtown Moscow. Thus, when Gorbachev moved to Moscow and became a Central Committee "secretary" in charge of Agriculture, he became, de facto, the policy maker and supervisor of Soviet agriculture, even though there was a minister and Ministry of Agriculture in the *de jure* government. This ministry's task was to carry out party agricultural policy, not to make it.

We should also note that by now, Gorbachev had really "arrived" in Soviet society. He was now fully a member of the Nomenklatura, the elite of the Soviet regime. This term, derived from the Latin *nomenclatura,* means "a list of designated positions, in a state ruled by a Communist Party, over which the Party has exclusive control." In other words, all positions of power, wherever located within the Soviet political, economic, and social system, were controlled by the party, and the party's central apparatus had the right to put trusted party members in those positions. Thus, the party reserved all power and privilege for itself, to the exclusion of all others. This was the "New Class" referred to by Milovan Djilas.[8] Thus, Gorbachev's rise to "Candidate" (nonvoting) membership in the Politburo, in November 1979, and a full voting member, in October 1980, was rather a foregone conclusion. He had the training, the experience, and the connections to get to the top, and the fact that he was 100 percent Russian was important, too. He was the youngest Politburo member at that time, and he only needed to wait. Leonid

Brezhnev, general secretary of the party since 1965, had long been in failing health, and he passed away on November 10, 1982. Another of Gorbachev's patrons, Yuri Andropov, took power but held it for less than sixteen months, himself dying on February 9, 1983. There was a short interregnum when the aged Konstantin Chernenko, who in fact was older than the deceased Brezhnev, took over, only to die as well, in March 1985.

The older generation had died off, and Mikhail Gorbachev, the well-situated youngster of fifty-four who was the product of the party itself, became the general secretary on March 12, 1985, at a plenary meeting of the Central Committee. Thus, Gorbachev was part and parcel of the political and economic system that he proposed to reform.

Boris Nikolayevich Yeltsin was also born in 1931, on February 4, in the village of Butko, Talitsky district, Sverdlovsk Province (an area now returned to its prerevolutionary name of Ekaterinburg). His parents, like Gorbachev's, were peasant farmers who were forced to join a collective farm. In 1935, driven by increasing poverty in the countryside, Boris's father moved the family to an industrial construction site and into one of the *obshezhitie* (common dwelling houses) still to be found in Russia. These buildings feature a single room for each family, with a common kitchen and a single toilet for all the families living there. Apparently, the major initial difference between Gorbachev and Yeltsin, as found in their respective biographical data, is that Yeltsin fancied himself somewhat of a youthful rebel, who was constantly in conflict with his rough father and oppressive teachers. Yeltsin even went so far as to blow off two fingers of his left hand while playing with a hand grenade, which he pilfered, allegedly at the possible cost of his life, from an arms depot.[9] After some struggle, young Boris finished secondary school in Sverdlovsk. He admits that he had already learned the utility of turning to the local party committee for assistance—he had early on discovered who held the power in the Sverdlovsk province. He entered the Civil Engineering Department of the Ural Polytechnical Institute, and in the normal five-year program, he won his Engineer degree (1955).

During Yeltsin's studies he traveled around the country, and it was then that he ran into released prisoners coming out of the slave labor camps. Yeltsin joined the Communist Party as a full member after he graduated and was already working as a construction site boss—that is, at a later age than Gorbachev. Further, he makes no mention of prior Komsomol work in his autobiography (also unlike Gorbachev). He mentions that party bosses had become too powerful and dictatorial and that they interfered even in construction activities, to the detriment of the economy. At age thirty-two (1963), Yeltsin had already become head of a large construction operation—the House Building Combine—and soon thereafter he switched to full-time party work as the party supervisor of construction in Sverdlovsk province.[10] Thus, again he differed from Gorbachev in that he had not spent his whole career in political work but rather had hands-on experience in construction for the Soviet state. It is also interesting to note that Sverdlovsk province is right on the border, as delineated by Russian geographers in the nineteenth century, between Europe and Asia. It is a place, nonetheless, in the heartland of Russian *lebensraum* and contains one of the great industrial achievements of the Soviet regime, the Ural Iron and Steel complex, the construction of which, beyond the reach of the Nazi war machine in World War II, was in good part responsible for Soviet victory in the "Great Fatherland War" (World War II).

On November 2, 1976, Boris Yeltsin became first secretary of Sverdlovsk Provincial Party Committee, reaching, like Gorbachev, the functional equivalency of governor in a U.S. state—on recommendation of the Central Committee in Moscow and a unanimous vote of local committee members. Unlike Gorbachev, however, Yeltsin had neither patrons nor previous experience in Moscow. Nonetheless, since both he and Gorbachev were provincial secretaries at the time they met, they entered into mutually useful relations on a personal basis, which was a common enough activity in the Soviet Union. In order for the Soviet system to function, one needed to supersede technicalities and, in an extralegal fashion, metal from the Urals found its way to Stavropol while Stavropol food reached Sverdlovsk. When Gorbachev went to Moscow permanently, Yeltsin was already his protégé and under his protection. On April 3, 1985, about a month after Gorbachev came to power, Boris Nikolayevich Yeltsin received his call to Moscow, to head up the construction supervision sector to the Central Committee's bureaucracy. Initially, he was under the direction of Central Committee Secretary Vladmir Dolgikh,[11] but in June, he took over the secretary job himself.[12] By December 22, 1985, Yeltsin was put in charge of the Moscow City Committee, the most important single party unit in the country, with 1,200,000 members.[13] Yeltsin now plunged into political work first and foremost.

NATIONAL TURBULENCE

By the end of 1985, both Gorbachev and Yeltsin were firmly in position to face the general national crises that confronted the USSR. Just what were these crises?

Features of the Old System: The Two Crises of Communism

The Moral Collapse. Karl Marx, and his alter ego, Frederick Engels, were, in good part, moral philosophers who railed against the evils of private property and the profit motive. If only these two evils could be eliminated, then barbarism could be eliminated as well and civilization would advance. They thought an emancipated "working class," toiling in cooperation rather than competition, would prove that the workers were a superior force, for they would create, first a socialist, and then a full-scale communist society. Neither

Marx nor Engels witnessed the seizure of power by their adherents, with the exception of the short-lived Paris Commune of January–March 1871. It took individuals like Lenin and Trotsky to take power in a major state and some-one like Stalin to establish the framework for the maintenance of power.[14]

We thus have two "men of words," Marx and Engels, who set the ideo-logical basis for communism; two "men of action," Vladmir Ilych Ulyanov (Lenin) and Leon Bronstein (Trotsky), who ran the revolutionary seizure of power; and one "consolidator," Joseph Vissarionovich Djugashvili (Stalin), who shaped the state and party apparatus, a structure that lasted from the 1920s until December 1991.

What did Stalin create? Joseph Stalin put together a political and an eco-nomic system. (The economic structure will be discussed later in this chap-ter.) The political system was based on very fine moral values and promised a wonderful future. Stalin postulated the end of monopolistic capitalism and imperialism. The core of the working class, the proletariat (the industrial workers themselves), would lead all the other workers, and the proletariat would take power and proceed to construct socialism, a process of building up industry on a cooperative basis. The hegemony of the proletariat would be exercised through its party, the Bolshevik Communist Party. A true par-liamentary democracy would develop. The government of the new Soviet state would draw up industrial development plans and carry them out and would ensure that agriculture became truly productive, culture would reach the people, health care and education would be generally available, and hous-ing would be the right of all. All adults, eighteen or older, would be able to vote, and younger people would be politically trained under the benevolent eye of the Communist Party. The state would control all internal and external trade and the distribution of goods, and prices for commodities would be determined for the social good of all the population, and not for profit.[15] On the bottom line, the moral principles of communism were supposed to be superior to capitalism, the driving force of which is exploitation. Commu-nism, after all, was to operate for the benefit of all the people; everything was to be owned by the people, and the party and the state would exist only for the benefit of all—not for private greed.[16]

The question, of course, is whether Stalin actually created such a society. The truth is that Stalin put together one of the most brutal totalitarian regimes the world has ever seen. It is not unreasonable to estimate that millions of people died as a result of Soviet communism and that a majority of their deaths can be attributed directly to the actions of Stalin. When this fact be-came generally known, both in the USSR and abroad, the moral underpin-nings of communism disintegrated.

The Economic Collapse. Marx and Engels were prophets of postindustrial-ization; that is, they thought that when a country had become fully developed by the bourgeoisie, it would be necessary to change over to socialism in order for civilization to advance. They did not, however, feel that it was the duty of a proletariat to develop a country, but rather felt it should take control of a state that was already completely industrialized. They specifically stated that the revolution would take place more or less simultaneously in the advanced countries of the world: the United States and Canada in North America and the states of Western Europe. When Lenin and Trotsky gained power in Russia (whatever their justification for doing so), they found themselves in possession of a backward, undeveloped area that did have potential for development. Lenin soon died and Trotsky was driven out; thus, it became Stalin's task to lay the plans for change. While Marx thought that the workers themselves could administer the economic system, Stalin thought differently. A huge state and party apparatus was constructed, which was to industrialize the Soviet Union at a rapid pace. The USSR, as Nikita Khrushchev later said, would overtake and surpass the capitalist West at a speed of development never before seen in history. In order to do so, Stalin put together a terrorist juggernaut, which crushed all real or apparent opposition and, for a twenty-five-year period, he ran an immense slave labor system. The principal features of this system were the following:

1. a central state economic planning bureau based in Moscow (Gosplan);

2. a centralized administrative apparatus, also in Moscow, for carrying out party policy—the over one hundred ministries of the government, which ruled over all aspects of Soviet life (totalitarianism);

3. a centralized party policy-making and supervisory apparatus (the Central Committee), which was subordinate to the fifteen-member Politburo and, ultimately, the general secretary;

4. a mechanism for repression that insinuated itself throughout the whole of the Soviet state, consisting not only of the party but also of the ordinary police, the secret police, the court system, and its "Procuracy" department; even the youth organizations and the bureaucrats themselves were part of a network of informers. Capping all this off were the execution squads, the slave labor camps, and the prisons.

This horrible structure did achieve some successes: the pre–World War II industrialization of the USSR and great advances in electrification, road and railroad construction, mining and metallurgy, electronics, and basic research. However, the results were not to the betterment of society and the common people's economic situation but rather to that of the military and the nomenklatura, and showy projects like space travel and jet airliners were sinkholes for state investments. The cost was horrendous in terms of lives, health, personal freedom, and even damage to the environment.

One of the worst features of the Stalinist method of "storming" to achieve results (ordering production regardless of the costs) was the total lack of concern about nature and the environment. This created disaster zones from

Central Europe, starting with the southern part of East Germany, all the way to the Pacific coast of the USSR, where nuclear waste was dumped offshore.[17]

However, Gorbachev and Yeltsin did not face Stalinism directly. Stalin had, after all, died in March 1953, and his chief henchman, Lavrenti Beria (alternatively head of the Ministry of the Interior and Ministry of State Security and, at the end, of both), was executed in December 1953, along with his principal assistants. Nikita Sergeyevich Khrushchev, who was himself deeply involved in Stalin's crimes, succeeded Stalin but then started a de-Stalinization campaign that brought the latter into disrepute. The goal of the campaign, of course, was to exculpate Khrushchev himself. Khrushchev, in his turn, also left power (October 1964), but in this case, he remained alive. He was forced out by high party officials who did not like either his attempts at reforming the Stalinist economic and political structure or his downgrading of Stalin and his "achievements," which affected all the Nomenklatura then in place.

Nikita Khrushchev and his son, Sergei, depicted Khrushchev's role in one way in the "Khruschev Remembers" series of books and in *Khrushchev on Khrushchev*,[18] while Pavel Sudoplatov and his son, Anatoli, in *Special Tasks,* gave quite another view.[19] With Khrushchev eliminated, the Soviet Union settled into twenty years of stagnation (*Zastoi*), from October 1964 to March 1985, a period of time forever that will be connected with the name of Leonid Ilich Brezhnev.

The leaders of the USSR from 1964 to 1985 were Leonid Brezhnev (October 1965–November 1982), Yuri Andropov (November 1982–February 1984), and Constantin Chernenko (February 1984–March 1985). However, since the last two General Secretaries of the Communist Party of the Soviet Union were in office for such short periods, both had no time or, in the case of Chernenko, any will, to make changes. Thus, for the sake of brevity, the whole twenty years is usually referred to as either the "Stagnation" or the "Brezhnev Period."

Leonid Brezhnev was born in Ukraine of Russian parents, in 1906. The way to power was opened to him when his superiors were purged in the 1930s. Always a career party worker, he represented those forces in the party that were quite comfortable with the Stalinist structure of the Soviet regime and the Stalinist way of doing things—albeit without the mass repression of party members associated with Stalin. Brezhnev and the Nomenklatura ousted Khrushchev and settled back down into the familiar routines.

During the Brezhnev period the system became stuck in a rut; no new initiatives were tried, and even the Soviet involvement in Afghanistan, in December 1979, was initiated almost as an afterthought. Conservatism was maintained among the ruling apparatus. No purges occurred *and* no prosecution took place—as long as one's incompetence and malfeasance were kept at a low level. A member of the party ruling elite was guaranteed a safe living and a safe retirement—and don't make waves or rock the boat were orders of the day.

Most members of the Soviet elite . . . had lived in constant threat of disgrace or oblivion during Stalin's lifetime. . . . Khrushchev had hired and fired freely. . . . To thousands of office holders . . . Brezhnevism translated into . . . the right to retain their positions indefinitely, barring gross incompetence or physical incapacity. Turnover at all levels was unhurried.[20]

Ideologically, the Stagnation period was self-identified as that of "Developed Socialism" or "Real Socialism." Deviation from set standards and attempts at reforms were suppressed, both internally (e.g., dissident writers) and in the Soviet bloc (Czechoslovakia in 1968, Poland in 1981) with sufficient, but not brutal, force; the show trials and executions of the Stalin period were not repeated. Psychiatric hospitals were used to "straighten out" those who would not conform.[21] The military gained an increasingly large share of the budgetary pie, and the minister of defense position went to a military man, along with a concomitant seat on the Politburo. Stalin was rehabilitated to a secondary place in Soviet history, while his role in World War II and the Soviet victory itself were glorified.

The party structure remained the same, as did the command economy; in addition, ideological purity was proclaimed and the military was honored as the protector of the Soviet state. The members of the security service (KGB or Committee on State Security) were portrayed as staunchly defending the socialist system from enemies both foreign and domestic. No reforms took place in industry, agricultural, cultural policy, or production for consumers. Everyone was equally a "Soviet" citizen, but the role of Russian history, language, and culture as being the leading history, language, and culture of all peoples of the USSR was emphasized (half the population was Russian; thus the other half, which indeed was made up of some 120 nationalities, obviously was not). Soviet control over its bloc of Central European nations (Poland, East Germany, Czechoslovakia, Hungary, Bulgaria, and Romania) and its influence on its allies in Africa, Asia (especially Vietnam, Laos, and Cambodia), and Latin America (especially Cuba and Nicaragua) continued unabated.

However, all was not well with the USSR. There was a general drop-off of vigor, a loss of direction took place, and by the early 1980s, the ship of state appeared rudderless. Agriculture, in particular, started to fail badly. While it is true that the USSR had some of the best grain-growing earth in the world (the "black earth," or *chernozem*), it nonetheless had less arable soil than the United States, which was two and a half times smaller, and the Soviet climate was always difficult. Imperial Russia had been able to feed itself and export foodstuffs, but the collectivized agriculture of the Soviet successor state could not. Soon, the USSR was importing tens of millions of tons of U.S. grain for hard currency payment. Technology, especially in computers, never really developed. Access to any type of computing capability, whether in industry or science, was meager at best. The production of quality goods was rare, and exports beyond the Communist bloc dropped off. Soviet products were of low quality and were purchased by domestic and satellite industries and consumers, who had no other choice.

Birthrates started to decline in the Russian population. Average life spans declined, too, as did levels of health care. Gridlock developed on the obsolescent rail system, and oil and natural gas production failed to achieve levels planned for in the crash (storming) plans issued by state agencies. Overall, industrial growth stagnated, and nearly all the leaders, with the major exception of Mikhail Gorbachev, were in their seventies.

Legacy of the Old System. In a certain sense, given the ideology basis and claims of the Soviet system (which was of the people and served the people), it is surprising that the whole thing was falling apart. Nikita Khrushchev had declared, at the Twenty-second Party Congress in 1961, that the USSR would overtake and surpass the West in rather short order, and in fact, the statistics (if they were true) seemed to bear him out, as growth rates averaged 5.4 percent annually between 1951 and 1970 (much higher than the U.S. growth rates).[22] At the height of Khrushchev's "virgin land" scheme, "Soviet farmers reaped the largest grain harvest in Soviet history."[23] The Soviet Union was the second of only two major players on the stage of world politics. The Soviets had been the first to leap into outer space, and they could threaten anyone on the planet with their nuclear weapons, which were mounted on intercontinental ballistic missiles. The USSR was like the proverbial idol with clay feet; its underpinnings were weak and liable to collapse.

Agriculture was failing despite the early success; the virgin land scheme had, for example, collapsed into a dust bowl. Life on the collective farm was poor and miserable, and everyone who could possibly flee to the city did so, leaving the old and infirm at home. Fertilizer, machinery, and good seed were in short supply. Even when there was a good crop, storage facilities were at a premium and grain was liable to be dumped directly on the ground next to a railway siding, without cover, and left to rot or be lost to the gnawing of the local rat and mouse population. Further, transit to the mill or market was not well coordinated, and wasteful and obsolete production machines and methods were used. It was thought that only 25 percent of a crop ever reached the consumers' plates.

Industry, which was planned from the center, was given to "giantism" (huge, inefficient complexes). Obsolete methods geared to large-scale, but low-quality, production, were the norm rather than the exception. Only certain areas of military production turned out high-quality goods: jet aircraft, artillery tubes, rocketry, tanks, armored personnel carriers, and rifles.

Propaganda for the system began to fall on deaf ears, as exhortations to "work, work, work" no longer aroused any enthusiasm.[24] Politics, for average people, became a sphere totally beyond them, something they had no influence on and, hence, no interest in other than taking part in perfunctory required political charades; that is, rallies and voting.[25] Real democracy was not even dreamed of.

POLITICAL PROFILE OF GORBACHEV AND HIS GROUP

On March 10, 1985, when Konstantin Chernenko died, Mikhail Gorbachev, the youngest of the eleven full-voting members of the Politburo, was fifty-four years old, a youngster among the septuagenarians. He had already started to articulate his new ideas publicly in February 1985, and he soon laid out a new program. As all political leaders do, Gorbachev started to replace his subordinates with "new" people, in this case, young and supportive comrades. Starting in April 1985, at a plenum of the Central Committee, he moved three people into full-voting membership in the Politburo (two without the intermediate "candidate" phase); "there had been no promotions of this kind for at least 20 years."[26] In July 1985, his principal rival, Grigorii Romanov, retired due to "ill health," while Boris Yeltsin moved to a Central Committee Secretary position. At the same time, Andrei Gromyko was pushed upstairs into the ceremonial Soviet presidency (technically, at that time, called "Chairman of the Presidium of the Supreme Soviet"—the head-of-state post in a parliamentary-type government), while Edward Shevardnadze, First Secretary of the Party of the Republic of Georgia, became Minister of Foreign Affairs in the government.

At the Twenty-seventh Party Congress in March 1986, two old Brezhnev supporters, who had left for retirement the previous month, were joined by 55 percent of the old Central Committee. In rolling fashion over the succeeding months, Brezhnev holdovers were weeded out of the party, state, and military apparatuses, and in September 1988, Andrei Gromyko retired from all party and state work while Gorbachev took over the state presidency—a position that he transformed over the next few years into one superior in power to the general secretary post itself. Thus, by 1990, Gorbachev had "formed a leadership team that reflected his personal qualities. It was younger. . . . [T]he average age was just 60, eleven years less than . . . Brezhnev's Politburo of 1982."[27] It was a leadership of educated, cosmopolitan politicians.

THE NEW PROGRAM—GRAND DREAM, POLITICAL REALITY

On coming to power, Mikhail Gorbachev published several works that laid out his program. One must understand, though, that the CPSU had at its beck and call a huge propaganda apparatus, which included paper mills, printing plants, editorial offices, translators for all the principal languages of the globe (and many minor ones), news bureaus, and a national and worldwide distribution system to get the word out. Because of the nature of the Soviet propaganda system, Gorbachev's statements, while noticed, initially had little credence in the West.

In 1985, Gorbachev's first work, *A Time for Peace*, which was addressed to both domestic and foreign audiences, extolling the first feature of his administration: world peace. The book was a compendium of articles, speeches, and interviews that presented Gorbachev's view that it was time to end the Cold War. He further pressed the issue in *The Moratorium*, another selection of speeches and statements, which in this case involved ending nuclear testing.[28]

The Russian word *perestroika* is a compound of *pere*—"re" in English—and *stroika*, meaning "construction." This signaled the recognition that the whole of the Soviet system had to be reworked, rebuilt, and "reconstructed." In order to do so, one had to establish *glasnost* (openness), encourage New Thinking (*Novoe Myshlenie*), and then democratize (*Demokratizatsia*).

Mikhail Gorbachev spelled this out very clearly in the Russian-language book *Perestroika*, which was issued by the Publishing House for Political Literature in Moscow in 1988.[29] This seminal work soon was published in all the major languages of the world, and the words *perestroika* and *glasnost* became well known. Two things should be noted immediately. One, Gorbachev clearly and distinctly felt that communism *could* be reformed; all that was needed was some tinkering with the system—a stand he apparently held until the fall of 1991, when it was too late. (Note that Boris Yeltsin had reached a different conclusion by 1989 and subsequently left the party in July 1990).

Second, the subtitle of the book, which was widely ignored by the popular press in the West, indicated that reconstruction would have to be based on New Thinking, and this applied, not only "for our country," but also "for the whole World." Let us now look at the clearly defined plan articulated by Gorbachev and his group of reformers. His book (of course, one should not really suppose that Mikhail Gorbachev actually wrote *Perestroika* but rather that a group of supporters and editors put it together for him to reflect his basic ideas) is divided into two parts. Part 1 deals with the concept of *perestroika* itself. As a requirement of Soviet literature, Gorbachev dutifully quotes Lenin to prove that his own ideas, while revolutionary in nature, are nonetheless revolutionary within the broad concept of Lenin on the need for revolutionary changes. More socialism would be created, along with more democracy. The Communist Party of the Soviet Union would be the source and guide for all economic and political reform in the Soviet Union—indeed, the Party is credited with starting *perestroika* and is charged with carrying the reform to a successful conclusion.[30] Next, Gorbachev goes on to claim that once Soviet society has joined in the movement for change, there will be new technical developments, economic expansion, and an all-round development of true democracy. Youth, women, professionals, and the governmental councils (Soviets) are all called on to develop and support Perestroika. In Part 2, Gorbachev expanded his ideas into "New Thinking and Peace," a discussion of the relationship of the Soviet Union to the world, and especially the West. He explained that the time for an ending of confrontation had come—now, we need coooperation. He also clearly placed himself in the "Westernizer" camp by seeking multilateral contacts with the West, and especially the United States, for trade and technology. He even went so far as to identify the USSR as a European nation by referring to "Our Common House" (i.e., Europe). Finally, he pleaded for an end to the arms race and general disarmament.[31]

This revolutionary reversal swung the USSR toward the West and out of isolation. For 500 years, since the rise of Moscovy in the fifteenth century, followers of two great orientations have fought to control the steering wheel of the Russian ship of state. The Slavophils thought that Russia was sufficient to itself, it did not need the decadent West for anything and was superior to it. The Westernizers, on the other hand, recognized Russia's weaknesses and sought new ideas, technology, and support from the West, with which they sometimes identified.

Thus, Gorbachev clearly aligned himself with the West, much to the chagrin of many in the Communist Party (which had been Slavophil, especially under Stalin). Gorbachev, however, was a great believer in the party's reformability. After all, he was its head, and he expected a party renaissance. He did not foresee that the dead weight of the party's terrible past and the inertia of its present bureaucracy and Nomenklatura would impede all his efforts. Yeltsin did foresee this, however.

As mentioned already, the Party was in the grip of a moral crisis, and the country was in an economic one. Slavophil elements, both in and outside the party, "lashed out at Gorbachev reforms, cosmopolitan society, the Western threat, nihilism, and Jews and praised Stalin as a true Leninist."[32] (Historically, the masses, and sometimes even the state, had attributed every evil in Russia to the Jews.) Gorbachev tried to reform the party by changing party secretaries on all levels and by reducing party interference in reforms taking place in the government and the economic arena. The Nomenklatura fought back by not carrying out change, if at all possible. Another consequence of the call for renewal and the reduction of oppressive measures was the reemergence of nationalism among the half of the population that was not Russian. The three Baltic republics, Estonia, Latvia, and Lithuania, which were forcibly annexed to the USSR in 1940, began to seek some freedom. The non-Russian Caucasian republics and national units began to squabble among themselves, while the Central Asian republics started to revive as ethnic units.

Mikhail Gorbachev was eventually attacked by some of his closest supporters, and between August 19 and August 22, 1991, a group of top leaders declared martial law and unseated him. The details of that badly planned and poorly executed coup need not concern us here. Suffice to say that while Gorbachev eventually survived the attempted overthrow, he was mortally wounded politically and could not recover.[33] While Gorbachev resigned from the party on August 24, 1991, and then banned it, acting on his power as the chief executive of the Soviet Union, it was too late, and the USSR started to come apart.[34] The Baltic states left the union and, on December 1, 1991, Ukrainians voted overwhelmingly, in a referendum, for independence. Boris Yeltsin preempted Gorbachev's idea of a new union treaty, which was to have been signed on August 20, 1991, but was not, by forming the so-called Commonwealth of Independent States in December 1991 and taking over the apparatus of the state and military within the Russian Federation. On December 25, 1991, Mikhail Gorbachev resigned as president of the now non-existent USSR.[35]

The (Non)Implementation of the New Program

Marshall I. Goldman, in his book on the former Soviet Union, included a chapter on Gorbachev's reforms entitled "The Reform That Never Was."[36] In it, he mentions the following failures:

1. Gorbachev lost internal credibility by hobnobbing with foreign kings, queens, presidents and popes.

2. His wife, Raisa, was perceived to have regal ways.

3. Gorbachev allowed the Central European Communist states to break away from Soviet control.

4. Military leaders resented their loss of power.

5. The Nomenklatura resented its loss of control.

6. National units within the USSR, once repression had been lifted, began to go their own way.

7. Gorbachev erred in believing that the Communist Party was reformable.

8. As a product of the system, he could not see that the whole system itself had to go.

9. None of Gorbachev's reforms had any positive effect on the daily life of citizens, and, in fact, decidedly negative results were obtained.

10. Gorbachev had no blueprint for change.

11. He tried for political reform first and economic reform later, the reverse of the highly successful experience of China.

12. He supported the state sector in the economy too strongly and too weakly encouraged privatization, creating reform gridlock.

13. A freeing of society, unfortunately, also meant the rise of organized crime.

14. Gigantomania (giantism) in economic enterprises could not be easily overcome, and centralized planning still controlled too much. "The transformation, espe-

cially the radical restructuring or even abandonment of those gigantic manufacturing monopolies, could not be achieved quickly or painlessly."[37]

15. A change in attitudes necessary for a real *perestroika* would require decades.

16. Reduction in oil production reduced the amount of hard currency available to Gorbachev's government.

17. The loosening of economic ties between the Soviet republics broke down long-standing economic arrangements.

18. When push came to shove, in August 1991, Gorbachev had no support and people shouted for "Boris," and not "Mikhail."

Boris Yeltsin

The fall from power of Mikhail Segeyevich Gorbachev was not unforeseen. In fact, many had predicted the coup attempt (but not its failure), and afterwards it was clear that Gorbachev was finished. Boris Nikolayevich Yeltsin's star was clearly in ascendancy as a result of the coup's collapse.

Yeltsin's first major office, which gave him national media attention in the USSR, was that of head of the Moscow city party apparatus: first secretary of the Moscow City Committee (the Gorkom). He was, *de facto,* the mayor of Moscow, replacing Viktor Grishin, who had ruled corruptly for eighteen years. Yeltsin plunged with a passion into the cleanup of Moscow's economic and political affairs. Television crews accompanied him as he made his rounds of stores and workplaces and purged incompetent and corrupt officials. By March 1987, he had replaced half of Moscow's party leaders and had arrested 800 corrupt retail trade officials.[38] He rode buses and the subway, visiting health clinics and schools. In short, he showed himself in every way to be a man of the people, someone with whom the average Russian citizen could identify with. His wife played no role whatsoever in politics (as is Russian tradition), and he boasted that he wore the pants in his family and was known to take a drink or two (or more) on occasion. Yeltsin ruffled a lot of feathers of high party officials, especially the number two man, Piotr Ligachev, and despite his rise to a Central Committee secretaryship and into the Politburo, they decided to get rid of him by pressuring him out. He resigned from the Politburo and was drummed out of it and the Moscow committee on November 11, 1987, when he was forced to publicly acknowledge his shortcomings.[39] He appeared to have been disgraced and headed into political oblivion. Though remaining a Central Committee member, he disappeared from the public eye for eighteen months into a government position as chairman of Gosstroi, the State Construction Agency.[40]

Boris Yeltsin's resurrection is a great exception in Russian history. However, as the perceived representative of the "little guy" in the age of *perestroika, glasnost,* and democratization, Yeltsin reappeared in both party and government politics. Despite a fleeting appearance at the Eighteenth Party

Conference, in June 1988, in rather dramatic circumstances, Yeltsin was not able to break out of "political exile" until he decided to run for the newly created "All Union Congress of People's Deputies" (a reformed legislative body of Gorbachev's making). Elections were held on March 26, 1989. The 2,250 delegates to the Congress of People's Deputies (a legislative body of the USSR as a whole, which was in existence from 1989 to 1991) were to meet only once a year, while a subgroup of 542, elected out of the larger body and called the Supreme Soviet, was to meet in spring and fall sittings of three to four months each. This unusually structured legislature, while this body existed, was headed up by a president of the USSR, Mikhail Gorbachev, who now had presidential powers resembling those of the president of France. During his final years in power, Gorbachev placed all his hope in this post as the indirectly elected head of the Soviet state.

Boris Yeltsin was elected to the All Union Congress, and in the next year, he made two decisive strategic moves. First, he resigned from the Communist Party (July 1990 at the twenty-eighth, and last, Communist Party congress). Second, he ran for, and was elected to, the Russian Congress of People's Deputies, the heretofore powerless legislature of the Russian Federation (Russia is two-thirds of the former Soviet territory, with a population of 151,000,000, about 85 percent of which is Russian). Yeltsin decided not to challenge Gorbachev for the USSR presidency but rather pushed forward in the Russian Federation to a position in the Russian Supreme Soviet (the subdivision of the Russian Congress) to achieve the chair of the presidium of the Russian Supreme Soviet; that is, to become the indirectly elected *de facto* president of Russia. He obtained this goal in May 1990. Despite fierce opposition from the party and Gorbachev, Yeltsin went further and held a referendum asking Russians whether they would favor direct election of the Russian president; the results were positive. "In the election held on June 12, 1991, out of six candidates, Yeltsin won 57.4 percent of the votes."[41] This was the first time Russians had ever been asked to elect their leader. Only Yeltsin, in all Russian history, could claim provable popular support. Gorbachev, on the other hand, had never been really "elected" to any party or government post by the general population. Thus, when the coup attempt took place in August 1991, only Yeltsin could—and did—rally popular support to resist it, and when the Soviet Union collapsed in December 1991, Yeltsin emerged supreme as the popular leader of the main successor state to the USSR, the Russian Federation.

NATURE AND SCOPE OF CHANGE

The nature and scope of change in the USSR (and, in fact, the disappearance of the Soviet Union) has been nothing short of mind-boggling. Sovietology, a social science discipline that arose in the West, and especially in the United States, in the post–World War II era, did not predict the collapse of the USSR.

Rather, it was supposed that there would be a very long period of struggle, perhaps for hundreds of years, between the East and West before the conflict would be resolved. After all, there appeared to be only two reactions to the great social, political, and economic upheavals caused by industrialization: Western free-market economics along with liberal democracy or Eastern command economics and totalitarianism. That one would collapse and the other emerge triumphant was unthinkable—but that is what happened. At least publicly the Soviet area has moved toward democracy and free-market economics.

Gorbachev's changes were unsuccessful, frequently wrong-headed, and nearly always incomplete. Certainly, some of his advisors, such as Abel Aganbegyan, had some fairly clear ideas about how to make changes; however, Gorbachev's timidity held them back.[42] The moral bankruptcy of the Communist regime came out during *glasnost*. Admission that Soviet forces had murdered 25,700 Polish prisoners in Spring 1940 (called, in part, the "Katyn Forest Massacre")[43] and the discovery of sites of other mass murders carried out by the NKVD (secret police) in Kuropaty (Belarus)[44] or Vynnytsia (Ukraine)[45] and other places really undermined whatever claim the regime had to righteousness. In fact, Robert Conquest's famous *The Great Terror* even found its way into a Russian translation.[46]

Gorbachev himself is singularly unpopular today. He has been treated roughly by the Russian government and has dropped from the world stage. Perhaps his plea at the great trial of 2017 would be that of incapacity to guide the reforms he unleashed; he could say he was the victim of one of those great movements in history that shook the very foundations of human organization. Marx had found such movements in the change from hunting and gathering to agriculture and from agriculture to industry—in this case, the movement was from authoritarian-totalitarian politics to democracy.

What Boris Yeltsin would plead in 2017, if a reversion to historic Russian centralism and authoritarianism were to occur, cannot be foreseen, for it is still in his power to guide that two-thirds of the former Soviet area, the Russian Federation, to a freer and more open society.

INTERPRETING BORIS YELTSIN AS LEADER

Boris Yeltsin, while also a Westernizer like Gorbachev, nevertheless is seen as a "real Russian," a man of the people who struggled up from poverty to become the first freely elected leader in Russian history. He stared down the coup plotters in August 1991 and forced the unpopular Gorbachev out by December. He is a pragmatist who recognizes that a military threat to the West is no longer possible. He is in command of the Russian armed forces, which took over as the successor to the Soviet army. He completed the withdrawal of military forces from Central Europe and the Baltic states, in September 1994. He has agreed to further reductions in nuclear weapons and has forced those Soviet successor states with nuclear weapons (Ukraine, Belarus, and Kazakstan) to agree to transfer them to Russia. Further, he has given support to Russians in the "near abroad" (Russians living in the fourteen other successor states of the Soviet Union) and indicated that he will protect them.

On the international scene, Russia gained the permanent seat, with veto power, on the United Nations Security Council that the USSR had held and has begun to reassert its influence in Europe and the Middle East. The so-called G-7 group, the seven most important economic powers on the planet (United States, Germany, Italy, France, Canada, Japan, and Great Britain) invited Russia to take part in its regular meetings in a sort of 7-plus-1 group. However, all is not well in Russia.

It is said that Bill Clinton, while he was running for the U.S. presidency, would often repeat to himself, "It's the economy, stupid," to remind himself of the primacy of America's economic woes. The same can be said for Yeltsin—it's the economy!

The *New York Times* of October 16, 1994, stated that it takes an average Russian 14 minutes of work to afford a pound of bread, an hour and 10 minutes for a half gallon of milk, 2 and a half hours for a pound of sausage, and 71 days to buy a television, while an American works 5 minutes of work for the bread, 9 minutes for the milk, 12 minutes for the sausage, and 6 days for a television set. Cash cannot be compared because Russians are using 1,000 ruble notes for small change and 3,000 rubles now equal $1 U.S. Recently, the ruble dropped 27 percent in value in one day. Where formerly, goods were scarce and lines were long but people had money, now there are no lines and goods are available but hyperinflation has made the money that people have nearly worthless.[47]

Yeltsin has had to fight tooth and nail for reform, even going so far as to prorogue the Russian Supreme Soviet (elected during Soviet times) by force before running new elections to the national legislature in December 1993.

Marshall Goldman has proposed that the following measures be taken to finally reform the Russian state in order to swing it firmly onto the side of free-market economics and democracy:

1. privatization should be pressed—state enterprises should be sold off to investors or stock should be distributed to workers in the enterprises;

2. agriculture should be taken over by private farmers;

3. entrepreneurs should be supported;

4. foreign investment and investors should be gladly received and not unduly burdened by state interference or regulation;

5. all prices should be freed of government control (this was partially achieved in January 1992);

6. the growth of organized crime (called the Mafia in Russia) should be halted;

7. a multiparty political system should be fostered (this is already in progress);

8. large-scale economic aid should be sought in the West.[48]

Further, while Goldman does not mention these problems, we must add that Russia should:

9. settle ethnic conflict with the 15 percent non-Russians who live in the Russian Federation;[49]

10. finally determine what role it wishes to play in international politics.[50]

There is no question that these steps need to be carried out. If reforms continue, the only problem is determining whether they should be gradually introduced or accomplished in one fell swoop—so-called shock therapy. Yeltsin, to date, has been able to hold on to power, keep the new legislature more or less in check, and fitfully introduce further reform. Whether he will be successful, we cannot know. Perhaps the answer will be heard in 2017.

NOTES

1. Richard Sakwa, *Gorbachev and His Reforms: 1985–1990* (New York: Prentice-Hall, 1990), p. 2.

2. See Robert Conquest, *The Harvest of Sorrow: Soviet Collectivization and the Terror of Famine* (New York: Oxford University Press, 1986).

3. Sakwa, p. 2.

4. See "Biography of Mikhail Gorbachev," in Mikhail S. Gorbachev, *A Time for Peace* (New York: Richardson and Starman, 1985), pp. 9–15.

5. Ibid.

6. Sakwa, p. 5.

7. See Merle Fainsod, "Constitutional Myths and Political Realities," in *How Russia Is Ruled* (Cambridge, MA: Harvard University Press, 1967), pp. 349–385.

8. See Michael Voslensky, *Nomenklatura: Anatomy of the Soviet Ruling Class* (London: The Bodley Head, 1980).

9. Boris Yeltsin, *Against the Grain: An Autobiography* (New York: Summit Books, 1990), pp. 21–32.

10. Ibid., p. 55.

11. Ibid., p. 71.

12. Ibid., p. 91.

13. Ibid., pp. 107–108.

14. John Clark and Aaron Wildavsky, *The Moral Collapse of Communism: Poland as a Cautionary Tale* (San Francisco: Institute for Contemporary Studies, 1990), p. 19.

15. See Joseph Stalin, *Leninism*, 2 vol. (New York: International Publishers, n.d. [1933]).

16. Ibid., 1:377–378.

17. See Murray Feshbach and Alfred Friendly, Jr., *Ecocide in the USSR: Health and Nature under Siege* (New York: Basic Books, 1992).

18. See Nikita Khrushchev, *Khrushchev Remembers* (1970) and *Khrushchev Remembers: The Last Testament* (1974), both published in Boston by Little, Brown and Co., and Sergei Khrushchev, *Khrushchev on Khrushchev* (Boston: Little, Brown and Co., 1990).

19. Pavel Sudoplatov and Anatoli Sudoplatov, *Special Tasks: The Memoirs of an Unwanted Witness—A Soviet Spymaster* (Boston: Little, Brown and Co., 1994). The elder Sudoplatov was high up in the Soviet Secret Service close to Beria, Abukhamov, Stalin, and Khrushchev from the middle 1930s to 1953. He was involved in planning Trotsky's assassination in Mexico in 1940.

20. Timothy J. Colton, *The Dilemma of Reform in the Soviet Union* (New York: Council on Foreign Relations, 1986), pp. 11–12.

21. Ibid, p. 13.

22. Marshall I. Goldman, *Gorbachev's Challenge: Economic Reform in the Age of High Technology* (New York: W. W. Norton and Co., 1987), p. 15.

23. Ibid.

24. Ibid., p. 30.

25. See Colton, pp. 32–67, and Zbigniew Brzezinski, *The Grand Failure: The Birth and Death of Communism in the Twentieth Century* (New York: Charles Scribner's Sons, 1989).

26. Stephen White, *Gorbachev in Power* (New York: Cambridge University Press, 1990), p. 18.

27. Ibid., p. 21.

28. See note 4. Also see Mikhail Gorbachev, *The Moratorium: Selected Speeches and Statements by the General Secretary of the CPSU Central Committee on the Problem of Ending Nuclear Tests (January–September 1986)* (Moscow: Novosti Agency Publishing House, 1986).

29. M. S. Gorbachev; *Perestroika i Novoe Myshlenie dla nashei strany i dla vsego Mira* [Perestroika and New Thinking for Our Country and the Whole World] (Moscow: Izdatelstvo Politcheskoi Literatury, 1988).

30. Ibid., pp. 55–56.

31. Ibid., p. 137.

32. Jonathan R. Adelman; *Torrents of Spring: Soviet and Post-Soviet Politics* (New York: McGraw Hill, 1994), p. 222.

33. See Bernard Gwertzman and Michael T. Kaufman, eds., *The Collapse of Communism* (New York: New York Times Co., 1991).

34. Ibid., pp. 549–550.

35. Michael Kort, *The Soviet Colossus: The Rise and Fall of the USSR*, 3rd ed. (Armonk, NY: M. E. Sharpe Co., 1993), pp. 329–330.

36. Marshall I. Goldman, *Lost Opportunity: Why Economic Reforms in Russia Have Not Worked* (New York: W. W. Norton and Co., 1994), chapter 1, "The Reform That Never Was," pp. 1–30.

37. Ibid., p. 16.

38. Ibid., p. 33.

39. Yeltsin, pp. 200–201.

40. Ibid., p. 202.

41. Goldman, *Lost Opportunity*, p. 47.

42. See Abel Aganbegyan, *Inside Perestroika: The Future of the Soviet Economy* (New York: Harper and Row, 1989).

43. Sudoplatov and Sudoplatov, appendix Five, pp. 476–478.

44. David R. Marples. "Kuropaty: The Investigation of a Stalinist Historical Controversy," *Slavic Review,* 53(2), (Summer 1994): 513–523.

45. Ihor Kamenetsky, *The Tragedy of Vinnytsia: Materials on Stalin's Policy of Extermination in Ukraine during the Great Purge, 1936–1938* (Toronto, Canada, and New York: Ukrainian Historical Association, 1989).

46. See Robert Conquest, *The Great Terror: A Reassessment* (New York: Oxford University Press, 1990).

47. Felicity Barringer, "When G-notes Are Small Change," *New York Times,* October 16, 1994, p. E3.

48. See Goldman, *Lost Opportunity,* chapter 4, "Economic Advice," pp. 64–93.

49. See Yuri Zarakhovich, "Russia: Fire in the Caucasus," *Time,* December 12, 1994, p. 36, for a report on one ethnic battle.

50. See Minton F. Goldman, ed., *Global Studies: Russia, the Eurasian Republics and Central/Eastern Europe,* 5th ed. (Guilford, CT: Dushkin Publishing Group, 1994), for the latest assessment of Russia's problems.

——— seven ———————————————

Rajiv Gandhi: Economic Liberalization in India

Rajiv Gandhi's accession to power following the assassination of his mother, Prime Minister Indira Gandhi, on October 31, 1984, reflected, on the one hand, firmly established democratic rules of transition of power in India and, on the other, a turbulence that had been building up in Indian politics for some years. The same characteristics of Indian politics were evident six and a half years later when Rajiv Gandhi perished, on May 21, 1991, at the hands of an assassin while campaigning for a political comeback.

By the early 1990s, India had achieved a certain measure of economic prosperity and had been self-sufficient in food production for fifteen years. The prosperity was the result in part of the Green Revolution (promoting a dramatic increase in food production) and in part the result of the economic liberalization started by Indira Gandhi after returning to power in 1980. The improved economy, however, had largely benefited the upper and middle classes and had further increased the chasm between the rich and poor of India. That alone probably was sufficient to destabilize Indian politics. Distributive justice had been a major theme of the political statements in India since its independence from Britain in 1947. The improvement in economy made this goal even harder to realize and increased the frustrations of the masses, contributing to political turbulence.[1] Besides the issue of distributive justice, the demands of the regional, linguistic, and religious groups showed no signs of abating and were often intermingled with the economic unrest.

In order to understand the turbulence in Indian politics and economic liberalization during the administration of Rajiv Gandhi (1984–1989), we first present an overview of India's politics and economy and then consider sources and manifestations of turbulence, a political profile of Rajiv Gandhi and his group, his new program, his mobilization of power, the implementation of his program, and the nature and scope of change it brought about.

THE NATIONAL POLITICAL-ECONOMIC CONTEXT

With 900 million inhabitants, India is the second most populous country in the world, next to China. Its religious, regional, linguistic, social, and economic diversity presents an ideal milieu for generating turbulence in politics. Hindus are the predominant religious majority, constituting more than 80 percent of the total population. Muslims are the largest minority, with 12 percent of the population, followed by the Christians (3 percent) and the Sikhs (2 percent). Other religions in India include Buddhism, Jainism, and Zoroastrianism. Although India officially is a secular country, religion plays a dominant role in politics. Some of the political parties are blatantly religious and increasingly militant. Religion is one of the major factors in voting. In the formation of any government, religion is always given consideration. While many Indians are tolerant of each other's religion, hostility between religions is on the increase and is a major cause of political violence in the country.

India's twenty-six states are primarily grouped on the basis of language. The Indian constitution recognizes fourteen languages, of which Hindi is spoken by the largest segment in the country—approximately one-third. Hindi is the official language and English, which is widely spoken by the educated Indians, is considered an associate official language. A majority of Indians feel a strong sense of loyalty to the language they speak and experience an affinity with their linguistic group. Such loyalties have contributed to unrest in the country and even led to riots and demands for secession.

Based on the principle of hierarchy, there are innumerable social divisions within Hinduism, the majority religion. Hindus follow a rigid caste system that divides them into four major groups and scores of subgroups within each of the four. Once born into a caste, a person is unable to change it, and most Hindus still marry within their caste group. Indeed, caste remains a major influence in their social and political life. The loyalty of the Hindus to the caste system is so strong that it often leads to conflict and, sometimes, to violence.

One group among the Hindus is considered outside the caste hierarchy and is known as *Harijans,* which means "God's Children." (Members of this group were earlier called "untouchables.") The Harijans constitute approximately 15 percent of the country's population and, despite a quota system in the Indian constitution to provide them with education, jobs, and even seats in the national and state legislatures, they face discrimination by the caste Hindus. Of late, they have become militant and have begun to demand, not only legal, but also social equality. In addition, India has numerous tribal groups, comprising 7 percent of the total population. Government jobs are reserved for these groups also.

India has made remarkable technological progress; however, it still is a largely agricultural country. Over two-thirds of India's workforce is employed in agriculture. It also has a growing, almost mushrooming, middle class. Estimates on the numbers of the middle class vary. Most analysts, however, consider India's middle class to be approximately one-fifth of the population. Since the economic gains have barely trickled down to the poor, many among the rich and middle-class Indians are concerned about the possibility of violent conflict between the haves and the have-less or have-nots.

India has pursued a policy of a mixed economy of public and private enterprises. Until recently, socialism was the preferred ideology of the country, and when moves toward economic liberalization were made, first under Indira Gandhi and then, more so, under Rajiv Gandhi, it was made clear that socialism was not to be abandoned. Since the early 1990s, however, like many other countries in the world, India has adopted a greater degree of capitalism in the economy than ever before.

Internationally, India initially aspired to be not only a regional, but a world, leader. For seventeen years after independence, India's foreign policy was guided by the British-educated nationalist leader and prime minister, Jawaharlal Nehru. In a speech delivered at Columbia University in New York in 1949, Nehru outlined the goals of India's foreign policy. Emphasizing that it would combine idealism with national interest, he stated:

The main objectives of that [a policy combining idealism with national interest] are: the pursuit of peace, not through alignment with any major power or group of powers, but through an independent approach to each controversial or disputed issue; the liberation of subject peoples; the maintenance of freedom both national and individual; the elimination of racial discrimination; and the elimination of want, disease, and ignorance, which affect the greater part of the world's population.[2]

Nonalignment became the central element of Nehru's foreign policy. He made it clear that it was not a policy of isolation or neutralism and was not born out of India's weakness. He wanted India to judge every issue on its merits and not take sides based on some previously signed treaties. In effect, this policy meant not signing an alliance with either the United States or the Soviet Union. It also meant being able to ask and receive foreign aid from both camps. Along with nonalignment, India espoused a policy of anticolonialism and antiracism and became a leader of the newly emerging African and Asian nations in the United Nations on these issues.

The policy of nonalignment increased India's prestige in the United Nations and world politics. During the Cold War period, India started moving closer to the Soviet Union, mainly to gain a bulwark against China, which had defeated India in a war in 1962. Friendship with the Soviet Union was also considered desirable in view of the American support of Pakistan, India's regional rival.

However, nonalignment has lost its appeal in the post–Cold War period. While Indian leaders still talk of a world role, they are primarily interested in maintaining hegemony within South Asia. India is indisputably the pre-eminent nation in this region. Militarily, it is far stronger than any of its neighbors, including Pakistan. India's strength is sometimes viewed as threatening its smaller neighbors. It becomes embroiled in every regional conflict, whether in Sri Lanka, Bangladesh, or some other country. India has, however, accepted (after some initial resistance) the principle of regional cooperation in nonmilitary areas. Seven nations of the South Asian region—India, Pakistan, Bangladesh, Sri Lanka, Nepal, Bhutan, and the Maldives—became members of the South Asian Association for Regional Cooperation (SAARC) through negotiations in the early 1980s. The goal of this organization is "collective self-reliance" in nonmilitary areas such as agriculture, health, education, and rural development.

India became a nuclear power in 1974. Evidence indicates that Pakistan also has become a nuclear power, thanks to help from China and other nations. The possession of nuclear weapons by the two rivals has the potential of destabilizing the South Asian region, and efforts are being made to prevent the use of nuclear weapons by either side.

NATIONAL TURBULENCE

Few Third World countries have experienced as much turbulence in politics as has India and yet maintained a stable democratic system. Indeed, India's emergence as an independent nation in 1947 was accompanied by turbulence. Massive communal riots between the Hindus and the Muslims in India and the newly created Pakistan (partitioned from India) left at least 200,000 people dead. As many as 12 million people, including one of the coauthors of this book, became refugees as a result of this partition, and both India and Pakistan were burdened with the responsibility of resettling them. The partition also caused a war between India and Pakistan over Kashmir, a territory in the northwest of the South Asian subcontinent.

Domestically, India remained relatively calm for the next two decades. The Congress was the single dominant party during this period. The opposition parties and independent candidates did run in elections but gained little power. The parliament and the executive were firmly in the hands of the Congress leaders. Political stability was accompanied by encouraging economic growth during these years. In the international arena, India had become a leader of the nonaligned group of nations. It fought two wars in this period—one with China (1962) and the other with Pakistan (1965). The war with China was over disputed border areas, and the war with Pakistan was again over Kashmir. While China captured some territory, the war with Pakistan ended in a stalemate.

Domestic politics in India became turbulent after the mid-1960s. India's stability was shaken, first by the death of its venerable prime minister, Jawaharlal Nehru, in 1964, and then by the split in the Congress Party in 1969. Weaknesses in the Congress Party had become apparent even before this split. For example, the party had lost some of its appeal for the masses and had suffered electoral setbacks in the 1967 elections, particularly in the states. At the same time, opposition parties and independent candidates had gained strength. If one major opposition party had gained enough support to present a serious challenge to the Congress Party, India might have developed a stable, two-party system, but this did not happen. Instead, a number of opposition parties emerged or improved their strength, thus presenting the possibility of unstable coalition governments if the Congress Party did not win. When the Congress Party was defeated in the national elections, first in 1977 and then in 1989, such coalitions were formed, making Indian politics even more turbulent.

Around the mid-1960s, India's economy also started to falter and a period of industrial stagnation set in. The worsening of the economy contributed to the turbulence in politics. When the economy started improving, the benefits mostly went to the upper one-fifth of the population. That made the poor, who constitute the vast majority, even more aware of their miserable conditions. Many of those who gained from the economic growth are also frustrated due to the "rising expectations" syndrome. Such frustrations, combined with the growing chasm between the rich and poor, are a major cause of turbulence in Indian politics.

Political uncertainties caused by the decline of the Congress Party and the emergence of less powerful other parties, and economic frustrations have contributed to the growing violence in Indian politics. Elites as well as the masses are responsible for the increase in political violence.[3] On the one hand, India presents almost a model of democracy in the Third World—a democracy in which the transfer of power by constitutional means is taken for granted and the possibility of a military coup is virtually nonexistent. On the other hand, the use of violence during elections to intimidate opponents has become an accepted rule of the game. Every major political party hires musclemen for this purpose. The result is that death and injury are as much a part of the Indian elections as is fundraising.[4]

Indian democracy lacks in the spirit of compromise that minimizes political violence. Neither the elites nor the masses have learned to resolve political and religious grievances through the institutions provided in the Indian political framework. While courts are not entirely ignored for resolving such disputes, better results are expected from demonstrations, strikes, and even riots.

Religion has also added to the turbulence in Indian politics. Fundamentalism has increased in Hinduism, Islam, and Sikhism—three of the major religions in India, whose followers constitute more than 95 percent of the population. Fundamentalism has not only increased communal strife, it has also contributed to secessionist demands, notably by the Sikhs. Demands for secession are not new in India, having started soon after its independence from Britain. Secession has been demanded, on grounds not only of religion but also of ethnicity and language. While secessionist demands based on ethnicity and language have been, for the most part, contained by the Indian leaders, in the future, the tide of religion may prove to be too forceful to control.

The Sikh demand for a separate country started in the early 1980s. The Sikhs are among the most advanced segments of the society and are in the majority in the northwestern state of Punjab, which many of them seek to make into an independent nation. Sikh separatism gained momentum because the national government neglected Sikh demands for political autonomy in Punjab; played one Sikh faction against the other; displayed an abysmal lack of foresight in sending troops into their holiest shrine, in the city of Amritsar in June 1984; and then tolerated a carnage against them following Prime Minister Indira Gandhi's assassination by her Sikh bodyguards in October that year. At the time of this writing, the Indian government appears to have defeated the Sikh separatists.

Another state where secessionist demands based on religion are strong is Kashmir. A majority of the people in this state are Muslims, a growing number of whom want to make their state into an independent country. A large number, however, have for over four decades demanded to incorporate it into Pakistan, which is mostly Muslim, by joining it with the part of Kashmir controlled by Pakistan. (Since 1947, one-third of Kashmir has been controlled by Pakistan and two-thirds by India.)

The conflict over Kashmir goes back to 1947, the year of independence for India and that of the creation of Pakistan. A major issue of contention remains the holding of a plebiscite in Kashmir, an idea that had been accepted by the Indian government under Prime Minister Nehru in 1947 and then called for in a UN Security Council resolution in 1949. A plebiscite vote by the Kashmiris could determine whether the two parts of Kashmir would continue to remain separate, with one part under India and the other in Pakistan, or whether both parts will join Pakistan (the possibility of both joining India is not even considered due to the predominance of Muslims in both parts of Kashmir) or together form an independent country. Such a plebiscite was never held mainly because of the Indian government's fear of losing Kashmir. Unrest in Indian Kashmir has greatly increased over the years, and the Indian government has attempted to repress it by force. Many Muslims, as well as Hindus, have fled the state. The Muslims cross over to the Pakistan side of Kashmir, while the Hindus move south into the rest of

India. There seems to be no possible solution to the Kashmir issue in the foreseeable future. Kashmir will, therefore, continue to destabilize India.

Caste is another major source of turbulence in Indian politics. The Indian caste system is one of the most complex social structures ever devised by a society. The four caste groups evolved in India centuries ago and became associated with different occupations. The highest caste is that of Brahmins or priests. Next in hierarchy come Kshatriyas (rulers and warriors), Vaisyas (merchants), and Sudras (people working on farms or in trades). Those who had menial jobs such as sweeping streets or mending shoes were kept outside the caste system, or varna (the Indian word for caste).

Members of different caste groups traditionally followed a rather elaborate set of rules. For example, the Brahmins were treated with deference by other groups. Those traditional rules of behavior are breaking down under the impact of modernization. New rules have not yet emerged in place of the old, and the result is tension in the society. Moreover, the social tensions have influenced politics. Thus, caste conflicts are apparent in almost every facet of Indian politics and have become a major source of political violence.

Higher castes in India are economically better off than the lower castes, who resent the economic disparity and demand the redistribution of economic resources. A major issue in contemporary Indian politics has been the demand of the so-called "backward" castes for the reservation of government jobs for the members of their groups. In 1993, a quota system was adopted for them in government jobs. The "advanced" castes resent the quota system for the Harijans, tribal groups, and "backward" castes. Complaints of reverse discrimination are common in India and are frequently expressed, not through lawsuits but rather through demonstrations and violence. The Harijans, who are often blamed for reverse discrimination, complain about the ill treatment that they still suffer at the hands of the caste Hindus. Furthermore, tribal groups have their own grievances and want a share of the political pie. The tribes in the northeastern parts of India have been particularly restless. Some of them formerly wanted to secede from India, but they now seem to be more interested in concessions from the Indian government that would provide economic benefits and political power within that country.

POLITICAL PROFILE OF RAJIV GANDHI AND HIS GROUP

Rajiv Gandhi was born on August 20, 1944, in Allahabad, a major city in the Hindi-speaking state of Uttar Pradesh, northern India. A scion of one of the most politically influential families in modern India, he was educated in an exclusive school in the northern hills of India and studied at Cambridge University in England from 1962 to 1965. Never a brilliant student, Rajiv Gandhi left Cambridge without earning a degree. Back in India, he became a pilot in the government's domestic airlines and remained indifferent to a political career until the accidental death in 1980 of his younger brother,

Sanjay, who had been the heir apparent to the family's political dynasty. The death of Sanjay left the older brother with no other choice but to enter politics.

Rajiv Gandhi grew up in a house of prime ministers and continued to live there with his mother even after his marriage to an Italian woman in 1968. Rajiv's mother, Indira Gandhi, had also grown up in the prime minister's (Jawaharlal Nehru's) house and continued to live there after her marriage. Upon Nehru's death in 1964, Indira Gandhi joined the Indian cabinet and then became prime minister, in 1966, on the death of Lal Bahadur Shastri, who had succeeded Nehru. Indira Gandhi remained India's prime minister until her assassination in 1984, except for a period of nearly three years (1977–1980).

Rajiv Gandhi's father, Feroze Gandhi, was a prominent member of the parliament who died of a heart attack in 1960, when he was only forty-eight. Even before Feroze Gandhi's death, Indira Gandhi had chosen to live with her father in the prime minister's house instead of with her husband in a parliament member's flat. Rajiv Gandhi and his brother, Sanjay (Indira Gandhi had no other children), thus grew up in close proximity to the center of political power in India.

Rajiv Gandhi wanted a nonpolitical career and perhaps would never have entered politics had his younger brother not died. It was the family pressure, or rather the pressure of his prime minister mother, that made him decide to run for parliament. Rajiv Gandhi won the parliamentary seat held by his late brother Sanjay and joined the parliament in August 1981, when he was barely thirty-seven.

Even though Rajiv Gandhi never held a political office before entering parliament in 1981, he showed a remarkably astute grasp of politics, which was clearly due to his political socialization within the family. Noninvolvement in politics, however, gave him a tremendous advantage of not owing anything to anyone. Even more important, he could not be accused of the corrupt political deals with which most Indian politicians are associated. This advantage prepared him to enact bold policy moves later, upon becoming prime minister.

Several of Rajiv Gandhi's close advisors came from his circle of friends from his school and college days and his years as an airline pilot. Paul H. Kreisberg wrote in a commentary published in *Foreign Affairs* in 1985:

Rajiv feels most comfortable with his own generation and with individuals whose backgrounds are similar to his own. His closest advisors and the key managers of his election campaign were his classmates at the elite Nehru Dun boarding school for boys or friends from his years as a pilot for Indian Airlines. But he has also promoted more traditional politicians in his general age bracket, such as V. P. Singh [V. P. Singh later became Rajiv Gandhi's rival and replaced him as prime minister], an attractive and shrewd Congress Party member of parliament in his mid-forties.[5]

A biographer of Rajiv Gandhi, writing about a prominent member of his government, noted:

Scindia, Minister of Railways in the 1984–89 Rajiv Gandhi's government, is the archetypal Rajivite: young, Oxford-educated (New College, Oxford), articulate, contemporary and passionately committed to building a modern, secular, prosperous India.[6]

Rajiv Gandhi was secular in his outlook, tolerant and respectful of all religions. He also showed commitment to social justice, but he was not a doctrinaire socialist. His economic policies were dictated more by pragmatism than by any ideology. When his economic reforms (introduced in 1985, they lowered taxes on the rich and on business) were criticized and he was called prorich, he changed the policy the following year. Antipoverty programs were now given attention and taxes were increased on such items as cars, television sets, and refrigerators, which are purchased by the affluent Indians.

Initially, Rajiv Gandhi had the image of an incorruptible leader. He was often referred to as "Mr. Clean." He wanted to bring computers and modern technology to India, which earned him the nickname "Computerji" or "Mr. Computer." His popularity, as reflected in the 1984 parliamentary elections, was indeed unprecedented. Even his legendary grandfather, Jawaharlal Nehru, never enjoyed such popular electoral support. The euphoria for Rajiv Gandhi, however, did not last long, in part due to the frequent policy changes he made and in part due to his alleged involvement in a major scandal involving kickbacks.

THE NEW PROGRAM

Rajiv Gandhi had a new political agenda for improving the Indian economy. He was no ideologue, but he could not break away from the socialist tradition of independent India. Thus, a commitment to the eradication of poverty and the improvement of antipoverty programs remained his major political slogans. At the same time, a greater degree of liberalization of the economy was introduced than ever before in India. Rajiv Gandhi's program also included reducing political corruption and strengthening the Congress Party.

In order to understand Rajiv Gandhi's new program and the political turbulence in India, it is essential to review the major economic and political changes in India since 1947, the year of the nation's independence. Independence was accompanied by the division of erstwhile India into India and Pakistan (on religious grounds), unprecedented violence and loss of life caused by the riots by the two largest religious groups (Hindus and Muslims), and a war between India and Pakistan over Kashmir. Despite such rocky beginnings, in just a few years, India settled down to a period of relative peace and prosperity. The leader of this era was Prime Minister Jawaharlal Nehru.

Nehru was a liberal intellectual who was born in a rich north Indian Brahmin family and educated in England. He believed in social justice, secularism, socialism, and centralized planning. Two other views competed with Nehru's ideology—those of Mahatma Gandhi and of Nehru's political rival, Sardar Vallabhbhai Patel.[7] Mahatma Gandhi believed in a decentralized economy based in villages and local industries. Patel distrusted socialism and was an advocate of capitalism. Gandhi was assassinated in 1948, and Patel died in 1950. The deaths of these two men left Nehru the undisputed leader of the country. Although Gandhian views were not entirely given up, and have, to some extent, remained a part of the Indian political economy until today, and although Patel's vision of private enterprise also guided the economy, it was Nehru's ideology of socialism and planning that became the core of Indian economics and politics.

Nehru's views formed the basis of the Industrial Policy Resolutions of 1948 and 1956, which were consensus-building documents and accommodated diverse political and economic interests in the country at the time. The Indian political economy adhered, to a considerable extent, to the principles laid down in these documents until the early 1990s. The Industrial Policy Resolutions assigned a dominant role to the public sector in the economy.[8] The state was to own and run public utilities such as electricity, water, and telephone services, as well as basic and heavy industries such as coal, steel, defense, and shipbuilding. A private sector was permitted but was kept under close government scrutiny. Private foreign capital was considered acceptable, but only if it met the government's guidelines of ownership and control.

Economic self-reliance was a major goal of India's initial economic efforts. This goal was to be achieved through what is known as import substitution.[9] In other words, less-essential goods for the consumers were to be sacrificed for the sake of more-essential goods for the economic development of the country. Goods such as cars and radios were considered less essential; such goods and items of daily necessity were to be produced at home. Products that were essential for the economic development or those for which the country lacked resources (e.g., heavy machines, oil, and food) were to be imported.

Concern for the poor remained a central theme, at least in policy statements and planning. Profit in the public sector was secondary. As a biographer of Rajiv Gandhi explained:

Back in the fifties, government investment in a core public sector in India had two goals: first, provision of employment for the poor as a measure of distributive justice; second, independence in the production of basic needs like coal, steel and cement. Profit was not a chief motive.[10]

Socialism has been a dominant theme in the political economy of India. Socialism meant distributive justice and a reduction in the concentration of wealth. These principles were incorporated in the Directive Principles of State Policy of the Indian constitution, promulgated in 1950. Like many other countries, however, India was not ready to redistribute its resources for the common good. Nehru, more than most other Indian advocates of socialism, understood this and settled for very limited progress in this area. Land reform was implemented half-heartedly and little redistribution was achieved. The rich were taxed at a very high rate, but they succeeded in evading taxes. An interesting viewpoint was expressed by James Manor who stated that "after independence in 1947, the liberal order might have broken down [in India] had Nehru pressed aggressively for the substantial social reform with which he had great sympathy. He believed that it was too early for such an effort to succeed."[11]

The socialism that emerged in India reflected the state's power in the production and regulation of the economy and not the social justice for which it also stands. Socialism created a mixed economy of public and private enterprises in India. One scholar, however, argued that "state participation in the industrialization of India [in response to Nehru's vision] had little to do with socialism. On the contrary, it provided the base and support necessary for a state-supported capitalist pattern of industrial development."[12]

Socialism and the mixed economy were sought through five-year plans, starting in 1951. The first plan emphasized agriculture more than industry and considered fertilizer plants and irrigation programs among the top priorities. In the second five-year plan, the emphasis shifted to industry, and in particular the production of heavy machinery and other capital goods. The third five-year plan moved the focus back to agriculture.[13]

The first fifteen years of planning, and particularly the decade from 1956 to 1966, are given much credit for improvements made in the Indian economy. One study called 1956–1966 "the golden decade of development" and noted the "massive industrial boom" in this period.[14] The authors of the study commented:

A growth strategy based on rapid industrialization through capital-intensive investment, import substitution, and emphasis on heavy industry provided opportunities for almost every industry to grow, and the lines between the public and private sectors became blurred.... Both the public and private sectors grew rapidly, and India appeared headed for an economic takeoff into self-sustaining growth.[15]

Such optimism is not shared by many scholars. India indeed made progress during the 1947–1966 period, especially if we consider that it had "started almost from scratch."[16] India's growth rate during the British colonial rule was negligible, so any improvement seemed impressive. For almost a half-century before India's independence in 1947, the growth rate was less than

1 percent.[17] Contrasted with such a low growth rate, "for the fifteen-year period of the three plans ending in early 1966, GDP increased by 3.8 percent per annum. Agricultural output rose annually by 2.8 percent per annum and industrial output by 7.3 percent per annum."[18]

Another set of economic statistics, however, tells a different story. While the national income grew at annual rates of 3.5, 4.7, and 2.6 percent during the first, second, and third plans, respectively, population growth stunted progress in per capita terms.[19] Per capita income during the first three plans grew at annual rates of 1.6, 2.5, and 0.3 percent.[20]

That India made progress during the first fifteen years of planning is generally accepted; it is the extent of progress that is debatable. By the end of the third plan, a deceleration in the Indian economy had started. Even before the plan ended, strains in the economy were evident. India had fought two wars in three years—with China, in 1962, and with Pakistan, in 1965. The wars had resulted in an increase in defense spending, thus straining the country's limited resources. At the same time, foreign aid had leveled off, further reducing India's economic capacity.[21] One scholar blamed import substitution for the deceleration of the industrial growth in India.[22] According to this viewpoint, import substitution satisfied demands of a relatively small segment of the affluent consumers, who were able to absorb the growth in products only for a limited period of time. As a result, such demand was exhausted by the mid-1960s, whereupon the deceleration in industrial growth started.[23]

The industrial growth rate from the mid-1960s to the end of the 1970s declined substantially and, according to most estimates, remained below 5 percent. In comparison to the other less-developed economies, this progress was considered disappointing by most economists. Countries such as Brazil, Mexico, and Pakistan had higher growth rates than India in this period.[24] Even if lower-performing less-developed economies such as those of Bangladesh, Haiti, and Uganda are considered, India ranked "just above the average performance" during this period.[25]

These fifteen years are considered a period of industrial stagnation in India by many economists.[26] It could be argued that India experienced a "dual phenomenon of deceleration and slow growth" in the industrial sector.[27] As Isher Judge Ahluwalia pointed out, "heavy industries, e.g., machinery, transport, equipment and basic metals, suffered a major slowdown in growth, while light industries such as food manufacturing and textiles never experienced a takeoff."[28] Overall, however, Ahluwalia also considered this period to be marked by industrial stagnation.[29]

A bright spot in the Indian economy during the period of industrial stagnation was the acceleration in food production brought about by the Green Revolution. The Indian government decided in the mid-1960s to revolutionize agriculture by increasing fertilizer production, expanding irrigation, and introducing high-yielding varieties of grain. The decision was to adopt a strategy of "agricultural development with balanced industrial support."[30] This ended a fifteen-year period of vacillation by the Indian government on agriculture in relation to industry.

The Green Revolution affected only about one-fifth of the agricultural land. However, the unprecedented growth in agriculture made India self-reliant in food by the mid-1970s. Two scholars on India noted the following in a book published in 1987:

Unlike most Third World countries, India invested in agricultural technology. Agricultural production since the mid-1970s has made India self-sufficient with regard to food, an achievement that distinguishes it not only from most Third World countries but also from the Soviet Union and most of Eastern Europe.[31]

Economic as well as political factors contributed to India's industrial stagnation. Although the two categories are interlinked, we can separate them for analytical purposes. The economic factors responsible for India's industrial stagnation were poor performance of the public sector industries, underutilization of the heavy industries, indifference to consumer products, restrictions on the import of foreign technology, two consecutive droughts (in 1966 and 1967), a leveling off of foreign aid, and, possibly, import substitution.[32] The Indian business community blamed "the dilution of demand because of [the] high level of prices," which reflected "partly the high cost of production and partly the high element of taxation."[33]

Isher Judge Ahluwalia, in his book on industrial stagnation in India, pointed to four factors that contributed to such stagnation:

(a) slow growth of agricultural incomes and their effect in limiting the demand for industrial goods; (b) the slowdown in public investment after the mid-sixties with its particular impact on infrastructural investment; (c) poor management of the infrastructure sectors, leading to severe infrastructural constraints; and (d) the industrial policy framework, including both domestic industrial policies and trade policies and their effect in creating a high cost industrial structure in the economy.[34]

Two wars that India fought in a short period of time, the first one with China in 1962 and the second with Pakistan in 1965, were among the major political causes of India's industrial deceleration as the wars led to an increase in defense spending, thus straining the country's resources. At the same time, American sympathy for India had decreased and India had started experiencing a decline in the volume of the American foreign aid. When Richard Nixon became president of the United States in 1969, that nation further distanced itself from India and tilted toward India's rival, Pakistan, which further reduced American aid to India.

Nixon's support of Pakistan against India was particularly evident during another war between India and Pakistan, which was fought in 1971 over the secession of the eastern province of Pakistan, which became the independent nation of Bangladesh as a result of the war. India had supported the secessionist province out of its security considerations in the region or, rather, out of a desire to maintain hegemony there. The war, however, aggravated India's economic problems, not only due to defense spending but also due to the influx of millions of refugees from Bangladesh into India. Two years after this war came the oil price escalation of 1973. The oil price increase of 1973, as well as that of six years later, further slowed the growth of the Indian economy. India continues to depend on imported oil for a substantial portion of its energy needs.

The growing divisiveness within India's political elites and political instability also contributed to the economic slowdown. India had become accustomed to political stability under the one-party dominant rule of the Congress Party. Congress, as it is usually called, was established in 1885 and later waged a struggle for India's independence from the British colonial rule. After India achieved independence, it became the single dominant party in the country. Its hegemony, however, was challenged by other political parties and shattered by the late 1960s, in part due to factional politics within itself. Jawaharlal Nehru, India's first prime minister, had kept the Congress Party united through his charismatic personality and a well-controlled system of patronage. However, after his death in 1964, the schism in the Congress, which had always existed, became marked, and by 1969, the party had officially split. At the same time, opposition parties gained power, particularly in the states.

The split of the Congress Party initially helped Indira Gandhi, who had become prime minister in 1966, to consolidate her power and win an impressive victory at the polls in 1971. However, within a few years, opposition to her regime, aggravated by the economic slowdown, led her to impose an authoritarian rule on India for a twenty-one-month period during 1975–1977. In 1977, the Congress Party, led by Indira Gandhi and known by the initial of her first name, Congress (I), was defeated, and the first coalition government—the Janata coalition—was formed in India. This coalition was defeated in the parliamentary elections three years later and Indira Gandhi's party again won power and returned her to her position as prime minister.

During the period of 1964 through 1980, i.e., between Nehru's death and Indira Gandhi's return to power, India wavered between policies of economic liberalization and government controls, including nationalization. Nehru's successor as Prime Minister, Lal Bahadur Shastri, is given credit for starting a liberalization program that continued for a few years into Indira Gandhi's first tenure as prime minister. This liberalization was opposed by the leftist segments of the ruling party as well as by some opposition parties. By the end of the 1960s, Indira Gandhi gave in to these pressures and reimposed government controls on industries. She also nationalized the insurance and banking industries. This socialist wave did not last long, and political pressures compelled the government to again relax controls on the industries. The liberalization continued under the authoritarian rule of 1975–1977.

The Janata coalition government (which came to power in 1977) attempted to return to India's economic policies of the mid-1950s. Its economic concerns were largely driven by the groups providing political support. As Atul Kohli wrote: "the policies [of the Janata government] were aimed primarily at satisfying the interests of agrarian and industrial capitalism."[35]

Some scholars believe that industrial stagnation continued for several years because it benefited certain groups. Prem Shanker Jha noted:

> The decisive cause of economic stagnation after 1966 is political and not economic. It is the rise to dominance of an intermediate class or stratum consisting of market-oriented peasant proprietors, small manufacturers, traders and other self-employed groups, which benefited from economic stagnation and had a vested interest in its perpetuation. The growing political power of this class was reflected in the steady reinforcement of economic controls on all industrial activity in the country until these applied a severe brake to the growth of output and employment in the organized sector.[36]

A similar view was expressed by P. N. Dhar in his analysis of the Indian economy. According to Dhar, "The slow-growth syndrome of India has benefited powerful interests spread over big farmers, small industrialists, trade union elite and several business groups operating in sheltered markets or trading in scarce commodities."[37] The economic slowdown thus resulted in the empowerment of certain groups. The economic controls from which these groups benefited came under attack with the return of Indira Gandhi to power in 1980.

The Janata government, which Indira Gandhi defeated in 1980, had emphasized cottage industries (for example, production of bricks in the house or backyard) and small-scale enterprises more than large-scale endeavors.[38] The economic changes introduced by Indira Gandhi were the precursor of her son's far bolder policies. Scholars and commentators agree that political expediency and, possibly, age (she was born in 1917) had made Indira Gandhi less an ideologue and more a pragmatic leader. She now wanted industrial growth, even though it meant giving less attention to social justice and the eradication of poverty. Economic liberalization under Indira Gandhi did not mean the end of government controls over industries or closing down of public sector industries. Instead, it signaled an era of fewer controls over the private sector. Bureaucratic controls such as licensing and price-fixing were relaxed in the private sector, exports were encouraged, and a more hospitable environment for foreign investment and technology was created. The changes thus "marked a significant shift away from the isolationist policies of the 1960s and early 1970s when self-reliance was a dominant theme."[39]

Rajiv Gandhi faced an India burdened by increasing political and religious violence and an economy which, following the policy shift initialized by his mother, needed further invigoration. While popular support provided the political environment for further innovations in the economy, his relative youth (Rajiv Gandhi was forty at the time he became prime minister), Western education, modern outlook, fascination with technology and computers, and commitment to a developed secular India were the motivating forces behind his agenda to introduce major economic changes.

In setting up his political program, Rajiv Gandhi did not merely carry forward what Indira Gandhi had started in the early 1980s but rather went much beyond it. Evidence indicates that he had indeed influenced Indira Gandhi's economic liberalization initiative.[40] A few scholars believe that Rajiv Gandhi's commitment to liberalization was "neither personal nor ideological" and that, unlike British Prime Minister Margaret Thatcher and U.S. President Ronald Reagan, he was a pragmatist.[41] Most scholars discount this viewpoint and argue that Rajiv Gandhi had a personal as well as an ideological commitment to his agenda for the country. His biographers portray him as an intensely private man who cared, not only for his personal and his family's interests, but even more for his country's interests. After having grown up in the shadow of his grandfather, Jawaharlal Nehru, it was virtually impossible not to have acquired an ideological commitment to economic development and social justice for India. Of course, like any realistic and ambitious political leader, he wanted to stay in power as long as possible. If that required some compromises, such as accommodating certain groups and making some policy changes, he showed flexibility in modifying his agenda. However, he never gave up his personal as well as ideological commitment to his program.

MOBILIZING FOR POWER

Any scion of the almost legendary Nehru family would need little effort to mobilize political support of the masses in India. Rajiv Gandhi had the added advantage of the sympathy generated by the assassination of his mother. Despite the lack of political experience and his relatively young age, Rajiv Gandhi was sworn in as the prime minister immediately after Mrs. Gandhi's death. Had he waited a few months to hold parliamentary elections, the sympathy factor would probably have lost some of its value. Rajiv Gandhi understood that, and held elections in December of that year (1984). His party won 80 percent of the parliamentary seats. Even his grandfather, Jawaharlal Nehru, whose sustained popularity among the Indian masses may not be matched again, never won by such a margin.

India is a Third World country and its people, or rather, the predominant Hindus, worship hundreds or perhaps thousands of gods. Indian masses are prone to elevate their leaders to an almost superhuman, god-like status. (Such an adulation of political leaders is far less likely in a Western society.) The euphoria created during and after the 1984 parliamentary elections did not resemble any earlier political event in independent India's history. Rajiv Gandhi was an untainted political leader who had no skeletons in his closet. "Mr. Clean" promised an honest government without corruption, which is an unrealizable dream in India or, for that matter, any other country. The Indian masses, however, believed in that dream. Rajiv Gandhi also promised economic growth through modernization, technology, and the use of computers and stressed his mother's ideal of eradicating poverty.

It is not only the majority Hindus who perceived this mortal to be god-like, albeit for a short period; the minorities also had faith in him. Rajiv Gandhi believed in his grandfather's goal of creating a secular India where people of different faiths could practice their religions and be tolerant of each other. Rajiv Gandhi had made it clear that he opposed discrimination against religious, tribal or caste minorities. The minorities believed in the promise, in part because his earlier life never gave any hint of religious or caste bigotry. Not a particularly religious person, he had married a Roman Catholic Italian woman whom he met in England and, perhaps genuinely, believed in the equality of all human beings, regardless of religion, tribe, or caste.

The business groups and middle classes supported Rajiv Gandhi because of the economic liberalization and reforms including lowering taxes (introduced in the beginning of his administration). When his reforms were opposed by the leftist groups and the Gandhians (followers of Mahatma Gandhi's philosophy) who wanted social justice based on higher taxes for the rich and attention to the villages and the poor, Rajiv Gandhi retracted from the course of reform. That move made him unpopular among the business groups and middle classes, which had initially supported him.

In a commentary published in *Foreign Affairs* in 1987, Paul H. Kreisberg wrote that by early 1987, "the honeymoon was over for Gandhi."[42] The state elections held in March 1987 indicated a substantial erosion in his political base—a third of the state legislatures earlier controlled by the Congress Party had been won by the opposition parties.

Minhaz Merchant, in his biography of Rajiv Gandhi, provided a detailed account of "the fall from grace."[43] Merchant listed

three unconnected events [that] nearly destroyed Rajiv Gandhi in 1987: . . . the Bofors scandal [involving the sale of weapons by the Swedish Company Bofors to India allegedly involving huge bribes to Indian politicians and officials], . . . the Nusli Wadia-Dhirubhai Ambani feud [the two were prominent Indian businessmen whose feud apparently involved Rajiv Gandhi] and . . . the Zail Singh-Rajiv Gandhi confrontation [Zail Singh was India's president and relations between him and Rajiv Gandhi were strained and grew worse].[44]

It appears that the elements were also against Rajiv Gandhi. India experienced a very severe drought in 1987, which affected its agricultural output and increased inflation. The drought was handled well by Rajiv Gandhi's government, but the hardships faced by the poor were serious enough to cause a further decline in Rajiv Gandhi's popularity. Merchant wrote: "By the end of 1987, the failure of the south-west monsoon had come to embody the failure of his regime."[45]

When Rajiv Gandhi became prime minister, the hopes of the Indian masses were raised more than ever before. Now the god-like leader appeared a mere mortal, who was not above the temptations of money allegedly gained through illegal means. Rajiv Gandhi was no longer the leader for whom Indians had hoped. Notwithstanding the achievements of his government in improving the Indian economy, his defeat in the elections appeared likely. Rajiv Gandhi's greatest opponent was a former political ally, V. P. Singh, who now promised a clean instead of a corrupt government, economic growth, and domestic peace between various religious and ethnic groups. Campaigning as the leader of a coalition of parties, Singh won the parliamentary elections in November 1989 and replaced Rajiv Gandhi as the prime minister. However, Singh did not survive in power for even two years, and elections were again held in the summer of 1991. Rajiv Gandhi now seemed ready for a comeback. Most polls did not predict a clear victory for any single party, but the Congress Party once again appeared to be the strongest. Had Rajiv Gandhi lived, he would likely have become the prime minister for the second time, possibly as the head of a coalition government. His assassination generated sympathy for the party. However, this did not result in a clear victory for the Congress Party, so a coalition government under the leadership of a Congress Party veteran, P. V. Narasimha Rao, was formed.

IMPLEMENTING THE NEW PROGRAM: THE POLICY DIMENSION

The economic liberalization policy introduced by Rajiv Gandhi, albeit haltingly, concentrated on reducing government controls over private industries, encouraging private investment, improving the quality of products and making them available at competitive prices, importing technology, reducing restrictions on imports, increasing exports, and simplifying the tax laws. The reduction of government controls in areas such as the licensing of industries and setting of production quotas encouraged competition and productivity. Industries could now decide what and how much to produce. Import duties were lowered and, in some cases, altogether eliminated. In general, the emphasis was on controlling tariffs rather than setting import quotas, as was prevalent in earlier regimes. Exports were encouraged through measures such as tax incentives.

Scholars debate to what extent Rajiv Gandhi's policies differed from those of Indira Gandhi. A sympathetic biographer of Rajiv Gandhi wrote that "Rajiv's free-market economic thinking was a break from Mrs. Gandhi's state-controlled, ideology-laden, socialistic economic policy."[46] Most experts on India, however, believe that the changes introduced by Rajiv Gandhi were significant but not a radical departure from the past policies. Commenting on the first two years of Rajiv Gandhi's government, Stanley Kochanek noted that "the changes he has introduced, however, retain the basic structure of regulatory system. They do not dismantle or replace it."[47] He further argued that many of Rajiv Gandhi's policies had been tried in the past with rather limited long-term success.[48] The *Economist* (a British magazine), in a survey of India published in May 1987, was far more critical of Rajiv Gandhi's liberalization policy.[49] According to the *Economist,* some critics altogether rejected the label of "liberalization" for Rajiv Gandhi's policy and called it "half-hearted, ill-thought-out tinkering."[50]

Rajiv Gandhi's policy may not have been completely innovative, but it certainly signaled a major change from the past. The socialist pattern of society on which India had started building an economic system in the 1950s was based on the concepts of centralized planning and social justice. While a private sector was permitted, the public sector was given predominance in the economic system. Tax laws were passed to make the rich pay for economic development and reduce the economic gap between rich and poor. Under this system, controls and licenses had created bottlenecks to sustained growth. The result was sluggish economic progress. Tax evasion by the rich and graft by the politicians and bureaucrats were accepted rules of the game. The liberalization introduced earlier had brought encouraging improvements in the economy but was not sufficient for stable growth. Rajiv Gandhi made a bold attempt to break away from the old system by expanding on the liberalization already in motion.

The Indian economic system of centralized planning, controls, and licenses had benefited certain groups, notably large-scale farmers, business groups sheltered by the government's protectionist policy, labor unions, bureaucrats controlling public sector industries, and the leftists, who were opposed to an extensive liberalization. The new liberalization policy was criticized by those groups and was often called prorich, mainly because it had lowered individual and corporate taxes, as well as the wealth tax, and had provided incentives to entrepreneurs. As a result of this criticism, some changes were made in the taxation policy and appropriation for antipoverty programs was increased. The essential course of Rajiv Gandhi's liberal policy, however, was not altered.

NATURE AND SCOPE OF CHANGE

Notwithstanding the turbulence in Indian politics, the verdict of most scholars is that the country made unprecedented progress during Rajiv Gandhi's term as prime minister. Commenting on the economic growth, Bhabani Sen Gupta wrote: "The first five years of Rajiv Gandhi's prime ministership were years of all-round improvement, the last two years particularly so."[51] Minhaz Merchant provided some details of the improvement:

Agricultural production in 1989–90 climbed to a record annual level of 180 metric tons, nearly thirty-five percent higher than the average level under Mrs. Gandhi's term in the early 1980s. [Rajiv Gandhi was voted out of office in November 1989. However, he could legitimately be given credit for the 1989–1990 progress.]

Industrial production grew at a compound rate of over twelve percent a year in 1985–90, Gross National Product (GNP) at nearly six percent a year. Inflation stayed below nine percent during the same period.

Despite the country's worst drought in 1987, GNP still grew at 2.5 percent in that year and by over nine percent in 1988–89.[52]

Rajiv Gandhi made the Indian economy market-oriented. However, his economic policy was centralist. When we call his economic policy liberal, we do not imply that he introduced liberalism in the European sense.[53] He did not, for example, seek to denationalize public sector industries, nor did he dream of introducing in India the social welfare programs of Europe. Instead, it was a program to reduce government controls over industries, reform taxation, and still keep some government subsidies (i.e., to higher education) and antipoverty programs. In those efforts, Rajiv Gandhi's success was more than moderate, but not dramatic. The country prospered and developed a large middle class, despite the severe drought of 1987, political unrest in Punjab, Assam (a northeastern state), and Kashmir, and protests by various interest groups at different times. In a 1988 report, the World Bank wrote: "Among the low-income countries, India and China stand out with strong growth, despite the worsening environment of the early 1980s."[54]

In some areas, Rajiv Gandhi's record is less than impressive. He did not succeed in making the public sector industries efficient. His antipoverty program made no significant progress in reducing poverty in the country. Indeed, since the rich and middle classes improved their lot, the chasm between them and the poor increased. The overall problem of distributive justice remained as unresolved when he left office as when he moved into it. He established a tenuous peace in Assam, but Kashmir and Punjab grew even more restless, and various ethnic and religious groups of India continued their feuds. His efforts to make peace with his neighbors—Bangladesh, Pakistan, and Sri Lanka—were also not successful. On the international level, he followed his mother's policy of leaning toward the Soviet Union and keeping a distance from the United States. His economic policy, however, did prepare the basis for the improvement in economic relations between India and the United States that occurred at a later date. More important, he laid the groundwork for the economic revolution with which Prime Minister P. V. Narasimha Rao's name has come to be associated.

Rajiv Gandhi's successor, V. P. Singh, was in office less than two years, most of which he spent battling his political opponents. He gave more attention to the agricultural sector than had been done under Rajiv Gandhi's government, but the economic policies of Rajiv Gandhi continued for the most part. Rao, who succeed Singh in 1991, brought dramatic changes in the Indian economic system. Rao had come to power after the collapse of communism in the former Soviet Union and Eastern Europe. Since socialism had been discredited, drastic economic changes faced less opposition than was the case under Rajiv Gandhi. Rajiv Gandhi, and even Indira Gandhi before him, had initiated significant economic reforms but were unable to sustain many of them due to the opposition of the groups adversely affected. Opposition to Rao's policy was weak largely due to the collapse of communism and the rapid introduction of privatization in several countries.

Rao's economic reforms, which were first incorporated in the Industrial Policy of 1991, carried further Rajiv Gandhi's policy of removing restrictions on industries. Rao abolished many such restrictions, sharply reduced the budget deficit, devaluated Indian currency to promote exports, cut direct export subsidies, and encouraged foreign investment.[55] Never since 1947 had India been so hospitable to foreign investment. A number of American companies, including Coca-Cola, Pepsi, IBM, Kellogg, and Ray-Ban, took advantage of the new opportunities in India. Rao's government also reduced subsidies to farmers (income tax is not levied on farm income in India) and proposed far-reaching changes in taxation. It began the process—perhaps the most difficult in the new policy—of closing down those public enterprises that were virtually bankrupt and had become economic liabilities.

Rao's policy has faced opposition, primarily from the leftist and nationalist groups. The leftist groups resent the shift toward privatization and foreign investment, while the nationalist groups are opposed to what they consider foreign influence in the name of investment. Experts consider Rao's policies irreversible. Of course, the real test of these policies will take a few years, when it is known which groups benefited from them and to what extent.

INTERPRETING RAJIV GANDHI AS LEADER

Rajiv Gandhi had emerged as India's leader in 1984 following the assassination of Indira Gandhi. The turbulent politics of India had disempowered certain ideas, institutions, and groups by that time. Such disempowerment, along with the sympathy generated by Indira Gandhi's death and the mystique of India's most celebrated political family, enabled Rajiv Gandhi to institute major reforms that became the precursor of Prime Minister Rao's much bolder economic policy.

Since the 1950s, India had pursued a policy of a mixed economy of public and private enterprises, of which the concepts of centralized planning and social justice formed the core. In practice, these concepts built an inefficient system of public enterprises and a plethora of government controls over private enterprise. As a result, after some industrial growth that lasted until the mid-1960s, the country experienced industrial stagnation for a decade and a half. Owners of large farms, industrialists sheltered by the government's protectionist policy, labor unions, bureaucrats in public enterprises, and leftists opposed to private enterprise had benefited during these three decades. When Indira Gandhi returned to power in 1980, she appeared less concerned about social justice and the eradication of poverty than about achieving economic growth through a reduction of government controls over private enterprise. Indira Gandhi's policies of the early 1980s had started an era of empowerment for the ideas of economic liberalization and of less concern for social justice. They benefited the business groups and a growing middle class. Rajiv Gandhi's economic policy promoted those ideas and the groups to an extent that was perhaps not envisioned by Indira Gandhi.

The empowerment of the idea of "clean" government was also a characteristic, although for only a short period, of Rajiv Gandhi's tenure as prime minister. Corruption in India, as in many other, especially Third World, countries, is widespread and an almost accepted rule of the political game. Rajiv Gandhi promised a corruption-free government. For a while, that idea caught on, and a large number of Indians believed that Rajiv Gandhi was, indeed, "Mr. Clean." That image of Rajiv Gandhi, however, did not last long, since his name was linked to one of the greatest kickback schemes of late twentieth-century Indian politics.

Rajiv Gandhi's campaign for a "clean" government, his youth, his promise of continuation of a secular India with reduction in sectarian violence, his program of a rejuvenated economy supported by technology, and, of course, the family connections and the sympathy generated by his mother's death made him, in 1984, the most popular political leader that India had witnessed since his grandfather, Jawaharlal Nehru, had governed the country as prime minister (from 1947 to 1964). Rajiv Gandhi won more seats in parliament than even Nehru had in any of the three elections in which he ran.

Rajiv Gandhi's pragmatism sustained his popularity for some time. When he introduced his tax policy in 1985, which favored the rich and business he was criticized for being pro-rich and, consequently, he changed that policy. As a result, taxes were increased on "luxury items" such as cars, television sets, and refrigerators and the antipoverty programs were given attention.

Rajiv Gandhi had raised the hopes of the Indian masses to an unprecedented level, and the latter elevated him to an almost god-like status. The country did prosper under him, but the economic gains were uneven. The vast majority of the Indians, who are poor, benefited little from the economic reforms. A severe drought in 1987 decreased food production, and the poor suffered greater hardships than the affluent segments of the society. At the same time, the press revealed details of a scandal implicating Rajiv Gandhi's political cronies and even himself in the sale of weapons by the Swedish company Bofors to India. Furthermore, sectarian violence showed no signs of abating. By the time the parliamentary elections were held in November 1989, Rajiv Gandhi's political stock had suffered such damage that his defeat was not a surprise to either political pundits or the average voters.

Less than two years later, Rajiv Gandhi appeared destined for a political comeback. Parliamentary elections were again being held, and the Congress Party was leading in the public opinion polls. During a campaign rally in the southern state of Tamil Nadu, on May 21, 1991, a female terrorist, who was affiliated with the Sri Lankan Tamil guerrillas, pretended to pay respect to Rajiv Gandhi by the traditional Indian method of touching his feet. However, this was a ploy to assassinate him, and a bomb strapped to the terrorist's body exploded, killing Rajiv Gandhi and several bystanders.

Sri Lanka's Tamil minority (an ethnic group) was demanding secession from the country to form an independent state of its own. Rajiv Gandhi was opposed and had sent Indian troops to Sri Lanka in 1987 to defeat the Tamil guerrillas fighting the government. He had also taken measures to crack down on the Sri Lankan Tamil guerrillas' operations in Tamil Nadu. The assassination of Rajiv Gandhi was the guerrillas' revenge against him. It also mirrored India's turbulence of the late twentieth century.

NOTES

1. Although official reports indicate a decline in poverty in India, a majority of the Indians continue to live in abject poverty.

2. Quoted in William J. Barnds, *India, Pakistan, and the Great Powers* (New York: Praeger, 1972), p. 48.

3. The discussion on political violence is based on an article by one of the coauthors. See Kul B. Rai, "India Remains a Powder Keg of Political Violence," *Hartford Courant,* June 5, 1991, p. D15.

4. This discussion is limited to political violence, not violent crime in India which, despite an increase in recent years, remains low in comparison to the United States.

5. Paul H. Kreisberg, "India after Indira," *Foreign Affairs,* Spring 1985, p. 876.

6. Minhaz Merchant, *Rajiv Gandhi: The End of a Dream* (New Delhi: Viking Penguin India, 1991), p. 165.

7. See Robert L. Hardgrave, Jr. and Stanley H. Kochanek, *India: Government and Politics in a Developing Nation,* 5th ed. (New York: Harcourt Brace, 1993), pp. 355–356.

8. For a brief history of the public sector in pre-1947 India, see R. K. Sinha and Sudama Singh, *Economics of Public Enterprises* (New Delhi: South Asian Publishers, 1983), pp. 19–23. For a summary of the various interpretations of the public sector's dominance in the Indian economy, see Baldev Raj Nayar, *India's Mixed Economy: The Role of Ideology and Interest in its Development* (Bombay: Popular Prakashan, 1989), p. 123.

9. For a brief discussion of the import substitution policy, see Debesh Bhattacharya, "Growth and Distribution in India," *Journal of Contemporary Asia,* 19 (2) (1989): 153.

10. Kathleen Healy, *Rajiv Gandhi: The Years of Power* (New Delhi: Vikas Publishing House, 1989), p. 240.

11. James Manor, "How and Why Liberal and Representative Politics Emerged in India," *Political Studies,* March 1990, p. 37.

12. Atul Kohli, *The State and Poverty in India* (New York: Cambridge University Press, 1987), pp. 64–65.

13. See K. V. Varghese, *Economic Problems of Modern India,* 2nd ed. (New Delhi: Ashish Publishing House, 1988), p. 267.

14. Hardgrave and Kochanek, p. 358.

15. Ibid., pp. 358–359.

16. Varghese, p. 10.

17. Ibid., p. 10.

18. P. N. Dhar, "The Indian Economy: Past Performance and Current Issues," in Robert E. B. Lucas and Gustav F. Papanek, eds., *The Indian Economy: Recent Developments and Future Prospects* (Boulder, CO: Westview Press, 1988), p. 6.

19. Varghese, p. 18.

20. Ibid., p. 18.

21. Dhar, p. 6.

22. Bhattacharya, p. 153.

23. Ibid., p. 153.

24. Isher Judge Ahluwalia, *Industrial Growth in India: Stagnation since the Mid-Sixties* (Delhi: Oxford University Press, 1985), pp. 2–3.

25. Ibid., p. 2.

26. See, for example, Prem Shanker Jha, *India: A Political Economy of Stagnation* (Bombay: Oxford University Press, 1980).

27. Ahluwalia, p. 7.

28. Ibid., p. 7.

29. Ibid., p. 32.

30. Hardgrave and Kochanek, p. 379.

31. Lloyd I. Rudolph and Susanne Hueber Rudolph, *In Pursuit of Lakshmi: The Political Economy of the Indian State* (Chicago: The University of Chicago Press, 1987), p. 11.

32. See Ahluwalia, pp. 8–9, 156; and Dhar, p. 6.

33. Ramkrishna Bajaj, *Indian Economy: Emerging Perspectives* (New Delhi: Allied Publishers Private Limited, 1986), p. 6.

34. Ahluwalia, p. 168.

35. Kohli, p. 91.

36. Jha, p. vii.

37. Dhar, p. 20.

38. For a discussion of the Janata government's policy, see Jha, pp. 191–198.

39. Hardgrave and Kochanek, pp. 365–366.

40. See Kreisberg, pp. 874–875.

41. Stanley A. Kochanek, "Regulation and Liberalization Theology in India," *Asian Survey,* December 1986, p. 1308.

42. Paul H. Kreisberg, "Gandhi at Midterm," *Foreign Affairs,* Summer 1987, p. 1056.

43. Merchant, pp. 206–218.

44. Ibid., p. 206.

45. Ibid., p. 238.

46. Merchant, p. 341.

47. Kochanek, p. 1289.

48. Ibid.

49. See the *Economist,* May 9, 1987, pp. 1–19.

50. Ibid., p. 11.

51. Bhabani Sen Gupta, *Rajiv Gandhi: A Political Study* (Delhi: Konark Publishers, 1989), p. 134.

52. Merchant, p. 325.

53. See Fredie A. Mehta, "Growth, Controls and the Private Sector," in Lucas and Papanek, p. 204.

54. Quoted in Sen Gupta, p. 134.

55. See "India's Revolution: Socialism Out, Free Market In," *New York Times,* March 29, 1992, p. 1.

—— eight ——————————————————————————

Deng Xiaoping: China's Economic Transformation

With over a billion people, nuclear weapons, and an invigorated economy, China is a virtual world power.[1] It has the third largest economy in the world, next only to the United States and Japan. The architect of the Chinese economic miracle is Deng Xiaoping who, starting in the late 1970s, introduced capitalism in China's planned economy. Prior to Deng Xiaoping's economic reforms, the country's economy and politics were controlled by Mao Zedong (1893–1976), one of the greatest leaders of communism, who established a Communist state in China in 1949.

The history of China since 1949 has been marked by ideological conflicts, economic experiments, and turbulence in politics. The turbulence transformed China's political and economic institutions and caused the deaths of millions of Chinese citizens. In order to understand the role of Deng Xiaoping in China's transformation and turbulence, we first present an overview of the economy and politics of China.

THE NATIONAL POLITICAL-ECONOMIC CONTEXT

China is a multiethnic state with fifty-six distinct nationalities. The most numerous and the dominant of these nationalities is the Han group, which constitutes 93 percent of the total population. The Hans control the economy and politics of the country and historically have subjugated other nationalities, whom they considered culturally inferior. The superiority complex of the Hans still prevails. A semiofficial but reliable source on China described the Hans as "more developed than the minority nationalities in the political, economic and cultural spheres."[2]

Of the minority nationalities, the Zhuang is the largest, with over 13 million members, while the Hui, Uygurs, Yi, and Miao number over 5 million each. The Manchus, Tibetans, Mongols, and Koreans, numbering between 1 and 5 million each, are also among the prominent groups. The smallest of the fifty-five minority nationalities is called Hezhen and has under 2,000 members.[3]

The minority nationalities were historically concentrated along the borders of China. The government recognized their concentration by creating autonomous regions; however, it has vigorously encouraged the movement of minority nationalities to other areas, and of the Hans to the autonomous regions. While tension between the Hans and the minority groups continues, it has not created the type of political turbulence that some other multiethnic states, notably the former states of Yugoslavia and the Soviet Union, have faced.

China has also avoided two other major sources of political turbulence, namely, religion and language. The first constitution adopted by Communist China (in 1954) granted freedom of religious belief to all citizens. Communism, however, advocates atheism, and the Communist government of China discouraged the practice of religion for at least three decades. Since 1979, however, a more tolerant attitude toward religion has prevailed. The government recognizes only five organized religions: Buddhism, Islam, Protestantism, Roman Catholicism, and Taoism.[4] The combined total of the followers of these five religions is less than 20 million.[5]

Religion, as understood in the West, has not been historically practiced in China, which, for example, never had an organized church or hierarchy of religious leaders. Religion to the Chinese is a code of ethics and customs, which is based on tradition and the teachings of the learned. Such an interpretation of religion has spared the Chinese turbulence in this area, and religious conflicts, which have killed millions in many countries, have been unknown in China.

While several dialects are spoken in China, the government considers Putonghua, or Standard Chinese, as the national language. The writing of the ideographic characters of the Chinese language has been made uniform. A phonetic alphabet called Pinyin has been devised and is used throughout the country. China has not faced the kind of conflict on language that is commonplace in India.

China has, however, experienced conflicts throughout its history, and twentieth-century Chinese history in particular has been plagued by violence. Chinese written history began 3,500 years ago. As in many other countries, several dynasties ruled over various parts of the country, and wars between kingdoms, often for territorial expansion, were common. The nineteenth century ushered in a period of Western commercial penetration, when the Qing (pronounced Ch'ing and also called Manchu) dynasty controlled most of China. Japan sought control over China at the same time and gained Korea, Taiwan, and some other Chinese territory following victory in a war with China in 1895. The Chinese resented foreign control and blamed the ruling Qing government for it. The unsuccessful rebellion against foreigners called the Boxer Uprising (1900), followed by the successful Wuchang Uprising (1911), led to the abdication of the monarch and the end of dynastic rule in China. A republic was established in 1912.

Pre-Communist twentieth-century China experienced a bloody civil war for more than two decades. The civil war began in 1926 between the Communists and the ruling Nationalists. The Chinese Communist Party had been founded in 1921. The Nationalist Party, called Kuomintang (KMT), was founded in 1912. Its greatest leader was Sun Yat-sen, who had played a pivotal role in ending the monarchy in China. Following Sun Yat-sen's death in 1925, Chiang Kai-shek had become KMT's leader. Even with the victory of the Communists and the fleeing of Chiang Kai-shek and the Nationalists to Taiwan, where they founded the Republic of China, turbulence in China continued. Turbulence in Communist China is detailed in the next section.

Like other Communist states, China has employed the facade of democracy in governmental structures. The first constitution promulgated in 1954 was followed by constitutions adopted in 1975, 1978, and again in 1982. China has a president who is head of state, a prime minister, a council of ministers, and a parliament, whose members are elected every five years. It is a quasi-federal country, which is divided into twenty-two provinces. There are, in addition, five autonomous regions and local government units such as cities and counties.

Power, even today, remains well-entrenched in the hands of the Communist Party, which has over 50 million members. Eight other political parties are permitted, but they are subordinate to the Communist Party and have no resemblance to the opposition parties of a democracy in the West. Conflicts in Communist China that created an environment of political turbulence have mostly arisen within the Communist Party hierarchy, and not in the other political parties or in governmental structures.

China's foreign policy also reflects some of the conflicts and dilemmas that it faces. China declares itself a peaceful nation in official pronouncements, and the Constitution of 1982 states:

China adheres to an independent foreign policy as well as to the five principles of mutual respect for sovereignty and territorial integrity, mutual non-aggression, non-interference in each other's internal affairs, equality and mutual benefit, and peaceful coexistence in developing diplomatic relations and economic and cultural exchanges with other countries; China consistently opposes imperialism, hegemonism and colonialism.[6]

In reality, however, China's foreign policy is guided as much by national interest as the foreign policy of any other country.

China started as a Communist state by aligning with the Soviet Union, its major benefactor at the time. A thirty-year treaty of "friendship, alliance, and mutual assistance" was signed by the two countries in 1950. In the 1950s, the Soviet Union was China's most important ally in the "struggle against Western imperialism," and its major trading partner. By 1960, however, severe strains, arising from ideological differences, border disputes, and the conflict over leadership of the Communist world, had developed between the two nations. The break was signified in 1960 by the Soviet withdrawal of its experts from China and the cancellation of a large number of aid and other agreements. For the next three decades, China and the Soviet Union feuded in the international arena through verbal skirmishes, occasional border clashes, and supporting hostile Third World countries by taking opposite sides. China also opposed what it called hegemonism by the Soviet Union and the United States.

During the period of conflict between China and the Soviet Union, the two countries not only maintained diplomatic relations, they also conducted trade and some cultural exchanges. The economic and cultural relations between them showed an improvement in the 1980s. The collapse of communism in the Soviet Union and Eastern Europe and China's steps toward capitalism have removed some of the major obstacles to the improvement of relations between the two sides.

The United States had first refused to recognize Communist China and officially held that position for three decades. The Republic of China (Taiwan) was recognized by the United States as the sole representative of China. The same position was taken by the United States in the United Nations, where Communist China was denied representation until 1971. In December 1978, the United States officially recognized Communist China and established diplomatic relations with that nation on January 1, 1979.

In the 1980s and 1990s, the United States became one of the largest trade partners of China. China enjoys most-favored-nation status in trade with the United States, which assures the lowest possible tariffs on Chinese imports into the United States. There are, however, some serious differences between China and the United States, arising from the less-than-satisfactory record of China on human rights, the reported Chinese sale of weapons and advanced technology to some Third World nations, and questionable Chinese practices in trade. These differences, and particularly the human rights issue, have on several occasions been raised in Congress and in the American media.

Although China was never as active as the United States or the Soviet Union in exporting ideology to other countries, it sought the leadership of the Third World and Communist nations, particularly in Asia, and carried out its own brand of interventionism. Starting with a direct role in the Korean

War, on the side of North Korea, in the early 1950s, China intervened, not only in East Asia, but also in Southeast Asia during the Vietnam War and, later, in South Asia, where it sided with the United States against the Soviet occupation of Afghanistan and supported Pakistan against India (with which it fought a war in 1962). China's interventions outside Asia were far less assertive.

NATIONAL TURBULENCE

The establishment of the People's Republic of China in 1949 was the outcome of a bloody civil war between the Nationalists (the Kuomintang or KMT Party), led by Chiang Kai-shek, and the Communists (the Chinese Communist Party), led by Mao Zedong. During the period of the Japanese invasion of China, which began in 1931, became full-scale in 1937, and ended with Japan's defeat in World War II in 1945, the Nationalists and the Communists had nominally formed a united front to fight the Japanese. The bitter struggle between the Nationalists and the Communists, however, continued during this period also. The early twentieth-century Chinese history prior to 1926 (the civil war had started that year) was not peaceful, either. A military uprising had led to the overthrow of the Qing (also called Manchu) dynasty in 1911 (the Qing dynasty had ruled China since 1644) and the establishment of a republic. The establishment of the republic did not diminish political turbulence in China and instead, ushered in another period of instability. This period is often referred to as the "warlord era," since local military leaders controlled different parts of the country. Sun Yat-sen attempted to bring some order, but he died in 1925 and the mantle of leadership passed to Chiang Kai-shek.

The post-1949 period in China has also been marred by national turbulence. Starting with the Chinese Communist Party's attempts to consolidate its power, the country has experienced several major upheavals that killed millions more Chinese citizens. (Although accurate estimates are hard to get, the loss of life during the first half of the twentieth century in China was very extensive.) We will consider three of these upheavals: the Great Leap Forward, the Cultural Revolution, and the Tiananmen Square Revolt. We must first discuss the reasons for national turbulence in Communist China.

Reasons for Turbulence in China

When China emerged as a Communist nation in 1949, the Communist Party needed to consolidate its power throughout the country. Opponents of the regime were dealt with harshly, and large-scale executions of the "enemies of the regime" were carried out. Most sources agree that hundreds of thousands of the Chinese were killed in this manner by the mid-1950s. While order was restored in just a few years, China continued to experience intermittent upheavals.

A major reason for such upheavals is the leaders' desire to promote fast-paced economic development and maintain stability in the society. Chinese leaders have embarked on several "political movements" to achieve these goals. A well-known writer stated: "Between 1949 and the end of the Cultural Revolution [1976], Mao launched no fewer than nine major political movements as well as several minor ones. And during each political movement a large number of Chinese people were wrongfully accused of crimes and thrown into prison."[7]

Communist rule, by its very nature, is repressive. It permits no opposition to the primacy of the Communist Party and the policies it espouses. Such authoritarianism generates discontent in the country, so repression becomes necessary. The violation of human rights becomes commonplace under these conditions. China has had an additional reason for continuing a repressive regime. The Chinese leaders and, perhaps, the vast majority of the Chinese people place a premium value on order in the society. Such thinking is the result of the chaos that prevailed in several periods in Chinese history. The memories of the events of the turbulent periods of the twentieth century are still fresh in Chinese minds. While most Chinese may accept the price of deprivation of human rights for order, especially if it is combined with increases in living standards and the quality of life in general, a sizable number of the people, particularly in the urban areas, resent dictatorial rule. The consequence is continuing political turbulence in China.

The Chinese economic growth, which was phenomenal indeed during the 1980s and early 1990s, ironically has contributed to turbulence. A familiar argument, which is valid in China, is that as living standards, literacy, and the information flow increase, so does the desire for freedom. In China there is another reason for turbulence related to economic growth. China introduced capitalism in its economy with a policy statement in 1978, while remaining a Communist country. A market economy has developed, but the public sector economy, although not as productive, also continues, and the government retains controls over the public as well as the private economies. By the late 1980s, some analysts started suggesting that China could not become any more capitalistic "without raising questions of radical systemic transformation."[8] The extreme scenario of the radical transformation is to accept the failure of communism and replace the command economy with a market economy. China is not yet ready for such a transformation. Thus, "a dispute about ultimate ends about socialism versus the capitalist order" continues.[9] Along with this debate, political turbulence also persists.

China has not only introduced radical economic changes, it has also started some equally radical social changes. No other social policy has generated as intense an emotional response from the people as the single-child family policy, which has been advocated by the government since 1979. The policy has been enforced far more strictly in the cities than in the villages. China's population growth rate has indeed declined, but opposition to the policy continues.[10] Minorities are officially exempted from the restriction of a single child, but this is not a blank check to have a large family, and minority reproduction is also kept under surveillance and, indeed, controlled. Exceptions have been introduced under which a Han Chinese can have more than one child; however, such exceptions are limited, and in general, the single-child family policy continues to exist and generates unhappiness among the Chinese.[11] Like many other traditional societies, the Chinese strongly prefer sons over daughters. One result of the single-child policy was the increasing use of the ultrasound scanner, which helped Chinese couples determine the sex of the fetus, so that a female could be aborted. A law passed in 1994, and put into effect in 1995, banned this practice, at least in theory.

The Great Leap Forward, 1958–1960

The new rulers of Communist China faced two major tasks: the restoration of order and the promotion of industrial as well as agricultural development. In the early 1950s, the Chinese government did restore order, and the Communist Party's control was extended throughout the country. Socialist reforms were introduced in social and economic areas. Women were declared equal to men and a nationwide land reform was implemented, taking land from the landlord class and redistributing it to the peasants. Industry, however, was given much greater attention than agriculture in the early and mid-1950s. The model used was that of Soviet central planning. Long-range planning was done in Beijing, while short-range planning and implementation were left to the provincial and local authorities. The first five-year plan (1953–1957) allocated more than half of capital investment to industry and less than 10 percent to agriculture. Cooperatives were set up for agriculture, thus collectivizing this sector. Industrial production in the public sector did expand during the first plan, but the agricultural gains were disappointing; besides, the centralized command economy of China lacked coordination between the national and local units. It was to remedy these problems that the Great Leap Forward policy was launched by Mao.

The goals of the Great Leap Forward were "more, faster, better, cheaper"—to impart ideological purity to the masses and arouse revolutionary fervor among them, increase industrial and agricultural production, and, above all, accelerate the transition from socialism to communism.[12] Agricultural cooperatives, which had been set up earlier, were now combined into vast communes, where not only production but also family activities such as cooking and child care became communal. According to the claim of the Central Committee of the Communist Party, in December 1958, "across China, 740,000 cooperatives had been merged into 26,000 communes. These comprised 120 million rural households, or 99 percent of the peasant population."[13] The peasants were even encouraged to set up backyard factories, which produced "shoddy, unsalable goods."[14]

The Great Leap Forward was a disaster and "within a year, the Chinese leadership retreated, blaming poor planning and the weather, but an ensuing famine in the countryside resulted in millions of deaths."[15] One source estimates that the famine "claimed 20 million lives or more between 1959 and 1962."[16] According to this study:

Half of those dying in China that year [1963] . . . were under ten years old. The Great Leap Forward, launched in the name of strengthening the nation by summoning all the people's energies, had turned back on itself and ended by devouring its young.[17]

The Cultural Revolution, 1966–1976

The Great Proletarian Cultural Revolution was the most turbulent period of over four decades in Communist China's history. A study on this revolution defines it "mainly in terms of violence and chaos."[18] Launched in the spring of 1966, the most noticeable havoc generated by the Cultural Revolution occurred in the first two years. The official date of the end of this revolution is 1976, implying that the death of Mao in that year ended the greatest of his campaigns.[19] The estimates of deaths in the Cultural Revolution range from 1 million to 20 million.[20] A much larger number of individuals, possibly up to 100 million, suffered from the violence and chaos of this tragedy.[21]

Divergent views have been expressed by scholars on the goals and causes of the Cultural Revolution.[22] It is generally agreed, however, that Mao felt the need for a major campaign in order to revitalize the "revolution." He believed that "the Chinese revolution was losing impetus because of Party conservatism and the lethargy of the huge and cumbrous bureaucracy, which had lost its ability to make "speedy or innovative decisions."[23] Those in positions of authority in the party who had taken "the capitalist road" were blamed in particular. Among the highest officials singled out for political attack were the State President, Liu Shaoqi, and the Party General Secretary, Deng Xiaoping. Liu, Deng, and their supporters were removed from office and publicly humiliated for adopting pragmatic economic policies, which were interpreted to be regressing China toward capitalism. The most important goal of the Cultural Revolution indeed was to restore the ideological fervor in the party.

It was not only factional party politics that caused the Cultural Revolution. There were also some deep-seated causes. Lynn White argued that "the specific causes of the Cultural Revolution as a mass movement lay in administrative policies used in the whole pre-1966 history of the PRC [People's Republic of China]."[24] Perhaps the most compelling specific cause mentioned by White is the policy of official campaigns. (The Great Leap Forward was the most important such campaign before 1966.) These campaigns "frightened citizens into avid compliance with state policies" and "legitimized violence."[25]

Starting with the cultural field, especially literature and art, the revolution spread into practically every area of Chinese life. Schools and colleges were closed during the height of the revolution and "cadre schools" were opened to teach ideological purity of communism, as interpreted by Mao. Young students, called Red Guards, were in the forefront of the revolutionary activity in killing and maiming the "reactionaries," destroying historic buildings and works of art, and openly criticizing their elders, including teachers and parents. The People's Liberation Army (PLA), whose head, Defense Minister Lin Bao, was the most important ally of Mao in the beginning of the Cultural Revolution, also functioned as the major vehicle to carry out this revolution.[26] Most accounts, however, give credit to the PLA for reining in the overenthusiastic radicals in the revolution and thus maintaining a semblance of order in the country.

THE TIANANMEN SQUARE REVOLT, 1989

The Tiananmen Square Revolt of June 1989 represents turbulence in China emanating from students rather than from the party leadership. The Great Leap Forward and the Cultural Revolution were both started by leadership; the Tiananmen Square episode instead was initiated by students.

By the late 1980s, the Chinese economy had improved enough to show visible signs of a better standard of living for the ordinary people. The entrepreneurs, as expected in any economy that introduces capitalism, had benefited far more than the average citizens. Economic gains invariably generate demands for freedom and democracy. That happened in China also. In addition, an improved economy increased the gulf between the rich and poor and brought far more corruption to China than the people had experienced under rigid communism. The growing chasm in income and the increased corruption made many Chinese citizens criticize the government and yearn for reforms.

Events in other countries also fueled the desire for democracy and freedom. A wave of democracy had spread throughout the Third World in the 1980s, and a number of countries had either adopted democracy or were on their way to that goal. At the same time, communism had begun to collapse in Eastern Europe and the Soviet Union. Not unexpectedly, such news, combined with the economic changes in China, made many Chinese seek freedom and reform in the society.

Some Chinese intellectuals wanted an end to repression and a general amnesty for the political prisoners. The Chinese students, as they had done on several occasions in the past, also joined the vanguard for change. The death, on April 15, 1989, of the former Party General Secretary Hu Yaobang provided an occasion for the students to express their demands. Hu was admired by the students for his lenient attitude toward the student demonstrations of 1986–1987 which had led to his dismissal. Thousands of students from the universities in Beijing staged a rally in the historic Tiananmen Square in the heart of Beijing on April 17.[27] The goal of the rally was not only to mourn Hu Yaobang's death but also to seek democratic reforms and an end to corruption. In just a few weeks, the ranks of student demonstrators swelled up to about a million, and students in over twenty other cities also staged protests.

There was little dialogue between the student leaders and the party hierarchy. Party General Secretary Zhao Ziyang was apparently sympathetic to the students, but the more powerful leaders, including Deng Xiaoping, Premier Li Peng, and President Yang Shangkun, considered the student revolt a threat to the regime and their personal power. Troops were mobilized and stationed in the outskirts of Beijing as well as in the city and near the famous Square now "occupied" by students.

The tragedy occurred in the early morning hours of June 4, when tanks literally rolled over the students in their way. Military action had been a possibility for some days and the vast majority of students had gotten out of the square. However, several thousand were present in the square at the time of the military action.

The media all over the world reported the deaths of hundreds, and possibily thousands, of students.[28] The Chinese government, however, considered the event a "counter-revolutionary rebellion" and according to its propaganda, "23 students had been killed accidentally outside the Square, while 5,000 soldiers were wounded and 150 of them had died."[29]

Repression in China continues. At the same time, the repercussions of Tiananmen Square still reverberate. The U.S. Congress annually granted most-favored-nation status to China for trade with reminders that unless the human rights record of China improved, trade concessions would be stopped. (Trade concessions and China's human rights record were virtually delinked by President Bill Clinton in 1994.) The U.S. Congress passed a law in 1993 granting permanent resident status to all those of the 49,000 Chinese students who were studying in the United States at the time of the Tiananmen Square tragedy and wished to stay here for fear of persecution in China.[30] Chinese students, particularly those who were studying abroad, continued to voice demands for democracy and freedom. China also lost its bid for hosting the Summer Olympics in the year 2000 due to its questionable human rights record.

POLITICAL PROFILE OF DENG XIAOPING AND HIS GROUP

Deng Xixian, who was known as Deng Xiaoping since about age twenty, was born in 1904 in a small village, Xiexing, in the district of Guang'an,

Sichuan province. His father, Deng Wenming, was a landowner. Deng Xiao-ping's mother was the first concubine of Deng Wenming, who had two other concubines and a wife.

Deng Xiaoping grew up in comfortable circumstances and, being the oldest son in the family, received special attention. After attending school for a few years, he traveled to France in 1920 as a work-study student. He stayed in France until early 1926, when he left for Moscow to study. Deng's stay in Moscow was short, and he returned to China in September 1926.

It is not clear how much studying Deng Xiaoping did during his sojourn in Europe. He is reported to have told author Edgar Snow that "he had not studied in France at all but worked as a laborer."[31] Deng did, however, start his training in practical politics when he was in France. Two years after the founding of the Communist Party of China, in 1921 in Shanghai, he became a leader of the Communist Youth League of China in France, and he joined the Communist Party of China the following year.[32]

Uli Franz, the German biographer of Deng Xiaoping, presented a sym-pathetic view of Deng's five years' stay in France. According to Franz, Deng learned the "French language, European manners, something of the nature of the West, and—the ABC's of Communism. A still rather diffusely rebel-lious landowner's son was transformed in France into a pragmatically think-ing and acting Communist."[33]

Very few political leaders of the world can match Deng Xiaoping's record in the number of party and government positions that he held. Three times in his career, starting as early as 1933, he suffered political ouster (the second time in 1966 and finally in 1976). Each time, following rehabilitation he be-came more powerful. Franz wrote: "I know of no politician of our century—neither in the East nor in the West—who has travelled as tortuous, as rocky, and yet as successful a life's course as Deng."[34]

On return from Europe, Deng Xiaoping started teaching at the Political Department of the Xi'an Military and Political Academy.[35] In three years, he had moved up to the position of political commissar for the seventh Red Army. In this position, he imparted political education and indoctrination in Communist ideology to the troops. Deng held the post of political commissar for the troops at various levels during the next two decades of the Communist Party's struggle for power in China. By 1945, he had become a member of the Central Committee of the Communist Party of China. Ten years later, he was elected to the highest decision-making body of the party, the Polit-buro, and in 1956, he became the party General Secretary. Maneuvering within the faction-ridden politics of the Chinese Communist Party, he was elected and reelected to several positions in his career. By the early 1980s, Deng had become the paramount leader of China.

Deng Xiaoping's seniors in the party included Mao Zedong and Zhou Enlai. He was as committed to the ideology of communism as those two leaders with one major difference—his pragmatism was not matched by either one. It was his quest for pragmatic economic policy that earned him Mao's disfavor during the 1960s and led to his second political ouster. Deng's greatest mentor in pragmatism was Liu Shaoqi, who had replaced Mao as the country's president in 1958 and had also earned Mao's disfavor in the 1960s. In bringing reform to China, Deng supported leaders such as Hu Yaobang and Zhao Ziyang, but he withdrew his support if such leaders did not attach the same importance to the societal order that he did.

Few people in China or outside doubt Deng Xiaoping's deep commitment to his country. It is also generally accepted that Deng believed in "collective prosperity and national strength rather than individual freedom."[36] In analyzing China's prosperity and poor record on human rights, a *New York Times* correspondent wrote: "Mr. Deng places a huge premium on order and . . . he is willing to destroy anyone who he believes might unravel it. Dissent, in his view, challenges not just the Communist Party but also China's best hope for modernization."[37]

THE NEW PROGRAM

The new economic program under the leadership of Deng Xiaoping began taking shape following the Eleventh Party Congress, held in 1977, at which Deng was reinstated after his third ouster. Major economic policies were adopted in December 1978 at the Third Plenum of the party's Central Committee. For almost three decades prior to this date, China's economic policy was determined by Mao's ideas more than by those of any other Chinese. Some scholars refer to the period 1958–1978 instead of 1949–1978 as the Maoist era.[38] Until 1958, China had followed the Soviet model for its economy. Mao abandoned the Soviet agricultural model in that year.

In just three years after the founding of Communist China in October 1949, Mao had succeeded in rehabilitating the country's economy. Industries and communications destroyed by the war were restored, land was taken away from the landlord class and redistributed to peasants, and inflation was checked. Political control of the government, or rather the party, was established throughout the country. The military and police functioned as the loyal allies of the party.

Following the Soviet Union, its ally and benefactor at the time, China launched its first five-year plan in 1953. Foreign aid in the form of loans was extended by the Soviet Union to the fledgling Communist government of China. The loans were relatively small in view of China's size and needs, but China could not expect aid from the capitalist United States. Technical aid in the form of advisors and technicians also came from the Soviet Union. Furthermore, trade between the two Communist countries increased.

China made impressive gains in the industrial area during the first plan, but progress in agriculture was disappointing.[39] Overall, the Chinese economy performed well in the 1950s. Mao wanted rapid gains in the economy.

In order to achieve his goal, Mao abandoned the Soviet model and embarked upon his ill-fated Great Leap Forward program. The disastrous Great Leap Forward decelerated the Chinese economy in both industry and agriculture. The growth rate of its net domestic product decreased "from 4.8 percent during 1952–59 to 1.4 percent per year during 1957–65."[40] The Great Proletarian Cultural Revolution brought further dislocations to the Chinese economy and slowed down the recovery that had started after the end of the Great Leap Forward. As a result, the Mao era brought little improvement in the living standards of the Chinese over the gains made in the early years of the Communist rule. Xue Muqiao wrote: "Between 1957 and 1977, living standards almost remained the same. The average wage was not raised, the peasants' food grain was not increased, and about one in every three peasants led a hard life."[41] Western scholars generally agree with Xue Muqiao's assessment. In his study of China's political economy, Carl Riskin noted that "the Chinese economy of the immediate post-Mao period was providing living standards that were not qualitatively higher than those of the mid-1950s."[42] The late Mao era had shown significant economic growth. However, if the entire two decades of 1958–1978 are considered, the growth rate of GNP per capita in China remained under 3 percent.[43]

Mao's communism had almost completely abolished private enterprise in industry and commerce by the late 1950s. Mao believed in the self-reliance of local economic units. Such a fragmentation of the economy, according to Thomas Lyons, may have been deliberate.[44] It assured, for example, the political support of the party cadres who controlled the local units. There is no doubt that Mao transformed China. However, the cost of such transformation was millions of Chinese lives. By the late 1970s, the Chinese leaders also accepted that Mao's economic policies were not adequate to meet China's needs. The political environment for a new program seemed available. Mao's supporters, led by the "Gang of Four" (including his wife), had been discredited and arrested. Deng Xiaoping, the pragmatist, had been reinstated to his previous positions in the party at the eleventh Party Congress in 1977. The post–eleventh Party Congress leadership was ready for a new program.

Mao had selected Hua Guofeng to succeed him after his death. Hua, therefore, became the party chairman when Mao died. Hua and Deng, however, had serious ideological differences on the economic recovery of China. In contrast to Deng's cautious approach, Hua wanted an unrealistically rapid economic recovery and believed that such recovery was possible by planning and a surge of revolutionary spirit. In early 1978, he "unveiled a grandiose ten-year modernization program for 1976–85; as two years had already passed, it was actually an eight-year plan."[45]

The ten-year plan revived emphasis on the so-called four modernizations in the areas of agriculture, industry, science and technology, and national defense. Zhou Enlai was the first Chinese leader to have stressed these modernizations three years earlier. The ten-year plan, with its focus on the four modernizations, was expected "to enable China to reach the 'front ranks' of the world at the end of the century."[46] Hua foresaw massive investment in the Chinese economy and the import of Western capital and technology. Carl Riskin summed up the major goals of the plan:

[By the end of the twentieth century] China was to have achieved parity or superiority with respect to the advanced industrial countries in output of major industrial products, basically automated their production, and mechanized 85 percent of major farm tasks.[47]

The ten-year plan collapsed within two years. D. Gale Johnson noted: "By 1980 it was clear that the economy was running into major difficulties as a result of unrealistic targets, a large negative foreign trade balance and a substantial government deficit."[48] The failure of this plan "contributed to his [Hua Guofeng's] replacement by Deng shortly thereafter. It also made it clear that there was no 'quick fix' to economic growth."[49] Deng Xiaoping succeeded in having Hua Guofeng removed from the party chairmanship in 1981. The following year, Hua was ousted from the Politburo. Deng emerged as the most powerful leader of China at the Twelfth Party Congress, held in 1982, and was ready to launch his economic program. Harry Harding stated that "Hua was, literally, betrayed by Deng Xiaoping, who had pledged his loyalty to Hua as a condition for his own political rehabilitation."[50] However, such betrayals are not uncommon in the power conflicts within China or other countries.

Deng Xiaoping's program was expressed through various speeches and statements that he made. The final volume of such speeches was published in late 1993.[51] Deng's program had two symbiotic features: economic and political. In the economic area, Deng reintroduced capitalism in China. In the Chinese rhetoric it was labeled "socialism with Chinese characteristics," and according to the editor of a major anthology of Deng's pronouncements, "this idea has become the general guiding principle for modernizing China."[52]

Deng was opposed to the "total westernization of China and adoption of the whole capitalist system of the West."[53] He supported the four modernizations and "was the moving spirit under Zhou in 1975 behind this new modernization thrust."[54] In a talk with a Japanese delegation in June 1984, Deng stated: "The minimum target of our four modernizations is to achieve a comparatively comfortable standard of living by the end of the century.... By a comfortable standard we mean that per capita GNP will reach U.S. $800."[55] In order to achieve this target, Deng supported private ownership of property with limits, profit as the guiding force behind production, and joint economic ventures with Western companies. Deng did not want the Chinese to forget that communism had to be improved through capitalism. In practice, however, his desire to modernize the country required China to forgo some of the central concepts of communism and move ahead on the capitalist road. The pragmatic Deng did not seem to care that much for the Communist economic system. One of his most quoted dictums was, "It does not matter what color the cat is so long as it catches mice." The Chinese are aware of this and, as John Stoessinger noted, "during the 1980s, the Chinese rediscovered the profit motive and did so with a vengeance."[56]

In the political arena Deng advocated political restructuring and "democracy." Political restructuring to Deng meant overcoming bureaucratism and providing stimulus to the "initiative of the people and of the grass-roots units."[57] Deng also prepared "to solve the problem of the rule of law in China as opposed to the rule of man and to straighten out the relationship between the party and the government."[58] He wanted the party to lead but believed in separating its responsibilities from those of the government.[59]

Deng considered democracy "an important means of carrying out our reform [of the political structure]."[60] He was not in favor of the Western-style democratic political structure in which any number of parties are permitted. He wanted democratic centralism instead of party competition.[61] In Deng's words, "China also has a number of democratic parties, but they all accept leadership by the Communist Party."[62]

Deng did not want to "simply copy bourgeois democracy, or introduce the system of a balance of three powers."[63] In other words, he did not want China to adopt Western-style democracy and certainly not the separation of powers system of the American democracy. Instead, he bluntly said, "We cannot do without dictatorship."[64] Deng called for adhering to "the Four Cardinal Principles, that is, for keeping to the socialist road, upholding the people's democratic dictatorship, upholding leadership by the Communist Party and upholding Marxism-Leninism and Mao Zedong thought."[65]

Deng's pronouncements supported development of intellectual resources, creative activity by writers and artists, and freer public expression. However, any freedom of this nature must be subjected to the party's leadership and, when in conflict with the socialist principles (as understood by Deng and his associates), must be suppressed. The Tiananmen Square events of June 1989 reflect his lack of concern for freedom as understood in the West. Earlier as well, Deng had behaved in a manner contemptuous of the Western style of freedom of expression. After briefly permitting freedom of public expression between 1978 and 1979 in the "Democracy Wall" campaign, he suppressed it.[66] The most famous political prisoner of that era was Wei Jingsheng, who was freed in September 1993, after being jailed for fourteen and a half years, but was rearrested in April 1994.

Deng Xiaoping favored closer economic and political ties with other countries, or, as he often said, "opening to the outside world." In his statements he stood "firmly for the maintenance of world peace, for the relaxation of international tension and for arms reduction—above all, the reduction of the superpowers' nuclear and other weapons."[67] He also said he was "opposed to all forms of aggression and hegemony."[68]

MOBILIZING FOR POWER

In just five years, from his third rehabilitation in 1977 to the ouster of Hua Guofeng from the party's Politburo in 1982, Deng Xiaoping mobilized enormous power in the party, government, and army, which made him the paramount leader of the country for the rest of his life. Deng was seventeen years older than Hua, the chosen successor to Mao; had far greater contacts within the party than Hua; and, above all, had a program for China's modernization that Hua could not match. Harry Harding noted: "Hua Guofeng faced, in Deng Xiaoping, a powerful political rival waiting in the wings of the party, with enormous personal prestige and an alternative program."[69] He further commented:

Step by step, Deng whittled away at Hua Guofeng's position, first by creating new positions for his own lieutenants, then by dismissing Hua's more controversial associates, and finally, when the time was ripe, securing the removal of Hua. Even as he sought their political defeat, however, Deng dealt with his opponents in a relatively humane manner.... [N]one was subjected to the political persecution that was the fate of Mao's defeated rivals during much of the chairman's rule.[70]

Some historians maintain that it took Deng Xiaoping barely three years from his rehabilitation to become the most powerful leader of China.[71] Deng's greatest trump card was his economic program. In a meeting held in February 1980, the Central Committee of the party rejected Mao's "politics in command" for Deng's "economics in command," hoping to turn China into an advanced nation by the year 2000.[72] Part of Deng's strategy included accepting some basic tenets of Mao's ideology, while rejecting the Mao cult and demystifying Mao.[73]

In mobilizing power to defeat his political opponents and support his program, Deng Xiaoping broadened his coalition as much as he possibly could. Deng's political career, which was much longer than Hua's, gave him an edge over Hua because of the former's experience and contacts. Deng's coalitions "included a much wider range of supporters [than Hua's] from diverse backgrounds: the technocrats, generals of the army, and the bureaucrats."[74] Deng also gathered public support in his favor and encouraged the commonly used practice of displaying posters to bolster his position. Whenever possible, he utilized the Chinese media to increase support for his program and employed some of the Chinese intellectuals to write for him.

China's unprecedented economic growth as a result of the introduction of market economics, favored by Deng Xiaoping, helped Deng to retain political support within the party, the government, and the army, the three institutions that control the country. Market economics was "enshrined in China's Constitution" in 1992.[75] Considering Deng's advanced age of ninety at this writing, it is unlikely he will lose the status he attained during his lifetime. A major concern of Deng was to continue his program. To achieve that goal, he appointed Jiang Zemin his successor in 1989.[76] Jiang, a former mayor of Shanghai, was raised to three of the most powerful positions in China: President, Communist Party Secretary, and Central Military Commission Chairman (this commission controls the army). Some analysts believe that Jiang lacks the charisma and stature enjoyed by Mao and Deng and that after Deng's death he may face the same fate that befell Hua Guofeng after Mao's death.[77]

IMPLEMENTING THE NEW PROGRAM—THE POLICY DIMENSION

Deng Xiaoping gradually developed policies to implement his program and was guided far more by pragmatism than any theory of development. His "socialism with Chinese characteristics" initially meant keeping the command economy with increasing features of the market economy. Starting in late 1978, when the Third Plenum of the Eleventh Central Committee was held, the Chinese policy emphasized reliance mainly on a planned economy with its regulation by a market economy.[78] By 1984, however, the principle of the primary reliance on the planned economy was abandoned. Three years later, the Thirteenth Congress of the Communist Party officially resolved the issue of the command versus market economy when it stated that "the order of importance of planning and market is no longer a point of emphasis."[79] Deng, however, kept reiterating that China would remain a socialist country, implying that a planned economy was never to be entirely abandoned.

Since four-fifths of China's population lived in the countryside, the first order of business in formulating and implementing economic policy was to reform the agricultural system. In contrast to a healthy growth of the industry in China during the 1965–1980 period, agriculture had done poorly. While industry grew at an average annual growth rate of 10 percent during this period, agriculture lagged far behind, with only a 2.8 percent growth rate, which necessitated large grain imports.[80] Three major reforms in agriculture were instituted after 1978: "a change of land ownership; an even more radical change in the size of farms; and a sharp increase in crop prices."[81] Communist rule had virtually abolished private land ownership and introduced collective ownership. In the mid-1950s, cooperatives of farmers were introduced with "an average size of about 200 families."[82] The cooperative system was replaced by communes during the Great Leap Forward period of 1958–1959. Although the communes continued, "by 1962 the system had reverted to being much like what had existed in 1956–57."[83] By that year, wrote Perkins, "the basic collective unit . . . had become the production team, a subunit of the commune with only 20 to 30 families. . . . This collective agricultural system remained intact with only modest changes until the end of the 1970s."[84]

The new policy—the "household responsibility system," introduced in 1979—was applied uniformly by 1983. Under this policy, each household was assigned an equal plot of land less than an acre in size. Officially, the land remained public; however, later policy changes made it virtually privately owned with rights of inheritance and even sale of the right to utilize the land. Each household had to sign a contract with the local representative of the government, which specified the crops to be planted by the farmers. Farmers were encouraged to specialize in producing certain crops or to engage in such noncrop endeavors as fishery and raising livestock. The most important feature of these contracts was that each household "had to provide its share of the agricultural tax due to the government, the agricultural products purchased by the state under the system of mandatory production quotas, and fees owed to the [local] collective."[85] The farmers could sell products above the quota in the open market or to the government at prices higher than the quota prices. There have been some changes in the agricultural policy, notably the abolition of the mandatory quota purchase of products by the state. The goal has been to reduce state control over farmers and to give them greater freedom in making decisions.

Deng Xiaoping changed the industrial system of China by reducing the role of Soviet-style planning and state-owned enterprises and increasing that of the market forces and privately owned businesses. Although industrial reform began immediately after the December 1978 meeting of the party, it gained momentum in October 1984, when a resolution to reform the economic structure was issued. Prior to 1984, significant reforms had already been made in the industrial structure, including the introduction of private enterprise, reduction of control over state enterprises, incentives for greater productivity, lifting of price controls over selected items and the introduction of an income tax on state enterprises. These reforms did not replace the command economy by a market economy. As C. Y. Hsu wrote, "in the process [of industrial reforms of 1979–1984], the government backed away from the bureaucratic command economy characterized by central planning and directives . . . to a position of planning through guidance."[86]

The reforms of 1984 accelerated the market economy in China. The reduction of state controls on the economy and expansion of private enterprises continued. Managers of public enterprises were given greater authority in hiring, promotions, setting pay, and even firing, which had remained uncommon in socialist China. The mixed economy of public and private enterprises abolished the monopoly system of the Mao era and introduced competition. Not only public and private enterprises competed against each other, competition between the public enterprises was also encouraged. Further progress was made in letting the prices of goods fluctuate in response to market forces. While market forces determined prices of industrial goods in the early 1950s, the introduction of central planning froze the prices of most industrial goods at the mid-1950 levels for the next twenty-five years.[87] The prices of all industrial products were not to be determined by the market economy. Instead, the government permitted a dual system when it set the prices of some goods but left the prices of an enlarging list of other products in the hands of the market economy.

Another major economic reform initiated under Deng Xiaoping's leadership was the open door policy toward the outside world to increase trade and attract foreign technology and investment. Except for trade transactions with the Soviet Union and Eastern Europe until its break with the Soviet Union in 1960, China for the most part followed a policy of autarky until the early 1970s. President Richard Nixon's visit to China in 1972 had led to the opening up of China's trade relations with the United States. The policy of the Communist Party, formulated in the December 1978 meeting, accelerated this process with the United States as well as with other countries, notably Japan. China attracted foreign investment through incentives of preferential tax treatment and increased authority to the local governments to negotiate foreign corporations' investments in China. Special economic zones were established to encourage production and exports. Internationally, China was also readmitted to the World Bank and the International Monetary Fund. The United States granted it most-favored-nation status, assuring the imports of Chinese goods at the lowest possible tariffs.

A controversial feature of China's open door policy was its increased arms sales to the Third World states, and in particular, the Middle East countries and Pakistan. Most analysts agree that Pakistan has developed nuclear weapons with the substantial help of technology and equipment from China. Another issue of contention is the human rights record of China. Many members of the United States Congress question the continuation of trade concessions to China because of its repression of freedom and imprisonment of political prisoners.

Reforms in agriculture, industries, trade, and foreign investment resulted in unprecedented growth of the Chinese economy. In the early 1990s, the economy appeared to be overheated, raising the fear of hyperinflation, as inflation had surpassed the 20 percent mark by late 1993. Deng Xiaoping, however, said in November 1993 that "development at a slow pace is not socialism," which implied a continuation of the high rate of growth of well over 10 percent for the Chinese economy.[88] At the same time the party's Central Committee, apparently with the blessing of Deng, made policy decisions in the areas of taxation, banking and state-owned industries. The changes in the tax policy, involving levying income tax on individuals and state industries, service taxes on professionals, and excise taxes on luxuries, would increase the government's revenue base.[89] The party also approved the establishment of the country's first central bank to control the money supply and grant government loans.[90] Furthermore, it decided to "begin converting some portion of China's state-owned industries into modern corporations that can attract outside investors."[91]

NATURE AND SCOPE OF CHANGE

Agricultural and industrial reforms and the opening up of China to the outside world for trade and foreign investment under Deng Xiaoping's leadership brought dramatic improvements in the Chinese economy and quality of life. Chinese farmers initially experienced an even greater change in their living standards than the urban Chinese. Dwight Heald Perkins noted that "the rise in real per capita consumption of the average Chinese farmer was greater during the 7 years after 1978 than in the entire previous 26 years (91 percent versus 76 percent)."[92] Private ownership of land and the substantial reduction in state controls over the agriculture were largely responsible for the increase in the availability of goods to the rural Chinese.[93]

The introduction of a market economy and the opening of the economy to international business have revolutionized the industrial sector. As a result, urban incomes are now substantially greater than rural incomes. Aggregate data as well as success stories of Chinese companies and joint venture enterprises (collaborations with foreign companies) are a compelling testimony to the progress of Chinese industry. Consider the example of Hainan province in the south, which was an "autonomous region under the control of Guangdong province and the Chinese military" until 1988.[94] It was an undeveloped island with little prospect of economic advancement. When it was made a province in 1988, a special economic zone was created there. Five years later, Hainan had become "a showcase for the nation's 'socialist market economy,' recognized throughout Asia for its Chinese brand of swashbuckling capitalism."[95] The tax breaks and liberal investment rules brought 5,700 foreign investors, largely from Hong Kong and Taiwan but some also from the United States and Germany, to Hainan in five years, and these investors poured $6.3 billion (U.S.) into the province's economy.[96]

Data from World Bank reports reveal an overall economic progress in China, which is unprecedented not only in that country but perhaps in any other country as well. During 1980–1991, the average per capita GNP growth rate in China was an unusually high 7.8 percent.[97] Some quality of life statistics are also equally revealing. The number of "the Chinese living in absolute poverty—lacking decent food, housing and clothing—dropped from 220 million in 1980 to 100 million in 1990."[98] In statistical terms, the percentage of the poor in the Chinese population decreased from 28 to 10.[99] China also made impressive gains in the areas of life expectancy and children's health and literacy. Life expectancy at birth in China increased from 55 in 1965 to 64 in 1977 to 70 in 1990.[100] The infant mortality rate per 1,000 live births declined from 90 in 1965 to 64 in 1977 and 29 in 1990.[101] The under–

age-five mortality rate per 1,000 live births also showed an equally impressive decline and stood at 34.5 in 1990.[102] Over 95 percent of the children were immunized for measles before age 1 in the early 1990s. China also made great strides in eradicating illiteracy—its adult illiteracy percentage was 27 in 1990.[103] India, the other population giant in Asia which also has made noteworthy gains in its economy by reducing state controls, encouraging private enterprise and attracting foreign investment, pales before the Chinese advancement.[104]

Some analysts find China's economic recovery so startling that they envision a giant Japan emerging in Asia. Mortimer B. Zuckerman, editor-in-chief of *U.S. News and World Report,* wrote in a commentary:

If China can maintain the same growth rate over the next two decades that it has managed in the past 10 years, real per capita income will be equal to that of Japan's in the '70s. China's gross domestic product would grow sixfold.[105]

Despite such optimism, several problems have emerged in China. Small agricultural holdings, "neglect of large projects formerly serviced by the commune, such as the mechanized pumping of the irrigation system and the use of heavy tractors for preparation of the land," and the vast reduction "in the ability of farm units to deal with natural calamities" are among the problems facing agriculture.[106] "A shortage of efficiency and quality, not any lack of speed or quantity" is a major weakness of the Chinese industry.[107]

Reform in China is responsible for the growing gap between the rich and poor, some counterclaims notwithstanding.[108] It has brought corruption to the Chinese life that makes China resemble a typical Third World nation. China, on the one hand, has had campaigns against economic crime, but on the other hand it tolerates, even accepts, corruption as a price for economic progress. Zhang Zhongli wrote:

Corruption in China's social [and] economic life has become quite rampant. . . . Unprecedented since the founding of the People's Republic of China are activities such as smuggling and trafficking in smuggled foods, payment and acceptance of bribes, tax evasion, financial swindling, and the like.[109]

It is commonly known in China that many of the children of those in power in the country have amassed enormous amounts of wealth by illegal means, but they escape any penalty due to the influence of their parents. An author on the Chinese political economy reported: "According to one Hong Kong trader, entire sectors responsible for China's export trade are controlled by veritable illegal 'holdings,' managed by the sons and daughters of generals and high level cadres."[110]

Reform in China remains confined to its economy and political restructuring. China has not introduced democratic reforms that generally go with economic progress. While the young in China appear restive for freedom, the government at the time of this writing is not showing any signs of loosening its grip over people's lives. Deng Xiaoping, it seems, accepted repression as the price for economic growth.

INTERPRETING DENG XIAOPING AS LEADER

Very few leaders in the world changed the lives of so many people as did Deng Xiaoping, and before him, Mao Zedong. While Mao had changed China by making the country Communist, Deng brought revolutionary changes to China by virtually disempowering the ideology of communism. Communes and cooperative farming were replaced by privately owned agricultural plots. The institutions regulating agriculture were not completely disempowered, but their authority was very substantially reduced to allow for capitalist ideas of initiative and profit to flourish. In the areas of industry, trade, and foreign investments in China, the transformation was equally dramatic. Private enterprises were established and competition was encouraged between the enterprises. While public enterprises continued to exist, their utility in "socialism with Chinese characteristics" began to be questioned.

The three institutions controlling China—the party, government, and army—continued to wield power under Deng's regime. New groups, however, emerged with a potential to compete with those entrenched in positions of authority. The new rich class of Chinese industrialists has close connections with those in the party, government, and army, but at this time does not by itself compete with them for influence. The growing number of Chinese citizens, especially the young, who question the repression of freedom by the government, could, however, emerge as a major force competing with the Dengites for power. Deng and his supporters favored rapid economic growth, but had little concern for the freedom of the people. With increased prosperity, the movement for bringing democracy, as understood in most countries of the world, will keep gathering momentum. The tide of the democratic wave in the former Soviet Union, Eastern, and Central Europe and a majority of the Third World nations will continue to strengthen the Chinese movement for democracy.

Deng Xiaoping mobilized power in support of his program with ingenuity and cleverness unmatched by most leaders in the world adept at maneuvering for power. An early start in politics and the long life he enjoyed enabled Deng to gain experience and make contacts that are rarely available to other leaders. Improvements experienced by the Chinese in their living standards made them support Deng's policies. Deng's expertise in removing his opponents from positions of authority, bringing his supporters to those positions and enlarging his coalition to include all elements wielding power as well as the general public buttressed his call for reform and, not incidentally, his place in history.

That China would continue on the capitalist path even after Deng Xiaoping's death appears certain. What remains uncertain is to what extent China would continue to be a stable nation. The tumultuous history of China with recent memories of massive loss of life makes the Chinese yearn for order in society. However, the possibility of the continuation of hyperinflation due to an overheated economy, the growing gap between the rich and poor, the rampant corruption, and the desire of a growing number of Chinese for freedom and democracy have the potential to again make China an unstable nation. If chaos were to recur in China, historians would blame Deng Xiaoping. If, on the other hand, China continues as a stable nation and prospers as expected, Deng Xiaoping will be considered a savior and one of the greatest leaders, not only in the history of China, but of the world.

NOTES

1. China became a nuclear power in 1964.
2. *Information China,* Vol. 3 (New York: Pergamon Press, 1989), p. 1247.
3. Ibid., p. 1248.
4. See *The Statesman's Yearbook 1993–94* (New York: St. Martin's Press, 1993), p. 363.
5. See *Information China,* p. 1306. Many experts consider 20 million too low a figure.
6. Ibid., p. 1311.
7. Nien Cheng, "The Roots of China's Crisis," in James A. Dorn and Wang Xi, eds., *Economic Reform in China: Problems and Prospects* (Chicago: The University of Chicago Press, 1990), p. 330.
8. See Jan S. Prybyla, "China's Economic Experiment: Back from the Market," *Problems of Communism,* January-February 1989, p. 17.
9. Ibid.
10. One of the coauthors (Kul B. Rai) was a visiting professor at Huanghe University in China in fall 1986. During that stay, Rai interviewed over fifty Chinese college and graduate students. Virtually all expressed opposition to the single-child family policy. However, many also said they had no choice but to follow it.
11. For a discussion of the single-child family policy in China, see Joyce K. Kallgren, "Politics, Welfare, and Change: The Single-Child Family in China," in Elizabeth J. Perry and Christine Wong, eds., *The Political Economy of Reform in Post-Mao China* (Cambridge, MA: Harvard University Press, 1985), pp. 131–156. Exceptions to the single-child family policy are discussed on pp. 147–148. See also *U.S. News and World Report,* September 19, 1994, pp. 56–57.
12. See Jonathan D. Spence, *The Search for Modern China* (New York: W. W. Norton and Co., 1990), p. 578.
13. Ibid., p. 579.
14. *Countries of the World and Their Leaders Yearbook 1992: A Compilation of U.S. Department of State Reports . . . ,* Vol. 1 (Detroit, Gale Research, 1992), p. 403.
15. Ibid.
16. Spence, p. 583.

17. Ibid.

18. Lynn T. White III, *Politics of Chaos: The Organizational Causes of Violence in China's Cultural Revolution* (Princeton, NJ: Princeton University Press, 1989), p. 4.

19. See ibid.

20. Ibid., p. 7.

21. Ibid., pp. 6–7.

22. See Spence, pp. 602–617, esp. pp. 603–604; and White, pp. 8–18.

23. White, p. 8.

24. Ibid.

25. Ibid.

26. Lin Biao later had a falling-out with Mao and is believed to have attempted a coup against him. According to the Chinese Communist Party's reports, he died in a plane crash in 1971 while attempting to flee China.

27. The idea for such a rally "originated with students in the party-history department at People's University in Beijing." See Spence, p. 739.

28. According to the revised estimates of the *New York Times,* the death toll ranged from 400 to 800. See Immanuel C. Y. Hsu, *China without Mao* (New York: Oxford University Press, 1990), p. 289.

29. Ibid., p. 290. Hsu extracted these statistics from issues of *Beijing Review* published in June and July 1989.

30. A not-so-altruistic motive of the U.S. Congress in passing this law was to entice thousands of the best and the brightest from China to settle in the United States.

31. Wolfgang Bartke, *Who's Who in the People's Republic of China,* 2nd ed. (Munich, Germany: K. G. Saur, 1987), p. 72.

32. For a chronology of Deng Xiaoping's life, see Uli Franz, *Deng Xiaoping* (trans. Tom Artin) (New York: Harcourt Brace Jovanovich, 1988), pp. 323–326.

33. Ibid., p. 55.

34. Ibid., foreword, p. ix.

35. Bartke, p. 72.

36. *New York Times,* September 7, 1993, p. A10.

37. Ibid.

38. See, for example, Thomas P. Lyons, *Economic Integration and Planning in China* (New York: Columbia University Press, 1987).

39. According to Xue Muqiao, a Chinese scholar, "During the 1st FYP [five-year plan] period, the annual rate of industrial growth averaged 18 percent [but] . . . the rate in agriculture was only 4.5 percent." See Xue Muqiao, *China's Socialist Economy* (Beijing: Foreign Languages Press, 1981), p. 178.

40. Subramanian Swamy, *Economic Growth in China and India, 1952–1970: A Comparative Appraisal* (Chicago: The University of Chicago Press, 1973), p. 83.

41. Xue, p. 176.

42. Carl Riskin, *China's Political Economy: The Quest for Development since 1949* (New York: Oxford University Press, 1988), p. 261.

43. The World Bank estimates growth rate of GNP per capita in China between 2.5 and 3.0 percent for the period 1957–1979. See Lyons, p. 344.

44. Ibid., pp. 275–276.

45. Ibid.

46. Riskin, p. 259.

47. Ibid.

48. D. Gale Johnson, *The People's Republic of China: 1978–1990* (San Francisco: ICS Press, 1990), p. 47.

49. George Rosen, "India and China: Perspectives on Contrasting Styles of Economic Reform," *Journal of Asian Economics,* 1 (2) (1990): 276.

50. Harry Harding, *China's Second Revolution: Reform after Mao* (Washington, DC: The Brookings Institution, 1987), p. 66.

51. See the *New York Times,* November 4, 1993, p. A3.

52. See Deng Xiaoping, *Fundamental Issues in Present-Day China* (Beijing: Foreign Languages Press, 1988), editor's note.

53. Ibid., pp. 167–168.

54. David W. Chang, *Zhou Enlai and Deng Xiaoping in the Chinese Leadership Succession Crisis* (Lanham, MD: University Press of America, 1984), p. 297.

55. Deng, p. 55.

56. John G. Stoessinger, *Nations at Dawn: China, Russia and America,* 6th ed. (New York: McGraw-Hill, 1994), p. 297.

57. Deng, p. 150.

58. Ibid.

59. Ibid.

60. Ibid., p. 195.

61. Democratic centralism means the election of higher political units by lower units and freedom of discussion before reaching a decision, but not afterward.

62. Deng, p. 195.

63. Ibid., p. 163.

64. Ibid.

65. Ibid., p. 171.

66. See David Bonavia, *Deng* (Hong Kong: Longman Group Far East, 1989), p. 229.

67. Deng, p. 62.

68. Ibid.

69. Harding, p. 57.

70. Ibid., p. 69.

71. See, for example, Hsu, p. 39.

72. Ibid.

73. Ibid., pp. 45–53.

74. Chang, p. 210.

75. *U.S. News and World Report,* November 22, 1993, p. 39.

76. See the *New York Times,* November 4, 1993, p. A3.

77. Ibid.

78. Zhang Zhongli, "The Chinese Economic Regulatory Mechanism in Transformation," *Journal of Asian Economics,* 1 (1) (1990): 37.

79. Ibid.

80. China's growth rate figures are from *World Development Report 1992* (New York: Oxford University Press, 1992), p. 220.

81. *Economist,* August 1, 1987, p. 5.

82. See Dwight Heald Perkins, "Reforming China's Economic System," *Journal*

of Economic Literature, June 1988, p. 605. An excellent summary of China's agricultural reform is on pages 605–613.

83. Ibid., p. 605.

84. Ibid., p. 606.

85. Harding, p. 103.

86. Hsu, p. 182.

87. See Perkins, p. 620.

88. *New York Times,* November 23, 1993, D6.

89. Ibid.

90. Ibid.

91. Ibid.

92. Perkins, p. 636.

93. Paul A. Cohen, "The Post-Mao Reforms in Historical Perspective," *Journal of Asian Studies,* August 1988, p. 533.

94. *U.S. News and World Report,* November 22, 1993, p. 39.

95. Ibid.

96. Ibid.

97. The World Bank statistics cited here, unless indicated otherwise, are from an article on China published in the *New York Times* on September 7, 1993, pp. A1, A10.

98. Ibid.

99. Ibid.

100. Statistics for 1965 and 1990 are from *World Bank Report 1992,* p. 280; and for 1977, from Perkins, p. 640.

101. Ibid.

102. *World Bank Report 1992,* p. 280.

103. Ibid., p. 218.

104. For a comparison of China and India, see the *New York Times,* September 7, 1993, p. A10; and Robert E. Dernberger and Richard S. Eckans, *Financing Asian Development 2: China and India* (Lanham, MD: University Press of America, 1988), pp. 1–11.

105. *U.S. News and World Report,* December 6, 1993, p. 100.

106. Hsu, p. 175.

107. See Harding, p. 120.

108. See, for example, Perkins, p. 639.

109. Zhongli, p. 41.

110. Wojtek Zafanolli, "A Brief Outline of China's Second Economy," in Stephen Feuchtwang, Akhtar Hussain and Thierry Pairault, eds., *Transforming China's Economy in the Eighties,* Vol. 1 (Boulder, CO: Westview Press, 1988), p. 138.

Leadership in the Age of Turbulence

The twentieth century has never been an easy time for political leaders. Frequently in this century, revolutionary changes have followed in the wake of such events as the two world wars, the onset of the Cold War, and decolonization, which have led to the political demise of individual leaders and, in some cases, entire regimes. The list of failed leaders includes such disparate figures as European monarchs, democrats of the interwar period, fascist dictators, and Third World elites supportive of colonial rule. Technological change relevant to political life has also occurred throughout the century, sometimes taking dramatic forms. Certainly, the scientific and technological developments that made possible the atomic bomb changed the meaning of warfare forever and contributed to the intensity of the Cold War. However, despite all these events, in the period before 1970 and prior to the "age of turbulence," the most basic economic and political relationships experienced only incremental change. Political actors continued to conceive of economic activity as a national endeavor that was susceptible to management by domestic political leaders, citizens received "national" communications that overwhelmingly emanated from domestic media and governmental sources, and the distance between leaders and citizens was preserved by government control over politically relevant information. Most important, challenges to political leaders were individual, nationally specific events, or in extreme cases, confined to the members of defeated alliances.

As the postwar period progressed, the general economic and political environment proved increasingly amenable to elitism, stability, and centralization. In retrospect, the period from 1945 to 1970 proved to be one of relative stability, having been shaped by a "long peace" between the major powers and the establishment of consensual regimes within most states. Even in the Third World, where the awareness of economic dependence and political vulnerability was strongest, the elites of most states received broad popular support for postwar programs of national economic development and state-building. From the perspective of political leadership, such events as the Cold War and decolonization constituted political reference points that served to legitimate a wide range of capitalist, communist, and Third World elites. Notwithstanding some notable exceptions, leaders and regimes in all three political worlds enjoyed comparatively long tenures in power.

After 1970, the onset of global turbulence dramatically increased the constraints on political leaders. The speed, frequency, and scope of economic and political change accelerated to unprecedented levels, and the political environment was increasingly characterized by high degrees of complexity, dynamism, and density (see Chapter 1).[1] New actors pursuing widely diverse interests interacted in an increasingly interdependent world. Driven by hitherto unimagined innovations in technology, turbulent change impacted nearly every political system, regardless of level of development, ideological commitment, or geopolitical position. In the environment of turbulence, the domestic and international relationships that had defined the postwar world either began to break down or were transformed entirely. These included the Cold War, the Bretton Woods system, the postwar economic arrangements of many states, postwar patterns of political mobilization, and the relationship between leaders and the governed. Of the subsequent changes, three proved to be the most important—the growth of international economic interdependence, the increased scale of mobilization, and citizen enhancement. These changes altered the economic and political roles of large segments of the population across the three political worlds and contributed directly to the dynamics of turbulence.

In the period of turbulence, political leaders as a category faced unprecedented obstacles to the exercise of power, which included: rapid changes in the international economic and political environments, mass insecurity, new levels of public knowledge about politics, heightened public demands from enlightened citizens, the mobilization of new groups and interests, and opposition from groups previously excluded from politics. They also faced the devolution of power from national elites to local groups, the global revolution in mass communications and global exposure to newsworthy events, the worldwide spread of democratic political forms, the decline in salience of most ideologies, the breakdown of political coalitions and constituencies, and a growing global skepticism of the ability of government to solve problems.[2] These conditions were not limited to specific states or regions but rather existed across three political worlds. In the age of turbulence, leaders faced increased demands and, generally, shorter tenures in office than their predecessors.

TURBULENCE AND INCUMBENT POLITICAL LEADERS

The evidence seems indisputable that the environment of turbulence was strongly biased against incumbent political leaders. Between 1973 and 1982, an alternation of power occurred in every Western state with a tradition of party competition. In addition, the entire communist party leadership of the states of the former Soviet bloc succumbed to the events of 1989–1991, and both peaceful and violent leadership changes swept large sections of the Third World, especially Africa and Latin America. Change did not stop there; in 1992–1994, "recycled" former communists, running under a variety of new party banners, returned to power in several successor states of the former Soviet Union. Why did the environment of turbulence so disadvantage incumbent leaders? Three factors seem especially important: timing, the effect of turbulence on existing political-economic arrangements, and the relationship between turbulence and group mobilization.

Timing

The onset of turbulence followed more than three decades of clearly defined, and frequently stable, political patterns at both the international and domestic levels. At the international level, the Cold War competition between the West and the Soviet bloc dominated all other issues and provided clear organizing principles of state behavior for at least three decades. These principles dictated the state's integration into one of the competing alliances, as well as heavy investment in national security. Even for those states that sought nonalignment, the requirement of expanding the state's military capabilities still held.

Political life at the domestic level also demonstrated a high degree of coherence. Domestic politics was dominated by the pursuit of economic programs designed to provide for both national and individual well-being. These programs took the form of the Keynesian welfare state in the West, the neo-Stalinist, centrally planned economy in the Soviet bloc, and a variety of programs for economic development and state-building in the Third World. Despite the diversity of these programs and the varying degrees of success they achieved, most were initially supported by an overwhelming domestic consensus, which included support for the concept of an expanded role for government and the idea that government bore a heavy responsibility for economic outcomes. The result was three decades of political centralization, in which governmental elites not only performed additional functions but also assumed responsibility for the general welfare of the population. Elites on both sides of the East-West divide sought to retain political power by demonstrating administrative competence and knowledge of events, convincing citizens of the predictability of outcomes, and assuring the general population that its quality of life would improve. Until the end of the 1960s, this style of politics was reinforced by the impressive rates of economic growth achieved by the advanced industrialized states of the West, most states of the Soviet bloc, and selected states of the Third World. Citizens came to expect favorable policy outcomes and political leaders who were capable of controlling events.

Following as it did in the wake of a long period of stability and relative affluence, the insecurity, uncertainty, and downward mobility that accompanied the onset of turbulence came as an additional shock. After 1973, it became increasingly difficult for governing elites to achieve uninterrupted policy successes, and compared to their predecessors, they appeared less competent and less able to master events. Communist leaders lost popular support when they were compared to leaders of the West, and many Western leaders of the 1970s and 1980s failed the test of popular comparison to their counterparts of the 1960s and before. The political environment of turbulence simply did not lend itself to a continuing record of policy success or the political "great deeds" necessary to sustain political support.

THE BREAKDOWN OF EXISTING POLITICAL-ECONOMIC ARRANGEMENTS

The practical effects of turbulence can best be understood by reference to their impact on the economic and political order. European political economists, and particularly members of the French Regulation School, have demonstrated the importance of "national" or "mobilizing projects" in achieving postwar political stability. Central to the national project was a societal consensus on the manner in which the nation's economic resources should be employed for production, including the general principles of work organization and technology use, and agreement on the manner in which the state should regulate economic and other social activities.[3] The national consensus encompassed all politically significant groups, and even the weakest members of society, such as welfare recipients in Western states, received some benefits. Of course, the objective elements of the national projects differed across the three political worlds, ranging from the Fordist model of industrialization and the political welfare state in the West to the Stalinist system of state economic planning in the communist states. Regardless of their content, however, the various national projects performed the same function in every state: they established a model of economic and political life so widely accepted as legitimate that political power relations, including state regulation, could occur without major confrontation.[4] The advantages of such consensus politics to incumbent political leaders were numerous. Leaders derived their political identities and support from identification with the national program. In addition, political discourse centered on a relatively limited range of alternative approaches for implementing the national project.

In the environment of political turbulence after 1970, the breakdown of postwar national projects resulted in a new political context that was increasingly devoid of consensus and coherence. The collapse of the communist regimes of Europe followed popular rejection of both the political and economic elements of the Stalinist model, and in the West, the abandonment of Fordism and criticism of the welfare state increasingly transformed the political economies of many states. As a result, leaders of diverse states confronted what has been termed "acute national identity crises."[5] Previously hegemonic ideas like Marxism-Leninism and Western Keynesianism were no longer capable of mobilizing majority support. Similarly, such interest groups as traditional industry, trade unions, and manual workers, on which incumbent leaders had depended for political support, were left greatly weakened by the arrival of the global marketplace and the information society.[6] Under the strain of economic change, many previously stable coalitions of the postwar period broke up into competing groups, each trying to avoid economic losses and the costs of adjustment to the new economic realities.

Turbulence and Political Mobilization

Changed patterns of mobilization and new group proliferation were among the most important manifestations of political turbulence. Increased political mobilization impacted virtually every political system, altering relationships at the national level and within local communities. Even in states where new groups were brutally suppressed or contained by policies of compromise, the proliferation of ethnic, religious, and regional groups can be readily documented.[7] The new patterns of mobilization were facilitated by breakthroughs in global communications and information, the global trend toward political liberalization (including the spread of democracy), and the dynamic of decentralization that was at work in many political systems.

There was certainly nothing new about political mobilization; people, at both an individual and a group level, exist in a continual state of defining and redefining themselves.[8] This process was revolutionized, however, in the age of turbulence. The condition of citizen enhancement, which was a result of the revolution in information technology, broke down patterns of political inertia, habitual behavior, and passive compliance to political authority. Ordinary citizens now had available to them instant knowledge of events from around the world, as well as detailed technical and scientific data that had previously been the monopoly of governmental authorities. Knowledge of the outside world that was derived from global radio and television was also an important catalyst for group mobilization. Contacts with the outside world provided groups with rival ideas and models of political life with which to challenge the political status quo. The daily television transmissions from the West into the states of Eastern Europe doubtless played an important role in the demands for political and economic change that swept the area in 1989.[9] Dissident groups also gained encouragement from a knowledge of like-minded groups in other countries and awareness of outside sources of support. In this context, Islamic fundamentalists in many countries have been strengthened by the awareness of similar groups throughout the Islamic world and the realization that theirs is now a "global movement." Further, in some cases the extensive international media coverage given to protests or acts of violence served to strengthen the cohesion, self-consciousness, and determination of groups as members became aware of their ability to "make history."[10]

The proliferation of groups challenged incumbent political leaders in several ways. At the most basic level, the new groups contributed to the political complexity with which leaders had to cope, promoted political polarization, and, frequently, unsettled authority relations between the government and the governed. This was especially true of subnational ethnic, religious, and regional groups seeking radical decentralization or revolutionary regime change. Regardless of their objectives, such groups offered *alternative collectivities* to which people could attach their loyalties, thus reducing the existing sources of support for incumbent leaders.[11] Even when such groups operated entirely within the existing legal and institutional framework, they still siphoned political support from traditional parties and interest groups. The threat to incumbent leaders was intensified by the fact that the mobilization dynamic produced two different sources of challenge, the first from subnational groups seeking devolution or the complete breakup of the state into smaller political units, and the second from supranational movements oriented toward global issues and seeking to transfer the state's sovereignty to international organizations or regimes.[12] In this sense, the attack on the position of state leaders was similar to the attack on the state itself.

SURVIVING TURBULENCE

As with any political competition, the ability of incumbent political leaders to retain power in conditions of turbulence was affected by a number of factors. These included the prevailing political culture, patterns of political support, and the legal and institutional framework, including the electoral system. It seems clear, for example, that Margaret Thatcher was aided throughout her career by an electoral system that converted her modest electoral pluralities into solid Conservative majorities in Parliament. Similarly, in the 1994 election, Helmut Kohl benefited from western German attitudes favoring continuity and stability over change. The most important factors, however, appear to be those related to the political economy, and particularly the position of the incumbent leaders in relationship to ascending or descending national projects. In most states, leaders associated with economic and political liberalization have benefited from the advantages of association with ascending national projects. Neoliberal models of society and economic organization have been presented as prescriptions for success in the new economic environment and have been used successfully to mobilize political support in a wide range of countries. In all three political worlds, neoliberal programs have gained the support of powerful economic interests oriented toward global trade and investment. Such groups were well placed to provide political leaders with financial resources, organizational skills, and moral support. Neoliberal political groups also benefited from global trends, including the general rejection of Marxism in the postcommunist world and the growing skepticism about the value of government regulation and welfare state programs in the West. In the Third World, the rejection of the New International Economic Order in the 1970s and the demise of the Soviet bloc in the 1980s left leaders with few options but to attempt to compete in the new global marketplace.

Incumbent leaders seeking to defend descending national projects like Marxism-Leninism or Keynesianism faced numerous obstacles and ultimately risked political marginalization. The changing nature of economic life deprived them of supporters, their postwar coalitions typically broke up into competing factions, and the leaders themselves frequently became identified with the failed agendas of the past. In cases ranging from the British Labour Party to Mikhail Gorbachev, the defenders of descending projects were opposed by the strongest and most energetic groups in society.

It has been suggested that in the environment of turbulence, the personal attributes of leaders assumed increased importance. According to this argument, the diminished usefulness of most ideologies and other traditional political appeals compelled leaders to assume increased responsibility for the formation and maintenance of majority coalitions. In addition, in the age of global information technology, the ability to articulate coherent and effective messages became critically important. One observer has argued that political leaders were constantly required to legitimize themselves and their programs in extraconstitutional forums, like media interviews and economic summits.[13] While political skills are always of value in any political interaction, the elements of turbulence were clearly beyond the control of even the most gifted political actors. Political acumen was a possible prerequisite to a successful career, but other variables, and particularly those relating to the national political economy, were the decisive factors. Rather than a "great man theory" of turbulence, the evidence suggests that one of the most important factors in surviving politically was the weakness of the opposition. The same forces that worked to reduce the political support of many incumbent leaders also frequently worked to the disadvantage of the opposition. Even in the most difficult circumstances, leaders survived when their level of support, albeit reduced, remained above that of the opposition. This understanding provided the rationale for a wide range of tactics ranging from the deintegrative policies of Margaret Thatcher to negative political campaigns in the United States.

THE CASE STUDIES

Margaret Thatcher

The career of Margaret Thatcher illustrates well the dynamics of disempowerment and empowerment at work in the age of turbulence. In the 1970s, increasing competition in the global economy and the world recession after 1973 accelerated the process of economic decline that had been underway in Britain for a century. In the environment of growing economic constraints, the consensus on the Keynesian welfare state (the national project that had prevailed since the 1950s) began to break down. Economic interests that were previously supportive of the Keynesian consensus became bitter rivals in the competition for diminishing pay, benefits, and subsidies. In addition, a growing segment of the population became convinced that the prevailing levels of government spending were barriers to successful economic restructuring.

In an environment of growing turbulence marked by strikes, service disruptions, and the proliferation of short-term interests, Margaret Thatcher assumed the leadership of the Conservative Party in 1975. Supported by the New Right faction, Thatcher worked to consolidate control within the party as well as within the three governments she headed between 1979 and 1990. Once in power, the Thatcherites advanced a coherent program of neoliberal and neoconservative policies, which formed the basis of a New Right national project to establish an "enterprise culture" and replace the declining Keynesian project. By employing a deintegrative electoral strategy, Thatcher won three successive general elections without ever receiving a majority of the popular vote. During the eleven-year tenure of the Thatcher governments, neocorporate structures were abandoned, most state enterprises were privatized, and government housing was sold to its occupants. These actions accelerated the demise of the Keynesian project and made it impossible to return to the postwar political-economic order. Popular support for many programs of the welfare state remained high, however, while some Thatcherite programs, such as the "poll tax," were rejected. The effort to establish a new national project based solely on Thatcherite policies was, therefore, not successful. Due largely to the weakness of the opposition Labour Party, Thatcher was able to remain in power until 1990, when a combination of a worsening economy, political mismanagement, and intraparty conflict over Britain's role in the European Community led Conservative Party leaders to force her resignation.

Helmut Kohl

The German reunification project introduced new elements of complexity and turbulence into the German political environment, and the Kohl government's role in the process demonstrates the difficulties of governing through turbulence. Helmut Kohl assumed the office of chancellor in 1982, a time when growing concerns about Germany's international economic competitiveness and increasingly volatile electoral patterns were already changing German politics. Benefiting from an improvement in the economy after 1982, Kohl survived the political turbulence of the mid-1980s and won reelection in 1987. In 1989–1990, the strategic withdrawal of the Soviet Union from Eastern Europe and the mass disaffection of the citizens of the German Democratic Republic from their regime brought the issue of reunification to the forefront of the political agenda.

In early 1990, the Kohl government perceived a historic opportunity for the rapid reunification of the two Germanys. In response it developed a series of forceful domestic and international policies to achieve this end. These policies successfully marginalized the West German opposition to early re-unification, accelerated the collapse of the GDR, and gained the approval of foreign states, including the Soviet Union, for the reunification process. In the end, reunification was achieved through the accession of the GDR to the Federal Republic of Germany, and West Germany's democratic and capitalist institutions were extended to eastern Germany. In December 1990, Kohl's center-right coalition won the first all-German election since 1932, in what was widely interpreted as a referendum on Kohl's handling of the reunifi-cation process.

In the period from 1990 to 1994, the efforts to consolidate the reunification process met with great difficulty. It soon became apparent that the Kohl government had seriously underestimated or deliberately understated the ec-onomic backwardness, environmental damage, and social problems in the former GDR. In the short run, Easterners became resentful of what they perceived as their "second-class" status and Westerners reacted negatively to the high costs of reunification, which increased their taxes, raised interest rates, and necessitated greater government borrowing. In addition, reunifi-cation added new elements of complexity and turbulence, including new par-ties and interest groups, a new electorate with uncertain political loyalties, five new Länder, new political institutions, increased political violence, and an expanded role for the federal government.

From 1991 to 1993, Kohl's center-right coalition paid a heavy political price. In addition to suffering losses in state and local elections, Kohl per-sonally trailed his Social Democratic rival in opinion polls throughout most of 1993. By early 1994, however, a combination of factors contributed to the improvement of Kohl's political fortunes. These included an improving econ-omy, a more realistic approach by the Kohl government to funding reuni-fication, a stronger government response to right-wing political violence, and the implementation of a more restrictive immigration policy. Kohl's coalition was victorious in the October 1994 elections, winning in most of the western states but losing in four of the five eastern Länder. The relative inexperience of the leadership of the rival Social Democratic Party and the reluctance of West Germans to vote for change were important factors in the victory.

Lech Walesa

As the leader of the dissident movement Solidarity, Lech Walesa was the symbol of national resistance to the Soviet-model project in Poland. Subsequently, as the democratically elected president of Poland, he became a central figure in the politics of postcommunism. Walesa's career, and events in Poland in general, assumed great international significance because Solidarity was the first noncommunist union to achieve legalization in the Soviet bloc. In addition, in the postcommunist era, Poland opted for a full transition from a command system to a market economy and thus became a model for other states. Lech Walesa was the product of a typical Roman Catholic upbringing and adult socialization as a Baltic shipyard electrician in the industrial workforce. He was drawn into the protest movement during the 1970s, elected to strike committees, and later arrested. From the mid-1970s, Walesa's influence increased within the protest movement, which now gained the support of students and intellectuals. As a rising leader, Walesa demonstrated toughness, sound political instincts, and a populist appeal to traditional patriotism and morality.

The environment of increasing turbulence in the 1970s revealed the extent of popular dissatisfaction with economic conditions, the government's lack of legitimacy among major segments of the population, and the dependence of the regime on Soviet power. Major demonstrations and strikes occurred in 1970–1971 and 1976. In the crisis of 1980, strikes and antigovernment demonstrations were expanded to include demands for an end to political repression and greater independence from the Soviet Union. In addition, striking workers were supported by dissident intellectuals and the Catholic Church increased its criticisms of some practices of the regime. In 1980, Solidarity briefly gained official recognition as the first independent union in the Soviet bloc, but following the imposition of martial law in December 1981, it was outlawed and most of its leaders were arrested.

During the 1980s, the regime of General Jaruzelski failed to establish the legitimacy of the Communist project. The performance of the economy continued to worsen, minor concessions failed to quiet the opposition, and the political crisis continued when strikes and protests flared again in 1988. In April 1989, the government was forced to legalize Solidarity and announce semidemocratic elections for a two-house legislature. In the elections of 1989, Solidarity captured ninety-nine of the one hundred seats in the new Senate and, through political maneuvering, also gained control of the lower house. Before the end of 1989, Poland had a noncommunist prime minister, a cabinet under noncommunist control, and an amended constitution, which ended the Polish Communist Party's dominating role. During 1990, the Polish

Communist Party was dissolved by its members, President Jaruzelski resigned, and Lech Walesa became the first democratically elected president of postwar Poland.

Once in power, it soon became clear that Solidarity was a coalition of extremely diverse interests that had been united only in their opposition to the Communist regime. Its constituent groups included such diverse elements as extreme nationalists, noncommunist leftists, devoted followers of the Catholic Church, and atheists. Political turbulence intensified in the post-communist environment as conflicts erupted between the twenty-five political parties, which advanced rival plans for the economy, foreign policy, church-state relations, and the solution of social problems. With the Solidarity coalition fractured, Walesa became the focus of popular frustrations over the pace of economic change and his personal popularity plummeted. In mid-1994, however, no other leader appeared to have sufficient support to take his place.

Mikhail Gorbachev and Boris Yeltsin

Mikhail Gorbachev was the central figure in the political turbulence surrounding the fall of the Communist national project in the Soviet Union. After a series of appointments and promotions within the Communist Party of the Soviet Union, including appointment to the Central Committee in 1970 and membership in the Politburo in 1979, Gorbachev rose to the position of General Secretary of the CPSU in March 1985. In 1988, he also assumed the state position of President of the USSR. After moving quickly to consolidate his power base, Gorbachev presented his program for ending the Cold War and addressing the failure of the command economy to move from heavy industry to high levels of mass consumption and then high technology.[14] Although the extent of stagnation was recognized in elite circles, the problem had never been honestly or publicly confronted. Gorbachev's program for ending the Cold War included new overtures in the areas of arms control and defense policy and, ultimately, the strategic withdrawal of the Soviet Union from Eastern Europe. To address the stagnation of the economy, Gorbachev proposed the opening of public dialogue (*glasnost*) to permit meaningful discussion of economic and social problems and then limited restructuring (*perestroika*) of economic and political institutions.[15] *Perestroika* was to involve a limited decentralization of decision making, the introduction of some norms of profitability, and the toleration of some private enterprise. Gorbachev remained a committed communist, whose objectives were to reform the communist political-economic order and raise the standard of living of ordinary citizens—not to destroy communism.

Gorbachev's program accelerated the emergence of political and social forces that destroyed the Communist project. His economic policies were inadequate to reform the economy and actually provoked an alarming drop in production. They did, however, provoke the opposition of traditional defenders of the regime within the state and party bureaucracies and in the military, which culminated in the failed coup of August 1991. Of far greater significance, the process of *glasnost* penetrated all segments of Soviet society and ultimately ignited previously supressed subnational forces. Beginning in the Baltic states, the mobilization of these forces provoked secessionist movements, intense ethnic and regional conflicts, and demands for a radical decentralization of the political system.

In the aftermath of the 1991 coup, Gorbachev's political position deteriorated rapidly. Political power shifted to Russian President Boris Yeltsin, who had been instrumental in the defeat of the coup, as well as to the leaders of several other republics. In December 1991, Russia, Belarus, and Ukraine created the Commonwealth of Independent States, which was later joined by eight other republics. This action signaled the end of the Soviet Union and the failure of Gorbachev's program to revitalize the Communist project. Yeltsin was left to face the increasingly turbulent environment of the post-communist era.

Rajiv Gandhi

Rajiv Gandhi assumed the position of Prime Minister of India in 1984, following the assassination of his mother, Prime Minister Indira Gandhi. In the election later that year, Gandhi and his Congress Party received a huge electoral mandate, reflecting the widespread expectation that he would implement needed major reforms. Gandhi, however, came to power at a time of increasing political turbulence, in which new social and political conflicts were building on older ones. These conditions led some sources to question whether India's democratic and parliamentary system of government, based largely on the British model, could manage the increased levels of political participation and societal conflict.

The traditional sources of turbulence that had plagued India since its independence in 1947 continued to be present. These included caste, religious, and linguistic conflicts; conflicts between the regions and the central government; and the chasm between the rich and poor. In the 1980s, religious and regional tensions escalated sharply with the development of a Hindu fundamentalist movement, the demand by Sikhs for an independent state, and growing unrest among the Muslims of Kashmir. The presence of these movements threatened to disempower the model of a secular state, on which India's political identity had been based since independence. In addition, the introduction of some liberal economic reforms by the Gandhi government provoked both resistance from groups committed to the older, socialist tradition and later criticism from business interests when some of these measures were abandoned.

In general, Gandhi's economic program generated unrealistic expectations of rapid improvements, which his modest policies could not satisfy, and by 1987, he had suffered a serious erosion of his political base. Corruption scandals involving Congress Party officials, intraparty feuds, reversals of policy, and the uneven results of his economic program damaged Gandhi's reputation as a reformer and political manager. In the 1989 parliamentary elections, Congress experienced a major defeat, winning only 197 seats. In the resulting parliament, in which no party had an absolute majority of seats, opposition leader V. P. Singh was elected prime minister. Between 1989 and 1991, Gandhi's political fortunes seemed to improve, and parliamentary instability necessitated the calling of a new election in 1991, which many expected Congress to win. Before the election could be held, however, Gandhi was assassinated while campaigning, apparently by Sri Lankan Tamil rebels seeking retaliation for India's intervention in Sri Lanka in 1987.

Deng Xiaoping

Deng Xiaoping built his political career during the tumultuous period of the Chinese Communist Revolution, rose and fell three times in the party hierarchy, and then attained a political stature that could be matched by only a handful of world leaders of the twentieth century. As a result of the economic reforms he introduced, China achieved unprecedented economic growth, hundreds of millions of Chinese citizens emerged from poverty, and some joined the middle class or even became rich in a land where private wealth had been scoffed at and those aspiring for it had been punished only two decades earlier. China's prosperity, however, created new tensions in the society. At the same time, some of the old tensions that had generated turbulence in China before and after the victory of communism remained.

The environment of turbulence in the second half of the twentieth century in China included ideological and power conflicts within the party; unrealistic programs for rapid economic progress; rivalry between the party, military, and the government bureaucracy; and ethnic feuds between the dominant Han and the minorities. While many of the old tensions in the Chinese society continued, new sources of turbulence were added as a result of the introduction of capitalism and the changing position of China in the world. Capitalism contributed to the exodus of millions of rural Chinese to the cities in search of jobs and fortune. Such a large-scale exodus, which was unprecedented in China's, or perhaps any other country's, history, constituted a potential cause of upheaval in the society. Other potential causes of upheaval in contemporary China included the growing gap between rural and urban incomes as well as between the incomes of those who have versus those who have less or have not, blatant corruption perpetrated by the politically powerful and their families, and the demands for freedom and democracy.

Deng Xiaoping's experiment in capitalism was, to some extent, the reverse of Mikhail Gorbachev's model for Russia. Gorbachev introduced political reforms first and then structural changes in the economy, while Deng brought economic transformation in China but ignored political reform. As the Chinese improved their living standards and became aware of the movement toward democracy throughout the world, some also demanded more rights from the government. Deng's response to such demands, as exemplified in the tragedy of Tiananmen Square in 1989, was control by force rather than negotiation and compromise. Deng's indifference to democracy and freedom was also evident in China's overall policy on human rights, and their violation in China continued unabated, international protests notwithstanding.

China's emerging status in the international economy and its enhanced political position in the world further exacerbated tensions within the country. Since investment in China is profitable and the Chinese market is huge, Western powers, including the United States, were unwilling to pressure China into granting human rights to its people. China's growing military power also made it less vulnerable to outside pressures. The conflict between the advocates of freedom and the Chinese government is, therefore, likely to continue. Unless Deng's philosophy of preference for force over compromise is given up and fundamental political changes are made, China will continue to experience turbulence in the foreseeable future.

NOTES

1. These points are central to the model of turbulence of James Rosenau; see *Turbulence in World Politics: A Theory of Change and Continuity* (Princeton, NJ: Princeton University Press, 1990), pp. 59–64.

2. For a discussion of many of these points and the problems they pose for political leaders, see Robin Wright, "The Leadership Revolution," in Christian Søe, ed., *Comparative Politics 1993/1994* (Guilford, CT: Dushkin Publishing Group, 1993), pp. 221–226.

3. Alain Lipietz, "Governing the Economy in the Face of International Challenge: From National Developmentalism to National Crisis," in James Hollifield and George Ross, eds., *Searching for the New France* (London: Routledge, 1991), pp. 18–21.

4. Ibid., p. 19.

5. For a discussion of this concept, see Rosenau, chapters 4, 6, 11, 14.

6. For a discussion of the relationship between new technologies, emergence of the global marketplace, and political change, see Eugene Skolnikoff, *The Elusive Transformation: Science, Technology, and the Evolution of International Politics* (Princeton, NJ: Princeton University Press, 1993), pp. 93–174. The impact of economic change on socialist constituencies is discussed by Christian Lemke and Gary Marks, "From Decline to Demise? The Fate of Socialism in Europe," in Christian Lemke and Gary Marks, eds., *The Crisis of Socialism in Europe* (Durham, NC: Duke University Press, 1992), pp. 1–20.

7. Crawford Young, "The Dialectics of Cultural Pluralism: Concept and Real-

ity," in Crawford Young, ed., *The Rising Tide of Cultural Pluralism: The Nation-State at Bay?* (Madison, WI: University of Wisconsin Press, 1993), pp. 3–35.

8. Ibid., p. 24.

9. For a discussion of the importance of the flow of communications in the demise of the Soviet bloc, see Skolnikoff, pp. 96–102.

10. See Rosenau, pp. 338–352.

11. Young, p. 16.

12. See Rosenau, pp. 388–415.

13. Wright, p. 225.

14. Thomas Lairson and David Skidmore, *International Political Economy: The Struggle for Power and Wealth* (Fort Worth, TX: Holt, Rinehart, and Winston, 1993), p. 162.

15. Jeffrey Goldfarb, *After the Fall: The Pursuit of Democracy in Central Europe* (New York: Basic Books, 1992), p. 240.

Selected Bibliography

CHAPTER 1. GLOBAL TURBULENCE: POLITICAL CHANGE AT CENTURY'S END

Chirot, Daniel (ed.). *The Crisis of Leninism and the Decline of the Left: The Revolutions of 1989* (Seattle, WA: University of Washington Press, 1991).

Geiger, Theodore. *The Future of the International System: The United States and the World Political Economy* (Boston, MA: Unwin Hyman, 1988).

Gourevitch, Peter. *Politics in Hard Times: Comparative Responses to International Economic Crises* (Ithaca, NY: Cornell University Press, 1986).

Haggard, Stephan and Robert R. Kaufman (eds.). *The Politics of Economic Adjustment* (Princeton, NJ: Princeton University Press, 1992).

Isaak, Robert A. *European Politics: Political Economy and Policy Making in Western Democracies* (New York: St. Martin's Press, 1980).

Johnston, R. J. and P. J. Taylor (eds.). *A World in Crisis? Geographical Perspectives* (Cambridge, MA: Blackwell, 1989).

King, Alexander and Bertrand Schneider. *The First Global Revolution: A Report by the Council of the Club of Rome* (New York: Pantheon Books, 1991).

Nelson, Joan M. (ed.). *Economic Crisis and Political Choice: The Politics of Adjustment in the Third World* (Princeton, NJ: Princeton University Press, 1990).

Overbeek, Henk. *Global Capitalism and National Decline: The Thatcher Decade in Perspective* (Boston, MA: Unwin Hyman, 1990).

Rosenau, James N. *Turbulence in World Politics: A Theory of Change and Continuity* (Princeton, NJ: Princeton University Press, 1990).

CHAPTER 2. THE NEW POLITICAL ENVIRONMENT: SIX CHANGED RELATIONSHIPS

Armstrong, Philip, Andrew Glyn, and John Harrison. *Capitalism since 1945* (Cambridge, MA: Blackwell, 1991).

Dalton, Russell J. and Manfred Kuechler (eds.). *Challenging the Political Order: New Social and Political Movements in Western Democracies* (New York: Oxford University Press, 1990).

Frieden, Jeffry A. and David A. Lake. *International Political Economy: Perspectives on Global Power and Wealth*, 2nd ed. (New York: St. Martin's Press, 1991).

Hall, Peter A. (ed.). *The Political Power of Economic Ideas: Keynesianism across Nations* (Princeton, NJ: Princeton University Press, 1989).

Kesselman, Mark and Joel Krieger (eds.). *European Politics in Transition* (Lexington, MA: D.C. Heath and Co., 1987).

Klare, Michael T. and Daniel C. Thomas. *World Security: Challenges for a New Century*, 2nd ed. (New York: St. Martin's Press, 1994).

Knox, Paul and John Agnew. *The Geography of the World Economy* (New York: Edward Arnold, 1989).

Lairson, Thomas D. and David Skidmore. *International Political Economy: The Struggle for Power and Wealth* (New York: Harcourt Brace Jovanovich College Publishers, 1993).

Lash, Scott and John Urry. *The End of Organized Capitalism* (Madison, WI: The University of Wisconsin Press, 1987).

Rosenau, James N. *Turbulence in World Politics: A Theory of Change and Continuity* (Princeton, NJ: Princeton University Press, 1990).

Ross, Robert J. S. and Kent C. Trachte. *Global Capitalism: The New Leviathan* (Albany, NY: State University of New York Press, 1990).

CHAPTER 3. MARGARET THATCHER: ECONOMIC DECLINE AND TURBULENCE IN THE UNITED KINGDOM

Buxton, Tony, Paul Chapman, and Paul Temple (eds.). *Britain's Economic Performance* (New York: Routledge, 1994).

Cloke, Paul (ed.). *Policy and Change in Thatcher's Britain* (New York: Pergamon Press, 1992).

Gamble, Andrew. *The Free Economy and the Strong State: The Politics of Thatcherism* (Durham, NC: Duke University Press, 1988).

Jessop, Bob, Kevin Bonnett, Simon Bromley, and Tom Ling (eds.). *Thatcherism: A Tale of Two Nations* (New York: Polity Press, 1988).

Kavanagh, Dennis. *Thatcherism and British Politics: The End of Consensus?* 2nd ed. (New York: Oxford University Press, 1990).

King, Anthony et al. *Britain at the Polls 1992* (Chatham, NJ: Chatham House Publishers, 1993).

Michie, Jonathan (ed.). *The Economic Legacy 1979–1992* (New York: Academic Press, 1992).

Riddell, Peter. *The Thatcher Era and Its Legacy* (Cambridge, U.K.: Blackwell, 1991).

Thatcher, Margaret. *The Downing Street Years* (New York: Harper Collins Publishers, 1993).

Young, Hugo. *The Iron Lady: A Biography of Margaret Thatcher* (New York: The Noonday Press, 1989).

CHAPTER 4. HELMUT KOHL AND THE GERMAN REUNIFICATION PROJECT

American Academy of Arts and Sciences. "Germany in Transition." *Daedalus,* Winter 1994.

Ash, Timothy Garton. *In Europe's Name: Germany and the Divided Continent* (New York: Random House, 1993).

Hancock, M. Donald and Helga A. Welsh (eds.). *German Unification: Process and Outcomes* (Boulder, CO: Westview Press, 1994).

Huelshoff, Michael G., Andrei S. Markovits, and Simon Reich (eds.). *From Bundesrepublik to Deutschland: German Politics after Unification* (Ann Arbor, MI: The University of Michigan Press, 1993).

Jarausch, Konrad H. *The Rush to German Unity* (New York: Oxford University Press, 1994).

Pond, Elizabeth. *Beyond the Wall: Germany's Road to Unification* (Washington, DC: The Brookings Institution, 1993).

Merkl, Peter H. *German Unification in the European Context* (University Park, PA: The Pennsylvania State University Press, 1993).

Smith, Gordon, et al. *Developments in German Politics* (Durham, NC: Duke University Press, 1992).

Stares, Paul B. (ed.). *The New Germany and the New Europe* (Washington, DC: The Brookings Institution, 1992).

Wallach, H. G. Peter and Ronald A. Francisco. *United Germany: The Past, Politics, Prospects* (Westport, CT: Praeger, 1992).

CHAPTER 5. LECH WALESA AND THE EMERGENCE OF POSTCOMMUNIST POLAND

Andrews, Nicholas G. *Poland 1980–1981: Solidarity versus the Party* (Washington, DC: National Defense University Press, 1985).

Clark, John and Aaron Wildavsky. *The Moral Collapse of Communism: Poland as a Cautionary Tale* (San Francisco, CA: Institute for Contemporary Studies Press, 1990).

Dziewanowski, M. K. *The Communist Party of Poland,* 2nd ed. (Cambridge, MA: Harvard University Press, 1976).

———. *Poland in the Twentieth Century* (New York: Columbia University Press, 1977).

Kaminski, Bartlomiej. *The Collapse of State Socialism: The Case of Poland* (Princeton, NJ: Princeton University Press, 1991).

Kurski, Jaroslaw. *Lech Walesa: Democrat or Dictator?* (Boulder, CO: Westview Press, 1993).

Stokes, Gale (ed.). *From Stalinism to Pluralism: A Documentary History of East Europe Since 1945* (New York: Oxford University Press, 1991).

Wandycz Piotr. *The Price of Freedom: A History of East Central Europe* (London and New York: Routledge, 1992).

Weydenthal, Jan B. de. *The Communists of Poland: An Outline History* (Stanford, CA: Hoover Institution Press, 1978).

World Bank. *Poland: Economic Management for a New Era: A World Bank Country Study* (Washington, DC: The World Bank, 1990).

CHAPTER 6. MIKHAIL GORBACHEV, BORIS YELTSIN, AND THE DEMOCRATIZATION OF RUSSIA

Aganbegyan, Able. *Inside Perestroika: The Future of the Soviet Economy* (New York: Harper & Row, 1989).

Conquest, Robert. *The Great Terror: Stalin's Purge of the Thirties* (London, Toronto, New York: Macmillan, 1968).

———. *The Great Terror: A Reassessment* (New York: Oxford University Press, 1990).

Fainsod, Merle. *How Russia Is Ruled* (Cambridge, MA: Harvard University Press, 1967).

Feshbach, Murray and Alfred Friendly, Jr. *Ecocide in the USSR: Health and Nature under Siege* (New York: Basic Books, 1992).

Goldman, Marshall I. *Gorbachev's Challenge: Economic Reform in the Age of High Technology* (New York: Norton, 1987).

———. *Lost Opportunity: Why Economic Reforms in Russia Have Not Worked* (New York: Norton, 1994).

Gorbachev, Mikhail. *The Moratorium: Selected Speeches and Statements by the General Secretary of the CPSU Central Committee on the Problem of Ending Nuclear Tests (January–September 1986)* (Moscow: Novosti Agency Publishing House, 1986).

———. *Perestroika i Novoe Myshlenie dla nashei strany i dla vsego Mira* [Perestroika and New Thinking for Our Country and the Whole World] (Moscow: Izdatelstvo Politcheskoi Literatury, 1988). (These and other Gorbachev works were distributed worldwide in many languages, both by the Soviet government and private publishers; see any version.)

Sakwa, Richard. *Gorbachev and His Reforms: 1985–1990* (Englewood Cliffs, NJ: Prentice Hall, 1990).

Stalin, Joseph. *Leninism* (2 vols) (New York: International Publishers, n.d. [1933]).

Sudoplatov, Pavel and Anatoli Sudoplatov. *Special Tasks: The Memoirs of an Unwanted Witness—A Soviet Spymaster* (Boston, MA: Little, Brown, 1994).

Voslensky, Michael. *Nomenklatura: Anatomy of the Soviet Ruling Class* (London: The Bodley Head, 1980).

Yeltsin, Boris. *Against the Grain: An Autobiography* (New York: Summit Books, 1990.

CHAPTER 7. RAJIV GANDHI: ECONOMIC LIBERALIZATION IN INDIA

Barnds, William J. *India, Pakistan and the Great Powers* (New York: Praeger, 1972).

Healy, Kathleen. *Rajiv Gandhi: The Years of Power* (New Delhi, India: Vikas Publishing House, 1989).

Kohli, Atul. *The State and Poverty in India* (New York: Cambridge University Press, 1987).

Kreisberg, Paul H. "Gandhi at Midterm." *Foreign Affairs,* Summer 1987.

Lucas, Robert E. B. and Gustav F. Papanek (eds.). *The Indian Economy: Recent Developments and Future Prospects* (Boulder, CO: Westview Press, 1988).

Merchant, Minhaz. *Rajiv Gandhi: The End of a Dream* (New Delhi, India: Viking Penguin India, 1991).

Nayar, Baldev Raj. *India's Mixed Economy: The Role of Ideology and Interest in Its Development* (Bombay, India: Popular Prakashan, 1989).

Rudolph, Lloyd I. and Susanne Hueber Rudolph. *In Pursuit of Lakshmi: The Political Economy of the Indian State* (Chicago: The University of Chicago Press, 1987).

Sen Gupta, Bhabani. *Rajiv Gandhi: A Political Study* (Delhi, India: Konark Publishers, 1989).

Varghese, K. V. *Economic Problems of Modern India,* 2nd ed. (New Delhi, India: Ashish Publishing House, 1988).

CHAPTER 8. DENG XIAOPING: CHINA'S ECONOMIC TRANSFORMATION

Chang, David W. *Zhou Enlai and Deng Xiaoping in the Chinese Leadership Succession Crisis* (Lanham, MD: University Press of America).

Deng Xiaoping. *Fundamental Issues in Present-Day China* (Beijing, China: Foreign Languages Press, 1988).

Dorn, James A. and Wang Xi (eds.). *Economic Reform in China: Problems and Prospects* (Chicago: The University of Chicago Press, 1990).

Harding, Harry. *China's Second Revolution Reform after Mao* (Washington, D.C.: The Brookings Institution, 1987).

Hsu, C. Y. *China without Mao* (New York: Oxford University Press, 1990).

Lyons, Thomas P. *Economic Integration and Planning in China* (New York: Columbia University Press, 1987).

Perry, Elizabeth J. and Christine Wong (eds.). *The Political Economy of Reform in Post-Mao China* (Cambridge, MA: Harvard University Press, 1985).

Riskin, Carl. *China's Political Economy: The Quest for Development since 1949* (New York: Oxford University Press, 1988).

Spence, Jonathan D. *The Search for Modern China* (New York: W. W. Norton and Co., 1990).

White, Lynn T., III. *Politics of Chaos: The Organizational Causes of Violence in China's Cultural Revolution* (Princeton, NJ: Princeton University Press, 1989).

CHAPTER 9. LEADERSHIP IN THE AGE OF TURBULENCE

d'Encausse, Hélène Carrère. *The End of the Soviet Empire: The Triumph of the Nations* (New York: A New Republic Book, 1991).

Goldstone, Jack A., Ted Robert Gurr, and Farrokh Moshiri (eds.). *Revolutions of the Late Twentieth Century* (Boulder, CO: Westview Press, 1991).

Kaminski, Bartlomiej. *The Collapse of State Socialism: The Case of Poland* (Princeton, NJ: Princeton University Press, 1991).

Lemke, Christiane and Gary Marks (eds.). *The Crisis of Socialism in Europe* (Durham, NC: Duke University Press, 1992).

Lipietz, Alain. "Governing the Economy in the Face of International Challenge: From National Developmentalism to National Crisis." In James F. Hollifield and George Ross (eds.), *Searching for the New France* (New York: Routledge, 1991).

———. *Towards a New Economic Order: Postfordism, Ecology and Democracy* (New York: Oxford University Press, 1992).

Rosenau, James N. *Turbulence in World Politics: A Theory of Change and Continuity* (Princeton, NJ: Princeton University Press, 1990).

Rustow, Dankwart A. and Kenneth Paul Erickson (eds.). *Comparative Political Dynamics: Global Research Perspectives* (New York: Harper Collins Publishers, 1991).

Sederberg, Peter C. *Fires Within: Political Violence and Revolutionary Change* (New York: Harper Collins Publishers, 1994).

Skolnikoff, Eugene B. *The Elusive Transformation: Science, Technology, and the Evolution of International Politics* (Princeton, NJ: Princeton Press, 1993).

Young, Crawford (ed.). *The Rising Tide of Cultural Pluralism: The Nation-State at Bay?* (Madison, WI: The University of Wisconsin Press, 1993).

Index

Adenauer, Konrad, 94, 97
Agenda of politics, 3, 4, 5
Ahluwalia, Isher Judge, 180, 181
Alternative collectivities, 226
Andropov, Yuri, 135, 151, 155

Balcerowicz, Leszek, 137
Breakpoint (historic) change, 27
Bretton Woods system, 25, 30–31
    International Monetary Fund, 30
    World Bank, 30, 137
Brezhnev, Leonid, 135, 151, 155–156
Brzezinski, Zbigniew, 142–143

Chernenko, Konstantin, 135, 155
Chiang Kai-shek, 197, 199
China
    Communist Party (CCP), 196, 199,
        205, 211, 213
    corruption, 215, 217
    Cultural Revolution, 199–200, 202–
        203
    democracy movement, 216
    Democracy Wall campaign, 209
    foreign policy, 198–199

Four Modernizations, 207–208
Great Leap Forward, 199, 201–203,
    207, 211
Hainan Province, 214
household responsibility system,
    212
human rights, 198, 206
Kuomintang (KMT), 197
national political-economic context,
    195–199
nationalities, 195–196
other political parties, 197
Red Guards, 203, 207
reforms of 1984, 212
religion, 196
single-child family policy, 200–201
Tiananmen Square Revolt, 199,
    203–204, 209
turbulence, 199–201
Citizen enhancement
    enhanced analytical skills, 9, 36–39
    political effects, 222, 225–226
Cold War, 26, 27, 28
    end of Cold War relationship, 28–
        30

Deng Xiaoping
  implementation of the new program, 211–214
  interpretations of, 216–217
  mobilizing for power, 210–211
  nature and scope of change, 214–216
  the new program, 206–210
  political profile, 204–206, 233–234
Dhar, P.N., 183
Disempowerment. *See* Empowerment and disempowerment
Djilas, Milovan, 150

EFTA (European Free Trade Association), 138
Empowerment and disempowerment
  general dynamic, 14
  groups, 14–15
  ideas, 17–19
  institutions, 16
  in Soviet bloc, 16
Engels, Frederick, 152, 153
European Community/European Union, 30, 138

Fainsod, Merle, 150
Federal Republic of Germany
  Basic Law, 87, 88
  CDU/CSU, 88, 94–98
  CDU/CSU–FDP coalition, 98
  democratic consolidation, 87–88
  economic development in, 88–89
  Free Democratic Party, 88, 95, 96, 97, 98, 104
  National Question in, 83
  political and economic context, 83–86
  postwar development of, 87–89
  post–World War II division, 86–87
  scope of change following reunification, 115–116
  Social Democratic Party (SPD), 88, 103, 104, 107, 108, 114, 115
  turbulence from reunification, 89–93
  in Western Alliance institutional complex, 86–87
Franz, Uli, 205

French Regulation School, 224
  concept of "national projects," 224–225, 226–227

G-7 countries, 165
Gamble, Andrew, 73
Gandhi, Feroze, 176
Gandhi, Indira, 169, 176, 182–184, 186, 190
Gandhi, Mahatma, 178, 185
Gandhi, Rajiv
  assassination, 169, 191
  implementation of the new program, 186–187
  interpretations of, 189–191
  mobilizing for power, 184–186
  nature and scope of change, 187–189
  the new program, 177–184
  political profile, 175–177, 232–233
Gandhi, Sanjay, 176
Gang of Four, 207
Genscher, Hans-Dietrich, 101, 105
German Democratic Republic
  Berlin Wall, 87, 102
  economic problems in, 93, 111–112
  exodus from (1989–1990), 90, 98, 99, 100, 103, 106
  "falling dominoes" in Eastern Europe, 99, 100
  founding of, 87
  loss of legitimacy, 90, 98, 100
  March 1990 election, 106
  and Mikhail Gorbachev, 87, 99, 100, 103, 105, 115
  New Forum and opposition movement, 100
  protest culture (1989–1990), 90, 102
  reunification negotiations with Federal Republic, 106–109
  Round Table process, 102
  SED (Socialist Unity Party of Germany), 87, 102, 104, 106
  STASI, 87, 100, 103, 110, 111
  turbulence in (1989–1990), 91–92
Gierek, Edward, 128, 134, 135
Glasnost, 2, 135, 159
Global capitalism, 32–33

Global radio and television. *See* New technologies
Goldman, Marshall, 161, 165
Gomulka, Wladyslaw, 127, 128, 133, 134
Gorbachev, Mikhail, 38, 42, 87, 97, 99, 100, 103, 105, 115, 147, 148, 157, 164
  biography, 148–149, 151–152
  coup against, 160–161
  national turbulence, 152–158
    economic collapse, 153–158
    moral collapse, 152–153
  new program, 158–162
  political profile, 158, 231, 232
Great Britain. *See* United Kingdom
"Great domestic political reforms," 2

Harding, Harry, 210
Heath, Edward, 52, 54, 55, 57, 61, 62
Hegemony
  in Cold War, 28–29
  ideological hegemony, 17, 18
Honecker, Erich, 99, 100
Hsu, C.Y., 212
Hu Yaobang, 203–204, 206
Hua Guofeng, 207–208, 210–211

India
  castes, 170, 175
    "backward," 175
    Harijans, 170, 175
  Congress Party, 172–173, 177, 182, 185–186, 191
  Green Revolution, 169, 181
  Industrial Policy of 1991, 189
  Industrial Policy Resolutions of 1948 and 1956, 178
  Janata coalition, 182–183
  mixed economy, 171, 179, 189
  nonalignment policy, 171–172
  political-economic context, 170–172
  political violence, 173–175
  religions, 170, 172, 174, 177, 184–185
  socialism, 187
  turbulence, 169, 172–175, 191

Information revolution, 40–41
Isaak, Robert, 4

Jaruzelski, Wojciech, 128, 129, 132
  martial law, 129, 135
Jha, Prem Shanker, 183
Jiang Zemin, 211
Johnson, D. Gale, 208
Joseph, Sir Keith, 54, 55, 61

Kashmir, 172–175, 177, 188
Katzenstein, Peter, 14
Keynesian welfare state, 20
  defined, 17
  in United Kingdom, 73–75
Keynesianism, 17, 34
  in United Kingdom, 46–50
Knowledge-based society, 9
Kochanek, Stanley, 187
Kohl, Helmut
  CDU/CSU–FDP coalition, 98
  early attitude toward reunification, 97–98
  mobilizing support for reunification, 106–109
  policies of
    approach toward the Soviet Union, 105
    asylum law, 114
    consolidation of reunification, 110–111
    German Economic and Monetary Union, 106–107, 112–113
    negotiations with Gorbachev (July 1990), 105
    March 1990 GDR election, 104
    Second State Treaty, 108–109
    solidarity surcharge, 114
    Ten-Point Plan, 98
  policy dimension: consolidating reunification, 109–114
  political-economic context of the Federal Republic, 86–89
  political profile, 93–98, 228–230
  and reunification project, 98–114
  scope of change under, 115–116
  victory in December 1990 election, 109

victory in October 1994 election, 114–115
Kohli, Atul, 183
Kosciuszko, Tadeusz, 123
Kreisberg, Paul H., 176, 185
Krenz, Egon, 100, 102

Ladd, Everett Carll, 3, 4
Lafontaine, Oskar, 107–108
Lenin, Vladimir Ilych Ulyanov, 153
Li Peng, 204
Liberal international economic order, 30
  See also Bretton Woods system
Lin Bao, 203
Liu Shaoqi, 202, 206
Lyons, Thomas, 207

Manor, James, 179
Mao Zedong, 195, 199, 201–203, 205, 207, 210–211, 216
Marx, Karl, 152, 153
Mass movements, 36–39
  proliferation of, 37
Mazière, Lothar de, 106
Mazowiecki, Tadeusz, 135
Merchant, Minhaz, 185–188
Modrow, Hans, 102, 103
Mulroney, Brian, 15

National projects, 224–225, 226–227
NATO (North Atlantic Treaty Organization), 138
Nehru, Jawaharlal, 171, 173–174, 176–178, 182, 184, 190
Neomercantilism, 31
  free-rider problem, 31
  non-tariff barriers, 31
New Right in United Kingdom, 47, 54–56, 58, 61–62, 66
New technologies, 5, 8, 19, 39–40
  global radio and television, 8, 9, 225–226
New Thinking (in Soviet foreign policy), 2
Newly Industrializing Countries (NICs), 32, 33
Nixon, Richard, 181, 213
Nomenklatura, 129, 150, 161

Pakistan, 172, 177, 180–181
Patel, Sardar Vallabhbhai, 178
Perestroika, 2, 36, 135, 159
Perkins, Dwight Heald, 211–212, 214
Pilsudski, Jozef, 125
Poland
  Communist Party (Polish United Workers Party—PZPR), 124, 126, 127, 130, 136
  General-Gouvernement, 125
  Katyn Forest Massacre, 125–126, 164
  KOR (Committee for Defense of Workers), 134
  national turbulence, 124–128
  partitions, 123
  People's Republic, 127
  police (Militsia), 137
  resistance to communism, 123–124
  Sejm (National legislature), 135
  Solidarity, 134, 136, 137, 138, 143
  Soviet model in, 130, 131
  state socialism, 131
Political actors, 3
Political agenda. See Agenda of politics
Political change, 1, 2, 3, 13, 14
  leaders and, 3–4
  long-term change, 9–11
  medium-term change, 11–12
  post-1973, 13–14
  short-term change, 12–13
Political mobilization, 225–226
Political relationships, 12
  breakdown of the Bretton Woods system, 30–31
  change in, 26–28
  defined, 25–28
  empowered citizens, 39–41
  end of the Cold War, 28–30
  fall of "postwar economic arrangements," 33–36
  onset of global capitalism, 32–33
  proliferation of mass movements, 36–39
  six key relationships, 28–41
Postcommunist states, 16, 35–36, 123–145, 147–168

Postwar economic order (settlement)
  defined, 33–34
  in Soviet bloc, 35–36
  in West, 33–35
Powell, Enoch, 54, 55, 60

Rao, P.V. Narasimha, 186, 188–189
Reagan, Ronald, 14–15, 96
Reunification of Germany
  accession (Article 23), 108
  consolidation of the reunification
    project, 109–115
  and December 1990 election, 109
  East-West cultural divide, 110
  East's transition to capitalism, 110
  First State Treaty, 106–108
  Kohl-Gorbachev talks (July 1990),
    105
  and March 1990 GDR election, 106
  policy trade-offs from, 99, 111
  and political turbulence, 89–90
  Second State Treaty, 108–109
  and Social Democratic Party, 107,
    108
  Solidarity Pact, 114–115
  Ten-Point Plan (Helmut Kohl), 98,
    101
  transition crisis, 110–112
  two-plus-four talks, 99, 104–106
  Unification Day, 108
Riskin, Carl, 207–208
Rosenau, James, 20, 21
Russia (Russian Federation), 162–166

Scharping, Rudolf, 114
Sen Gupta, Bhabani, 187
Shastri, Lal Bahadur, 176, 182
Singh, V.P., 176, 186, 188–189
Snow, Edgar, 205
South Asian Association for Regional
  Cooperation (SAARC), 172
Stakhanov, Aleksandr (fictional Russian
  leader in 2017), 147–148
Stalin, Joseph Vissarionovich Djugash-
  vili, 153
Stoessinger, John, 209
Soviet bloc, 1, 3, 11, 15, 18, 19, 20, 36

Soviet Union, 1, 2, 3, 5, 8, 14, 15, 18,
  19, 26, 147–168
  Communist Party of, 147–162
  Gosplan, 154
  security police (KGB—Committee
    on State Security), 156
  technological time warp in, 8–9
Strauss, Franz-Josef, 95, 96
Subnational movements, 38, 225–226
Sun Yat-sen, 197, 199
Supranationalism, 38–39, 225–226
Surviving turbulence, factors in, 226–
  227

Thatcher, Margaret
  and context of economic decline,
    50–52
  implementation of policies, 65–71
  interpretations of, 66, 74–76
  mobilizing for power (career
    stages), 61–65
  nature and scope of change under,
    71–74
  and New Right faction, 54–56
  policy failures of, 70–71
  political profile, 52–54, 228
  resignation, 64–65, 71
  scope of change under, 71–74
  specific policies
    deintegrative electoral policy, 58,
      72–73
    economic record, 73–74
    and European Community, 65
    housing policy, 69
    labor relations policy, 68
    local government finance, 68–69
    macroeconomic policy, 67–68
    national electoral program, 56–57
    neoliberal economic policy, 66–
      67
    neoliberal social policy, 66–67
    poll tax, 69, 71
    privatization, 69–70
    share (stock) ownership, 70
    taxation and deregulation, 70
    statecraft of, 59–60
Thatcherism
  authoritarian-populist appeal, 56

crises of the economy, governance,
and the Conservative Party, 57–
61
defined, 56–57
monetarism, 67–68
as national program, 56–57
neoconservative and neoliberal influences, 54–56
policy dimension, 65–66
political and electoral strategy, 58,
72–73
Third World, 18, 41
ideological heterogeneity in, 18
Trotsky, Leon Bronstein, 153
Turbulence (political)
characteristics of political turbulence, 20–21, 221–227
in China, 199–201
defined, 20, 21
in Federal Republic of Germany,
89–93
in India, 169, 172–175, 191
onset of political turbulence, 222–
224
in Poland, 124–132
and political economic arrangements, 224–225
and political mobilization, 225–226
in Soviet Union/Russia, 152–158
theory of James Rosenau, 20–21
in United Kingdom, 50–52

Union of Soviet Socialist Republics
(USSR). See Soviet Union
United Kingdom
Conservative Party, 47, 48, 49, 50,
57–58, 60–61, 61–65, 75–76
economic decline in, 45–47
European Community member-
ship, 50

fall of postwar settlement, 50–52
Keynesian welfare state, 47–50, 74–
75, 76
Labour Party, 62, 63, 64, 72–73, 75,
76
New Right, 47, 54–57, 61–62, 66
political turbulence in, 50–52
postmaterialist values in, 46
scope of change under Thatcher,
71–74
Winter of Discontent, 62
United States, 14–15
agenda change in, 4

Walesa, Lech
biography, 133–135
implementing new program, 140–
141
interpretation as leader, 142–143
mobilizing for power, 138–140
nature and scope of change, 141–
142
political profile, 133–136, 230–231
program, 136–138
Wei Jingsheng, 209
Weimar Republic, 85
White, Lynn, 202–203

Xue Muqiao, 207

Yang Shangkun, 204
Yeltsin, Boris, 147, 148, 162–163
biography, 151–152
interpretation as leader, 164–166
nature and scope of change, 163–
164
political profile, 164–166, 232

Zhao Ziyang, 204, 206
Zhongli, Zhang, 215
Zhou Enlai, 205, 207–208
Zuckerman, Mortimer B., 215

About the Authors

DAVID F. WALSH is Professor of Political Science at Southern Connecticut State University in New Haven.

PAUL J. BEST is Professor of Political Science at Southern Connecticut State University in New Haven.

KUL B. RAI is Professor and Chairman of the Political Science Department at Southern Connecticut State University in New Haven.

ISBN 0-275-95166-9

9 0 0 0 0 >

EAN

9 780275 951665

HARDCOVER BAR CODE